D0536380

Organizational
Behaviour
in Hotels and
Restaurants

Organizational Behaviour in Hotels and Restaurants

An International Perspective

Yvonne Guerrier

SELKIRK COLLEGE LIBRARY

DISCARDED

DATE: DEC 0 7 2021

SELKIRK COLLEGE LIBRARY
TENTH STREET CAMPUS

JOHN WILEY & SONS, LTD

Chichester • New York • Weinheim • Brisbane • Singapore • Toronto

Copyright © 1999 by John Wiley & Sons Ltd,
Baffins Lane, Chichester,
West Sussex PO19 1UD, England

National   01243 779777
International (+44) 1243 779777
e-mail (for orders and customer service enquiries): cs-books@wiley.co.uk
Visit our Home Page on http://www.wiley.co.uk
                    or http://www.wiley.com

All rights reserved. No part of this publication may be reproduced, stored in a retrieval system, or transmitted, in any form or by any means, electronic, mechanical, photocopying, recording, scanning or otherwise, except under the terms of the Copyright, Designs and Patents Act 1988 or under the terms of a licence issued by the Copyright Licensing Agency, 90 Tottenham Court Road, London, UK W1P 9HE, without the permission in writing of John Wiley & Sons Ltd., Baffins Lane, Chichester, West Sussex, UK PO19 1UD.

Other Wiley Editorial Offices

John Wiley & Sons, Inc., 605 Third Avenue,
New York, NY 10158-0012, USA

WILEY-VCH Verlag GmbH, Pappelallee 3,
D-69469 Weinheim, Germany

Jacaranda Wiley Ltd, 33 Park Road, Milton,
Queensland 4064, Australia

John Wiley & Sons (Asia) Pte Ltd, 2 Clementi Loop #02-01,
Jin Xing Distripark, Singapore 129809

John Wiley & Sons (Canada) Ltd, 22 Worcester Road,
Rexdale, Ontario M9W 1L1, Canada

Library of Congress Cataloging-in-Publication Data

Guerrier, Yvonne.
    Organizational behaviour in hotels and restaurants : an
international perspective / Yvonne Guerrier.
        p.   cm.
    Includes bibliographical references and index.
    ISBN 0-471-98650-X (alk. paper)
    1. Hotel management.   2. Restaurant management.   3. Organizational
behavior.   I. Title.
TX911.3.M27G77   1999
647.94'068—dc21   99–13331
                                                                       CIP

British Library Cataloguing in Publication Data
A catalogue record for this book is available from the British Library

ISBN 0-471-98650-X

Typeset in 11/13pt Palatino by Mayhew Typesetting, Rhayader, Powys
Printed and bound in Great Britain by Bookcraft (Bath) Ltd, Midsomer Norton, Somerset
This book is printed on acid-free paper responsibly manufactured from sustainable forestry, in which at least two trees are planted for each one used for paper production.

Contents

Acknowledgements

Many people have contributed in some way to this book. I am grateful to numerous academic colleagues whose ideas have influenced my own. I would particularly like to thank my colleagues at South Bank University, not just for their ideas and perspectives but also for their support when I was hiding away writing. I would like to thank Iain Stevenson for encouraging me to write the book and Claire Plimmer for her advice, support and deadlines. Many thanks also to Joan Richards for her careful reading of and supportive comments on the manuscript.

Most of all I would like to thank all my students, past and present, postgraduate, undergraduate and those on short courses. Their comments, ideas and examples have frequently found their way into the book and it could not have been written without them.

1 Introduction

Organizations are puzzling places. Why is it a pleasure to work in some organizations and torture to work in others? Why is it sometimes difficult to motivate people to work hard? How can one persuade people to work together as a team? What is the best way of designing an organization structure? How can I persuade my boss to listen to my wonderful ideas? This book is about these real organizational problems that we all face at some time during our working lives.

In this book, organizational behaviour is looked at in the context of one sub-set of organizations, hotels and restaurants. It is also a book which attempts to take an international perspective. In the Introduction we will look first at the nature of organizational behaviour; second at the justification for a specific study of organizational behaviour in hotels and restaurants; and third at what it means to take an international perspective. It will then outline the content of the book and the approach taken in writing it.

What is organizational behaviour?

Organizational behaviour is the academic study of organizational processes using social science methodologies and approaches. The purpose of organizational behaviour is to help people understand human behaviour in organizations and, therefore, ultimately to operate more effectively within organizations. Chapter 2 looks in detail at what this means. However, at this point it is important to explain what this book does not attempt to do.

This is a book about organizational behaviour and not human resource management. The term "human resource management" is used in different ways. It sometimes refers to the activities of human resource specialists (otherwise known as personnel specialists) and sometimes to the activities of line managers in relation to managing staff. There is some overlap between organizational behaviour and human resource management when used in the latter sense. However, organizational behaviour is essentially about understanding organizations, not managing organizations; on the assumption that if one understands something then one can start thinking about how to manage it. So the emphasis here is on basic principles and processes, not on specific techniques. This book will not tell you, for example, how to design and implement a rewards package for a group of staff or how to implement an empowerment programme. But it will help you to think about how staff are motivated by various types of rewards and why certain rewards packages may not always have the consequences intended. It will tell you why empowerment programmes may be an effective method of motivating staff and help you to think about whether they would work with a particular group of staff. This book therefore attempts to provide a grounding in the basic models and approaches that are needed to progress to further study of human resource management and organizational change.

Why organizational behaviour in hotels and restaurants?

This book is designed primarily for those students who are studying hospitality management, hotel management or hotel and catering management at degree level, both undergraduate and, as an introduction to the subject, postgraduate. Whilst there are many excellent general textbooks in organizational behaviour available, students on hospitality programmes often find it easier to understand the relevance of a topic if specific hospitality examples are used, as is the case here. This textbook is also able to focus on those aspects of organizational behaviour which are of particular importance to the hospitality industry. For example there is a chapter looking specifically at the interactions between service providers and customers that would not be found in a general textbook on organizational behaviour.

Students studying for degrees in tourism management, leisure management and retail management will also find much in this book which is of relevance and interest to them. These industries have much in common with the hospitality industry and although most of the case studies and examples that are used are based on hotels and restaurants (the occasional tourism or retail example has crept in), in many cases you could substitute, say, travel rep for receptionist or sales assistant or airline cabin crew for waiter without straining credulity.

Anyone picking up this book who has no previous interest or background in the hospitality industry will find that hotels and restaurants provide a wonderful playground in which to explore how organizations work. Hotels and restaurants are very diverse organizations, ranging from the family-run guesthouse to the global corporation (e.g. McDonald's), through the five star prestigious hotel to the staff canteen. This diversity allows the investigation of a wide range of organizational problems and issues. We can look at service operations (reception, restaurant) as well as production operations (kitchens) and the relationship between the two. Unit size varies from the one-person sandwich bar to the 1000-bedroom resort hotel employing as many staff. There are single unit operations, multi-unit operations and multi-brand operations. We can study traditional male/female work roles and how different ethnic and cultural groups work together. We can study simple low-skill and low-status jobs (kitchen porter, fast food worker) and the management of highly skilled professionals (celebrity chefs). We can study how culture affects organizations, because hotels and restaurants can be found in some form everywhere in the world. We can study how work and organizations have changed through history, because hotels and restaurants, or at least ways of providing hospitality to travellers away from home, have existed throughout history. We can study commercial operations and non-commercial operations (e.g. prison catering, "hotel" services in hospitals). A further advantage of writing about organizational behaviour in the context of hotels and restaurants is that we all have some experience of these organizations, as guests if not as employees. It is easy to appreciate the problems that people working in them may face in a way that we cannot if, say, we were studying a merchant bank where we may have only a vague understanding about what work people are actually doing.

Why an international perspective?

This book claims to take an international perspective. Why, and what does that mean? Many of the existing textbooks in this area are specifically focused on the experience in one country. So British textbooks tend to be based on the British experience and American textbooks on the American experience etc. In many ways this is a sensible approach. One should write about what one knows and if you are British, as I am, you know most about Britain.

However, hospitality organizations exist all over the world and increasingly people from all over the world are studying hospitality management. Many of you reading this book will spend at least part of your career working in a country different from the one in which you were brought up. Even if you do not, you may find yourself working for a company owned by people from a different country or working alongside managers or staff who come from a different country. You will almost certainly have customers and guests who come from a different country. It is the premise of this book that not to take an international perspective is no longer an option. As Adler (1991) argues:

> the term *international* can no longer be relegated to a subset of organ-
> izations or to a division within an organization. Definitions of success
> now transcend national boundaries. In fact the very concept of domestic
> business may have become anachronistic.   (p. 4)

There is another important reason for taking an international perspective: to fight our own parochialism. To quote Adler (1991) again:

> Parochialism means viewing the world solely through one's own eyes
> and perspective. A person with a parochial perspective does not recog-
> nise other people's different ways of living and working nor that such
> differences have serious consequences. People in all cultures are, to a
> certain extent, parochial.   (p. 11)

Even if we never venture out from our own culture and never come into contact with people from other cultures (which in the modern world is increasingly unlikely), recognizing that other people have different ways of living and working can teach us something about our own way of living and working. It can teach us that the "way things are done here" is not inevitably the way things *have* to be done because in other places they are done quite differently. An international perspective helps us to interpret our own, domestic organizations more clearly and this, as I will show, is what organizational behaviour is about.

However, there are practical problems in trying to take an international perspective. It is still the case that most writing on management

and on hospitality management comes from an Anglo-Saxon tradition. Most of the authors I will quote are American or British, more rarely Canadian or Australian. There is an increasing number of studies of other cultures, and I will draw on these where they exist, but the coverage is patchy. I will also draw on case studies from my own experience of consultancy assignments in a variety of countries or from my students' personal experiences. Again the coverage of these is patchy. In some chapters, there will be a lengthy discussion of the British or American experience because that is where there is research to discuss. I am sure that, especially if you are not British, you will see examples of my "British" assumptions creeping through. We are all parochial to some extent; we cannot help seeing the world through our own culture and experience (I will examine this issue in depth in Chapter 4).

To summarize, because this book has an international perspective does not mean that it is just about multi-national companies. Its premise is that, in an increasingly global economy, we all need to understand more about working and living with people from different cultures. If nothing else, thinking about how things are done in other parts of the world, helps us think more clearly about "how we do things here". But it is impossible to produce a book which is truly international in focus; inevitably as an author what one writes is determined by one's own experience and the material available.

The content of the book

Chapters 2, 3 and 4 define the basic principles that underlie the rest of the text. Chapter 2 looks at the nature of organizational behaviour, what it is and how it helps people "read" organizational situations. It explores some of the reasons why the academic study of people in organizations is problematic and provides some tips for studying organizational behaviour.

Chapter 3 looks at the distinctive nature of hotels and restaurants as organizations and as places to work. Hotels and restaurants are variously described as being part of the hospitality industry, part of the service sector and part of the leisure industry: how do notions about the nature of hospitality, the nature of service and the nature of leisure help build an understanding of hotels and restaurants? The chapter then looks at work in hotels and restaurants and some of the reasons why, even with the worldwide growth of the hospitality industry, jobs within this sector often carry a low status. It looks at the way in which labour markets in the hospitality industry operate.

Chapter 4 examines culture. It explores what culture is, where our cultural assumptions come from and how they affect our behaviour. It then focuses on the way in which national culture affects managers and organizations. Finally, it looks at the extent to which organizations have cultures so that working for one hotel group may feel different from working for another.

The next three chapters look at a set of issues connected with the management of people within organizations. Chapter 5 examines motivation at work. It reviews the psychological theories about why people put effort into their work and the approaches that can be used to motivate people. It explores the relationships between motivation, job satisfaction and job performance. Finally, it looks at money as a motivator.

Chapter 6 explores the processes of working in groups and leading groups. It examines the psychology of group behaviour and the different roles that people play within groups. It reviews various theories of leadership and considers the relationship between leadership and power. It explores the way in which culture affects our perceptions of leadership. Finally, it examines what can be done to improve group working and leadership in hospitality organizations.

Chapter 7 uses the ideas from the previous chapters to explore the way jobs can be designed and organizations structured. Is it better to design simple jobs that anyone can do or enriched jobs that people find interesting to do? How can jobs be linked together to produce a flexible organization? Should organizations be designed as centralized, hierarchical and mechanistic structures or as decentralized, flat and organic?

The next set of chapters looks at different sub-groups within organizations.

Chapter 8 studies managers in the hospitality industry. It considers the nature of management work and looks at the skills needed by managers in the hospitality industry and the controversies about what skills are needed. It explores the way that management work is changing, and the barriers facing women and certain ethnic groups in developing management careers.

Chapter 9 looks at service providers and their relationship with customers. It considers the problems of controlling service staff (e.g.

how you "manage" a smile) so that they please customers. It considers the ways in which serving customers is a form of theatre with the service provider giving a performance which includes conveying the correct emotional response. This leads to a discussion of the downside of service work: dealing with stress and harassment from customers.

Chapter 10 looks at the relationship between hospitality organizations within the wider environment. It examines the population ecology perspective on organizations which uses the Darwinian notions of the survival of the fittest. It explores the reasons why organizations may need to collaborate with each other and why they sometimes find themselves in conflict with wider community values. It discusses the negative impacts that organizations can have on their environment and also the ways in which they can be socially responsible.

Finally the short concluding chapter looks at the future of hospitality organizations and at the study of organizational behaviour in hotels and restaurants, picking up on themes from the previous chapters.

Writing style

The main text in each chapter will take you through the principal issues and the content of the key theories that you need to be familiar with. But the text is interspersed with boxed examples which have been chosen to illuminate the key issues, to show how they relate to real hospitality work examples and to stimulate you to think more deeply about the subject matter. The main points are summarized at the end of each chapter. Here you will also find a series of activities and questions that have been designed to deepen your understanding of the issues and suggestions for further reading.

Without writing an encyclopaedia, it would be impossible to do justice to all the theories and ideas that could, rightly, be included in a textbook on organizational behaviour in hotels and restaurants. This book is a selection of theories and ideas and inevitably it is, to some extent, a personal selection. I take the view that the study of organizational behaviour is more about developing one's skills in reading organizations than about memorizing yet another theory of leadership or motivation. (This argument is developed further in Chapter 2.) If you are already familiar with this area of study and I have omitted your favourite theory I apologize but I hope you will find something else in the book which will challenge, interest or even infuriate you. If you are new to the subject area I hope the book will encourage further exploration. This is only a starting point.

2 Ways of seeing organizations

Introduction

Organizations can be confusing and frustrating places to work, as the cases in Box 2.1 demonstrate. Why is a job in one organization a delight, whilst the same job in another organization is a misery? Why can't I get my managers to implement my excellent ideas? Why do my staff dislike me even though I've really tried to do the best for them? Why don't they do what I tell them to even though I have formal authority over them? Why don't my colleagues support me when all I want is to do a good job? How do I design a management structure which ensures that everyone is heading in the same direction and acting consistently without being accused of being a control freak who never allows the team to use their initiative and develop their own ideas? Should I take a stand against colleagues whose behaviour is wrong and unethical, or should I compromise my principles and try to achieve my goals in a more subtle way?

This chapter will look at the ways in which the study of organizational behaviour can help us to understand how organizations work, and improve our ability to manage the difficult dilemmas which we inevitably face.

Box 2.1   Working in organizations: some case examples

Case 1

When Lamin returned to his home in West Africa after studying Hospitality Management for four years in England, he was proud to be the first local to be appointed as assistant manager at the Sunny Bay hotel.

The general manager was a European expatriate. Lamin was keen to improve standards in the hotel and to give the local staff opportunities to develop their skills and knowledge. He set up a small training room in the hotel and started running short courses on food and wine. He was adamant that everything should be done properly so when a post in the kitchen became vacant he ignored all the pleas from the staff who wanted him to consider their brother or their cousin. Lamin insisted on a fair and objective selection procedure.

During Ramadan, virtually all the staff were fasting during the daylight hours; only those few staff who were Christians were exempt. Although Lamin had been brought up a Muslim, he decided not to join the fast himself. He would not have the energy to complete his work properly, he reasoned, and of course his English wife and his general manager weren't fasting. However, he did ensure that the hotel restaurant opened a little later than normal in the evening so that staff had time to eat before the evening shift. A notice was posted on the restaurant door to this effect.

Lamin sensed that he was not well liked by some of the staff but, if you are a manager, you are bound to be a little unpopular. However, when the receptionists deliberately failed to inform him about the arrival of a visitor although he had expressly told them where to find him and that it was important he was contacted immediately the visitor arrived, he began to suspect that his problems were more serious.

Case 2

Marie was delighted to be appointed commis chef in a very prestigious and traditional kitchen. But it was an all-male operation. "We had a woman once" one of her new colleagues told her. "She wasn't any good. Chef doesn't really believe in employing women in the kitchen but Human Resources has told him he has to operate an equal opportunities policy so he didn't have any choice with you. I'm not prejudiced myself of course."

It was a very masculine environment. All the talk seemed to be about sport; a topic Marie knew nothing about. There were pin-ups of women on the office wall; some new ones were added for Marie's benefit. She was never invited to any of the social gatherings outside work. And she was aware that she was being tested the whole time, given particularly demanding tasks and watched in case she made a mistake.

Marie was determined to make a success of the job. She felt as if she would be letting down all her fellow working women if she failed. But she was increasingly miserable and anxious and that was affecting her job performance.

Case 3

Eileen was an area manager for a chain of branded pizza restaurants. She went to visit Phil, a bright young unit manager. "I've got some really good ideas for doing some local promotions" Phil told her, "connected with some special Pizza toppings. Look, I've worked out all the details. Give me the go-ahead and I can try it out next week. The staff are really enthusiastic. We thought we might adapt the uniforms in line with the theme as well."

"Hold on" said Eileen, "This is a branded restaurant. You know that all decisions about menu items and promotional activities are made by Head Office. It may be a great idea and I'm happy to take it back to the marketing department but I can't give you approval to go ahead, I don't have the authority. And you certainly can't change the uniforms. The whole point of a brand is that all the units are the same. The customer knows exactly what to expect."

"It's so frustrating" said Phil. "I'm close to my customers. I know what they want much more than anyone at Head Office. What do you want me to do? I'm supposed to be a manager but all I'm allowed to do is check that things are done according to Head Office procedures. Even if I get promoted to your level I still won't be able to change things because it is very plain that you don't have any authority either."

Reading organizations

Effective managers and professionals in all walks of life, whether they be business executives, public administrators, organizational consultants, politicians, or trade unionists, have to be skilled in the art of "reading" the situations that they are attempting to manage.

This skill usually develops as an intuitive process, learned through experience and natural ability. . . . For this reason it is often believed that effective managers are born rather than made, and have a kind of magical power to transform the situations that they encounter.

If we take a closer look at the processes used, however, we find that this kind of mystique and power is often based on an ability to develop deep appreciations of the situations being addressed.

(Morgan 1986, p. 11)

As the quotation above explains, everyone who works in an organization has to develop some skill in "reading" that organization. We need to try to work out how people will react to our actions. This is certainly true for managers who need to know how best to improve things and to get things done. But it is equally true for more junior staff who also need to figure out how things work within the organization that employs them and how to make things work for their benefit. ("Do I really need to get in on time in the morning?" "What happens if I take a little longer than allowed for my lunch break?")

"Reading" an organization is not quite the same as "reading" a balance sheet. A distinction may be made between "hard" skills (those technical skills that we require in order to do our jobs) that are about logic and finding a clearly defined right answer, and "soft" skills, which are about our understanding of and empathy towards people and human situations. So learning to read a balance sheet, or solve a statistical problem, or work a particular software package on a computer are all "hard" skills. But the possession of these "hard" technical skills is not sufficient to make a good manager or even a good employee. Any of you will surely be able to come up with at least one example from your own experience of a person who possessed superb technical skills but was a disaster in a job because he or she lacked an understanding of how to handle human situations and organizational issues. This is an issue frequently explored in fiction. To take one example, the premise of the television series "Star Trek" was that Mr Spock, although he was intellectually superior, would not have been as effective a star ship captain as Kirk because he lacked the crucial understanding of human behaviour.

As Morgan points out in the quotation above, there is a tendency to think that people who are exceptionally good at "reading" organizations have magical qualities; that they are "born" and not made. But we define "reading" organizations as a "soft" *skill* and this implies that it is a learned behaviour. No-one, after all, is born knowing how to motivate a member of their team or how to influence their boss; we learn to do these things. This does not imply that everyone can become equally skilled at managing human beings; any more than saying that football or ballet are learned skills implies that everyone could be a World Cup footballer or prima ballerina. It merely suggests that we can all improve our "soft" skills.

How do we learn how to "read" organizations? We can do this in a number of ways:

- **Through intuition and experience**. As the quotation from Morgan argues, most people learn how to work in and manage organizations through experience. From childhood most of us are introduced to the experience of functioning in organizations: in school, in college, in social clubs, in part-time jobs, even in the family. So by the time we take our first permanent job, we have already learned quite a lot about organizational life and we continue to learn as our careers progress.

- **Through fiction and the media**. Many plays, films, novels and television programmes also deal with these "soft" skills of how to manage people and situations and may provide models about how to cope with certain problems or indeed about how not to approach a situation. Fly-on-the-wall documentaries may also provide interesting insights into organizational life.

- **Through the popular management literature**. If we do not know how to deal with a management problem, we can look for advice to one of the many management gurus. Books like *The One-Minute Manager* (Blanchard and Johnson 1982) and *In Search of Excellence* (Peters and Waterman 1982) all tend to focus on the people management side of business life. I will examine the nature of the advice provided by these popular management texts later in this chapter.

- **Through studying organizational behaviour**. This book is designed to help you improve your skills in "reading" and understanding organizations through the study of organizational behaviour.

What is organizational behaviour?

The study of organizational behaviour is the study of organizational processes using social science methodologies. Although many organizational theorists would claim that organizational behaviour is now a discipline in its own right with its own theories and body of knowledge, it is based in the social science disciplines of psychology, sociology and, to a lesser extent, anthropology and political science.

I made the point earlier that "reading" an organization is not like "reading" a balance sheet. I also stated that most people learn the soft skills of managing people intuitively and instinctively. To what extent can a scientific approach be used to understand human behaviour? Could Mr Spock, or a highly sophisticated computer, learn through the application of the scientific method, to understand, predict and control human behaviour in the same way that he could understand the physical chemistry of the universe or the workings of a highly complex machine? In order to understand something about the nature of the social sciences we need first to understand something about the nature of the physical sciences.

Of paradigms and scientific revolutions

The dictionary definition of science is that it is "knowledge ascertained by observation and experiment, critically tested, systematised and brought under general principles" (*Chambers English Dictionary*). Science progresses through a gradual process of investigating a phenomenon, developing a theory about it, testing that theory, rejecting it if the test does not support it or developing it if the test does support it, gradually moving closer to establishing the objective truth about the phenomenon.

Or does it work like that? A classic book by the social scientist Thomas Kuhn (1970), looking at the history of science, argued that science did not progress in this gradual incremental way. He argued instead that science normally progresses within a set of shared assumptions about how the world is. These basic assumptions are not questioned; and any research that seems to question these assumptions is rejected except during a period of scientific revolution when the old assumptions or paradigm are rejected and a new paradigm takes its place. So pre-Copernicus and Galileo, the assumption was that the Sun rotated around the Earth and all medieval science was based on this assumption. In the nineteenth century, all physics was based on Newtonian principles; then Einstein overturned these basic views about how the universe functions. The switch to a new paradigm is a period of emotional turbulence almost akin to a religious conversion as scientists who have made their careers under the old assumptions do not want to give up the old paradigm without a fight.

The key point here is that normal science operates within set of shared assumptions about the way the world is: a *paradigm*. Scientists working within the same paradigm may disagree in their interpretation of detail but they will not differ in their basic understanding of how to approach a problem. Supposing I have a backache and I visit two doctors to ask their advice. They may give me different advice but that will be a matter of interpretation. They will agree that my body should be viewed as a collection of muscles, organs and bones and that it is to these that they should look for the cause of my backache. But suppose instead I go to a doctor and to a Chinese acupuncturist seeking a cure for my backache. Either, neither or both may be able to help me but they will do so from very different assumptions about how to understand my body. One sees my body as a purely physical system of bones, muscles and organs. The other is interested in the flow of unseen energy, *chi*, around my body. Two doctors can have a useful debate about my treatment, two acupuncturists can have a useful debate but a doctor and an acupuncturist so differ in their fundamental view of the world it is difficult for them to talk to each other in a medical context.

Social science and conflicting paradigms

Kuhn's theory of science presumes that there is only one dominant paradigm at any given time. Paradigms may change but if you take a snapshot of scientists in any given field at any one point in history they will all broadly share the same set of assumptions about how the world operates. However, in social science, it may be argued, it is possible for conflicting paradigms to exist simultaneously. Consulting five organizational behaviour specialists about a problem in a organization may be rather more like consulting a doctor, an acupuncturist, a witch doctor, an osteopath and a herbalist about my back pain rather than like consulting five doctors.

Morgan (1986) claims that different writers on organizations will give different advice about how to manage organizational problems because they use different metaphors to understand what organizations are like. We use a "metaphor" when we explain one element of our experience in terms of another. So when we say that an organization is like a machine, we are not saying that an organization *is* a machine, merely drawing attention to the ways in which it is machine-like. Metaphors always provide a partial understanding; they illuminate some aspects of experience at the expense of others. It is like the old Indian story of the six blind men and an elephant:

The first man feels the tusk, claiming the animal to be like a spear. The second, feeling the elephant's side, proclaims that it is more like a wall. Feeling a leg, the third describes it as a tree; and a fourth, feeling the elephant's trunk, is inclined to think it is like a snake. The fifth, who has seized the elephant's ear, thinks it is remarkably like a fan; and the sixth, grabbing a tail, says it is much more like a rope.

(Morgan 1986, p. 340)

In Box 2.2 I look at the way that this relates to how one would tackle organizational problems by describing how seven different organizational analysts using Morgan's different metaphors for understanding organizations would advise Lamin from Case 1 (Box 2.1)

Box 2.2   Metaphors for understanding organizations

The organization as machine
An organization is a set of interlocking parts, each of which contributes to the whole. It is important to ensure that each part is appropriately connected to each other part and that it is clear what its function is. Thus it is important to ensure that organizational structures are clearly defined and that there are clear job descriptions and lines of authority and responsibility.

Advice to Lamin: You are quite right to introduce more formal and bureaucratic structures such as formal selection and recruitment procedures. Your staff are only trying, sentimentally, to hang on to more primitive and less efficient forms of organization. Keep going, even in the face of opposition.

The organization as a living organism
Organizations are living beings that exist in an environment, that are born, grow, develop, decline and die. The organization's success depends on its capacity to adapt to the environment. The role of management is to help the organization achieve the "best fit" with the environment.

Advice to Lamin: Your instincts, that the hotel needs to change some of its management practices in order to compete, are good. But you have not sufficiently taken into account the needs and wants of your staff. You need to pay more attention to the way you implement change, attempting to bring your staff with you rather than impose change on them.

The organization as a brain
Organizations process information and are learning systems. We can look to the design of the brain for ideas about how to design organizations. The ideal organization is a holographic system where each sub-system

has the capacity to perform every function for itself; an organization made up of autonomous self-organizing groups.

Advice to Lamin: Your commitment to training and development is laudable. However, all your emphasis is on telling your staff what to do and what to learn rather than on encouraging them to take responsibility for their own learning. Involve your staff in decision making, allow them to take on more management responsibilities within the team. Don't do everything for them, allow them to do more for themselves and you will be surprised how resourceful and productive (and supportive of you) they will become.

The organization as a culture
Organizations are social constructions; members share values, norms, rituals and beliefs which direct their behaviour. Effective organizations develop cultures which support the achievement of their goals.

Advice to Lamin: You have run into trouble because you have tried to impose western values and management culture within a West African country where the cultural norms are very different. You have compounded the problem by transgressing the cultural norms yourself by not fasting for Ramadan. You may gradually be able to change the work culture in the hotel but you will have to proceed very carefully and you have not made a good start.

The organization as a political system
Different sets of interests, conflicts and power plays shape organizational life. Organizations, like societies, need to consider how they should best be governed. Managers, indeed all organizational members, need to learn to use their power to best advantage.

Advice to Lamin: Although you have formal authority, in other respects your power base is weak. Your lack of age and experience weakens your authority. In comparison, if they work together, your staff, as you have seen, can be effective in resisting you. You need to work out ways of building up your power if you are to operate effectively in this hotel.

The organization as a psychic prison
People are not fully aware of their true situation and true motives for action. In organizations our behaviour is often determined by our unconscious mind, by repressed desires and preoccupations, although we pretend that we are acting rationally.

Advice to Lamin: Your actions indicate that you are an anally-retentive control freak. Your staff's actions suggest that they too have problems relating to you as a father figure. Find yourself a good analyst.

The organization as instrument of domination
Organizations are potentially exploitative. They use their employees, their host community and the world economy for their own ends. We need to consider organizations from the perspective of exploited groups and not just from the perspective of the bosses.

Advice to Lamin: You are siding with the bosses; with the western-owned multi-national hotel company which has set up in your country for the benefit of the western tourists who are the hotel's main guests. Most of the money that is made goes back to Europe; it does not benefit the local economy. Is it any wonder that your staff dislike you?

Each of the ways of looking at organizations described here give some interesting insights into the way that organizations work but poor Lamin will be quite confused as the advice provided is quite different and in some cases contradictory.

Stop

Which of the above explanations to Lamin do you find most convincing? Are there any explanations that you do not like? Why? Your preferences will say something about how you see organizations and your value system. If you identify with management you may be attracted to thinking of the organization as a machine, or a living organism. If you are stuck in a job you dislike and coping with a difficult boss, the notion of an organization as a psychic prison or an instrument of domination may seem appealing.

To complicate matters further, there is another respect in which social scientists and organizational behaviour specialists, in particular, tend to disagree with each other. They disagree not just about the ways of thinking about organizations but also about ways of collecting information about organizations, about how to conduct research in the social sciences.

Organizational behaviour is not just about thinking up metaphors for understanding organizations. It is based in research; in a systematic process of investigation of organizational phenomena. But how should one conduct this research? Can we investigate human behaviour in organizations in the same way as we investigate atoms or rocks or plants?

It is useful to distinguish between two different approaches towards research in the social sciences; the *positivist* approach and the *phenomenological* approach. To illustrate these two approaches, refer to Box 2.3 which has extracts from two different academic articles on tipping.

Box 2.3   Research on tipping: alternative approaches

The results of these studies indicate that tipping is positively related to consumers' service evaluations, but that this relationship is weak. Evaluations of the service encounter accounted for only 1–6% of the variance in bill-adjusted tips in these studies. The positive relationship between tipping and service . . . supports the belief that tipping is motivated by a desire to equitably compensate or reward servers. . . . Previous studies may have failed to find significant effects because they did not have enough statistical power to reliably assess such a small effect. The weakness of tipping's relationship to service evaluations also raises serious doubts about the efficacy of tips as incentives.

(Lynn and Graves 1996, p. 10)

Intersender conflicts between organization and client become even more problematic in cases where the client has direct or indirect means of control over the service giver. One of the commonest means of control of subordinate service role occupants is the tip. In roles where it is normal to receive a tip and where the tip constitutes a major part of the service giver's earnings like waiters, taxi drivers and hairdressers, the subordinate service role occupant has to comply with the conflicting demands of two bosses, both of whom can directly reward him or withold their rewards. . . . We can hypothesize that intersender conflict in subordinate service roles will be directly related to the extent that the client has control over rewarding and sanctioning of the role occupants' behaviour.

(Shamir 1980, p. 749)

The positivist approach to research assumes that doing research in the social sciences is like doing research in the natural sciences. The first example in Box 2.3 is an example of research conducted within the positivist tradition. The researchers developed a set of hypotheses about tipping behaviour: for example, that the larger the size of the bill the bigger the tip would be, that customers from ethnic minorities would leaver smaller tips than white customers, that customers would tip more in proportion to their satisfaction with the service. The researchers then designed two studies to try to test these hypotheses.

In the first study they asked guests in a restaurant to answer questions about the value of their meal, their rating of the service provided and the amount of the tip they left. In the second study they asked a waitress to keep a record of variables such as the gender pattern of the guests at a table, whether she thought that they appreciated the service, the bill and the tip. The results were analysed using statistical techniques and finally the researchers drew conclusions from their results such as those given in the boxed example. The positivist tradition is about measuring behaviour as carefully and objectively as possible; the presence of statistical analysis in the paper generally indicates that it is research conducted in this tradition.

The second example is based in the phenomenological tradition of social science research. Here the emphasis is not so much on measuring behaviour as on trying to understand what behaviour means. Again the researcher based his conclusions on empirical research, i.e. he did go out and collect some data. In this case he asked service givers and clients to tell him their stories about "good" and "bad" examples of service (in technical terms the technique is called the "critical incident method"). But nowhere in the paper does he attempt to count the number of incidents of one type and the number of incidents of another type. Instead he uses the incidents to help him understand how service givers relate to clients. The incidents help him to develop an insight about tipping: that tipping means that the service giver is torn between two bosses. In the positivist tradition, the researcher starts with the hypothesis and then finds a way of testing it. In the phenomenological tradition the researcher starts with some data and then builds a model or hypothesis from it.

Looking at elephants

At this point if you are feeling confused this is not surprising. I have attempted to summarize, very briefly, some basic philosophical debates about the nature of organizational behaviour which it can take years of study to fully understand. The key point to remember is that not all organizational behaviour specialists agree with each other about how to understand organizations, how to do research in organizations and how to solve organizational problems. Does this mean that organizational behaviour is useless? If academics can't even agree with each other what is the point of studying the subject after all?

Let us return to the story of the blind men and the elephant. This story assumes that there is a sighted person looking on who can see that an elephant is, in some respects, like a wall or a tree or a spear but that it is much more than that; he or she can capture much more of the "elephantness" of the elephant. Will organizational behaviour specialists in time gain their sight; become less like the blind men struggling towards partial and contradictory understandings of an organization and more like the sighted person able to capture more of the essence of the creature?

Some writers would argue that organizational behaviour is indeed progressing towards a more sophisticated understanding of how organizations work; that, as Kuhn suggests in relation to the natural sciences, older paradigms have been abandoned and new paradigms adopted. One of the main American textbooks on organizational behaviour (Vecchio 1995) describes the development of the subject area in these terms. It is true that in attempting to emphasize that there is no "one best way" of reading organizations I have understated the degree of consensus and common ground that exists between many organizational behaviour specialists. We no longer tend to think of organizations as machines but as organisms, brains, cultures and political systems. It is possible to integrate many of the ideas from these approaches: to accept that organizations have to interact with their environment, have to process and use knowledge, have norms and rules of behaviour and that people jockey for power and position within them. All of these ways of thinking about organizations will be represented in this book and they can fit fairly happily alongside each other.

But another opinion is eloquently expressed by Morgan (1986) who argues that we will never be able to grasp the full complexity of organizations:

> . . . we do not really know what organizations are, in the sense of having a single authoritative position from which they can be viewed. Whilst many writers on organizations attempt to offer such a position . . . the reality is that to an extent we are *all* blind men and women groping to understand the nature of the beast. Whilst we may be able to share our different experiences and even come to some consensus, we will never achieve the degree of certainty that is implicitly communicated in the Indian tale by the idea that it is they who are blind and we who have sight. (p. 341)

What organizational behaviour specialists have in common is that they attempt to use serious research using social science methodologies to understand organizational processes; they recognize that organizations are complex and difficult to understand and they do not pretend that there are easy or even right answers to organizational problems. In these respects the academic study of organizations is very different from popular management writing.

Management gurus

> Popular science is often perhaps associated with the simplified presentation of the findings of scientific research. But the popular literature of management has more in common with popular fiction than it has with serious management science. Popular management literature no more intends to popularize academic management theories than Jackie Collins aims to present Guy de Maupassant's moral tales in a simplified way in her novels about sinful women in Hollywood. Management books are written to sell, not to support the production of scientific knowledge.
>
> (Bjorkegren 1996, p. 163)

Popular management writing is big business. Books like *In Search of Excellence* and *The One-Minute Manager* have sold millions of copies around the world. It appears that many managers and management students turn to popular management texts for advice about "reading" organizations. Yet there is an uneasy relationship between popular management writers and academics studying organizational behaviour. One may think, as the quotation above suggests, that it is the role of management gurus to simplify academic writing on organizations for the benefit of the general public. This is not necessarily the case.

In order for a popular management book to become really successful the author has to suggest that there are simple, effective and universally applicable solutions to organizational problems and solutions that the book will pass on (Thomas 1989). In this sense, a popular management book is like a popular novel: there has to be a happy ending. But, as I have shown, most academics in the field of organizational behaviour would deny that it is easy to teach someone to manage an organization better or indeed that there is one best way to manage an organization. They, therefore, tend to regard popular management texts as fraudulent; as books that one would be better off not reading.

There are management gurus and management gurus. The works of writers like Charles Handy and Rosabeth Moss Kanter, academics who have achieved "guru" status, are fascinating and are quoted several times in this book. As a student, it is important to be aware that popular management literature is not the same as academic management literature. Popular management writers are in the business of selling books and this means selling simple solutions: the type of solutions that many academics do not believe can work. And although many popular management books quote academic research in an attempt to give credibility to their work, they do not have to treat that research as rigorously as an academic writer would.

Learning about organizational behaviour

At this stage, some readers may be thinking "how interesting, I never knew that hospitality management could be so philosophical". However, others are no doubt thinking to themselves "Elephants, Galileo, Jackie Collins: what has all this to do with running a hotel?" People learn and like to learn in different ways; in particular, we differ in the extent to which we are interested in abstract concepts and ideas.

According to David Kolb (Kolb *et al.* 1979), the learning process can be conceived of as a four-stage cycle. This cycle can be joined at any point. For illustration, I will start the cycle with:

- **Concrete experience:** something happens that has an impact and causes a person to take notice. Returning to the case of Lamin (Box 2.1), a "concrete experience" is that his staff fail to let him know that a guest has arrived despite them being asked to tell him immediately. This experience leads the person to:

- **Observation and reflection:** the person reviews the episode, what led up to it, how he or she dealt with it, what it all meant. Lamin will reflect on his relationship with his staff and may recall other incidents that suggest that all is not as it should be. This leads to:

- **Formulation of abstract theories and concepts:** the person develops a theory or idea to explain what happened. So Lamin needs to come up with a theory to explain why his staff dislike him. There is a variety of theories and ideas that he can come up with, as has been shown in Box 2.2. The final stage is:

- **Active experimentation:** the person needs to test out the theory in practice. So if Lamin has decided that his staff dislike him because he has not consulted them enough about the changes he is implementing in the hotel he may decide to encourage them to share their ideas and concerns with him at a next training session. This action will provide another "concrete experience" leading to another recurrence of the learning cycle.

There are several important lessons about the learning process that can be gained from Kolb's learning cycle:

- Learning is not something separate from life and something which occurs only at school, college and university. Everyone is learning from experience all the time.

- The process of learning is like the process of doing science. "Experience", "reflection", "theory building" and "experimentation" is equally a description of the four stages in the scientific process.

- Being practical and being theoretical are not opposing states. Even people who do not think of themselves as being great conceptual thinkers use theories all the time in order to guide how they act. Suppose a waiter has to deal with a difficult and angry customer. He may tell himself "this person is not angry with me. He must have had a hard day and he wants to take it out on somebody." This is the waiter's theory about why the customer is angry and it guides how he feels and the way he acts towards the customer. Theories are not necessarily grand and sophisticated. We may not even be conscious of what our theories are. But everyone needs theories in order to decide what to do next. As the psychologist Kurt Lewin said "There is nothing so practical as a good theory".

To learn effectively means going through all the stages in the learning cycle. A person will not learn from experience if he or she does not reflect on that experience and try to formulate ideas from it. On the other hand, abstract theories and ideas are no use if they are not translated into practical actions. However, most people are more comfortable with some parts of the cycle than others (Kolb *et al.* 1979; see also Honey and Mumford 1992).

- **Activists** like to learn through concrete experience. They tend to be empathetic and people-oriented and like to respond to specific examples. If you like to learn intuitively through knowing what it *feels* like to handle a particular situation, for example by acting out the situation in a role-play exercise, you are probably an activist.

- **Reflectors** like to learn through reflective observation. They tend to be introverts who shy away from active learning methods; the people who want to *watch* other people role-playing a situation or solving a group problem rather than be part of the group itself. If you like learning through listening to lectures, reading books or watching others, you are probably a reflector.

- **Theorists** are excited by abstract conceptualization. If you like logic, ideas and theories; if you were fascinated by the earlier discussion on the history of science and positivist and pheno-menological approaches, you are probably a theorist.

- **Pragmatists** like to learn through active experimentation. They want to know how they can use and apply their learning in prac-tice. Pragmatists like to learn through *doing* (they are usually extroverts); through project work and practical assignments. If your main concern is what practical use you can make of your learning, you are probably a pragmatist.

There are self-assessment questionnaires that you can use to analyse your own learning style (see Kolb *et al.* 1979 and Honey and Mumford 1992) but you will probably recognize yourself in these descriptions. You may recognize yourself in more than one description as you may be strong at more than one stage in the learning cycle.

Many prospective and current hospitality managers have a "prag-matist" learning style. However, the study of organizational behaviour requires skills as "reflectors", "theorists" and indeed as "activists". As Kolb *et al.* (1979) point out, when managers (or prospective managers) meet academics both groups can be frustrated:

SELKIRK COLLEGE LIBRARY
TENTH STREET CAMPUS

Managers who "act before they think – if they ever think" meet the scientists who "think before they act – if they ever act". Research on learning styles has shown that managers as a whole are distinguished by very strong active experimentation skills and are very weak on abstract observation skills. Business school faculty members usually have the reverse profile.   (p. 49)

We can all benefit both from building on our own natural learning style and by extending our repertory of methods of learning and recognizing the value of other ways of learning. At the end of each chapter in this book I have included a series of exercises based around each stage in the learning cycle. Make use of these to help you understand the points that are being made. You may wish to start with those exercises that fit your own learning style: so, for example, if you are a natural pragmatist you might like to start with the "in practice" exercises. However, do not avoid the exercises that are contrary to your natural style. So if you are a natural pragmatist but not a natural reflector ensure you also do some of the "reflection" exercises.

Because many students are confused about how to study organizational behaviour the next section contains some detailed advice about what to read and how to read to support your studies of this subject. For some students much of what follows will be obvious and familiar; but even advanced students sometimes need to be reminded about basic study skills.

Tips for studying organizational behaviour

Box 2.4   Watch what you read

A student was set an assignment to write about the role of a manager in the hospitality industry. It was the evening before the assignment was due in and she was desperate as she hadn't written anything yet and all the recommended books had already been taken out of the library. She searched through the shelves and, hidden at the bottom, she discovered a dusty volume entitled *Hotel Administration*. Saved. She had a source for her essay. Diligently she copied down the main points including "the role of the assistant manager in the hotel is to stoke up the boiler every morning". The book had been written in 1935.

What do you read?

To study organizational behaviour successfully you need to read. But what do you read? As Box 2.4 demonstrates, all books are not equally appropriate.

There are three main types of material that you will encounter:

1. Textbooks
2. Professional journals/trade press
3. Academic books and journals.

Each of these have their uses and limitations. I will take each in turn: looking at what they are, their advantages, their limitations and recommending how you should make use of them in your studies.

Textbooks

What they are: Books, like this one, which aim to support the studies of students following a programme of study.

Advantages: If you are a student, a textbook has the advantage that it is aimed specifically at you. A textbook aims to give a general introduction to a subject area, explaining what the main theories and ideas are. It is useful for providing you with a mental map of a subject area and to supplement and support the input from your lecturer.

Limitations: Because textbooks attempt to provide an introduction to a subject area they will not be sufficient if you need to go into more depth. All textbooks, as all books and articles, reflect the strengths, weaknesses and prejudices of their authors. These strengths, weaknesses and prejudices may not be the same as those of the person who is teaching you organizational behaviour.

Tips for choosing and using textbooks: A textbook is the best place to start if you are new to the subject area. When choosing a textbook, be aware of the level at which it is pitched: a book aimed at 16-year-old college students will not be appropriate if you are studying at Masters level. Be aware of the age of the book. In the field of organizational behaviour the fundamental theories change relatively slowly so a previous edition of a textbook may still be useful to you. However you should be wary of books that are more than ten years old. (Look for the date of publication on the left-hand page after the title page. A new edition means that the book has been updated and revised; so a three-year-old edition of a book originally published in 1986 is acceptable.) If you are following a formal programme of study take your lecturer's advice about choice of textbook and if in doubt ask him or her if a certain book is appropriate.

General textbooks on organizational behaviour can usefully supplement the material in this book. My recommendations about general organizational behaviour textbooks are provided at the end of this chapter.

Trade press and professional journals

What they are: Magazines and journals which are published on a weekly, monthly or quarterly basis aimed at people working in a particular industry or profession. They are designed to keep practitioners up to date about current developments and concerns that are relevant to them and provide a forum for debate and exchange of opinion. The types of journals that may be relevant to this subject area are those aimed at hospitality managers – *Caterer* (in the UK), *Hotels* – as well as those aimed at general managers/business people – the *Economist, Management Today, Fortune*.

Advantages: You may find some useful case study examples and supporting material in the trade press. The material you find will be current and articles tend to be short and easy to read (as they are generally written by professional journalists).

Limitations: Many of the points that were made above in relation to management gurus and the popular management literature are also relevant in relation to the trade press and professional journals. Articles do not have to be researched and justified as rigorously as the articles in academic journals. Some may be simplistic and opinionated.

Tips for using the trade press and professional journals: Use these journals to find examples of current practice and topical issues but look at any articles critically; in particular be aware of whether an article is just based on someone's opinion.

Academic journals and books

What they are: These are books written primarily for academics and there are also a number of journals that are written by academics for other academics and serious students in a particular area. There are journals published across all fields of management. The most relevant to this book are the specialist organizational behaviour journals, including journals like *Organization Studies* and *Organization*, and the specialist hospitality management journals, including *International Journal of Hospitality Management, International Journal of Contemporary Hospitality Management, Cornell HRA Quarterly* and *Hospitality and Tourism Research Journal*. Papers are only accepted for academic journals through a process of peer review, whereby academics judge the quality of the papers submitted. Some journals require a more "academic" approach than others. In the hospitality field, *International Journal of Contemporary Hospitality Management* and *Cornell HRA Quarterly* tend to carry shorter, more practical articles making them more accessible to practitioners as well as academics.

Academic journals are only available in university and college libraries. As the number of titles has proliferated and journal subscriptions are expensive, most libraries are unable to stock every single journal relevant to a subject. However, any academic library will be able to obtain a copy of a published article even in a journal it does not stock, provided you have the full reference. This does take time and can cost money.

Advantages: If you want to look in depth at any topic you have to refer to academic articles. This is where you will find the latest research on a subject and the fullest discussion of theoretical ideas. Because of the way in which articles are scrutinized before they are published you can be confident that any papers you read in academic journals are reasonably sound, i.e. that the ideas in them are well argued and the research has been conducted competently (this does not mean you have to agree with everything in the article).

Limitations: As academic journals are written for academics the prose style used can make them difficult for students to understand. (Box 2.3 includes extracts from academic articles and illustrates how they tend to be written.) There are some tips in the next section on ways of coping with turgid prose. Also, because it takes on average eighteen months to two years from the time when a paper is submitted to a journal until it is published and the research on which the paper is based may have been conducted a year or two before the paper is submitted, academic articles are never absolutely current. Nowadays you may find some more current academic papers available on websites.

Tips for using academic journals: First year undergraduate students may be able to get by on textbooks alone but students in later years of undergraduate courses and Masters students have to learn to find their way around the journals. Find out what titles that are relevant to your studies are stocked by your library. If you are daunted by the most academic journals, start by reading papers in the more accessible journals.

How to read: coping with turgid text

Academic writing in the field of social science can be difficult to read. There are both rational and cynical explanations for this. The rational explanation is that academics are writing about complex ideas to an audience of other academics. They need to define their terms in very precise ways; this inevitably involves using jargon and they need to demonstrate how everything they argue is well backed up with evidence. This means that papers are packed with references to other people's work and with descriptions of complex statistical techniques and so on. It is impossible to write more simply without distorting the arguments. The cynical explanation is that academic careers depend on publications in academic journals and one increases one's chance of being published if one writes in an "academic" style, i.e. make what one writes as obtuse and difficult as possible. There is probably some truth in both of those explanations.

Students have to learn to cope with academic writing as it is. So the following tips may be helpful in approaching your reading.

- Use textbooks and lecture notes to give you an overview of an area so you understand what are the most important ideas and theories. You can also use these to find out what supplementary reading you should undertake. (There is advice about further reading at the end of each chapter of this book.)

- Try and find out as much as you can about what you are reading. As a minimum you should know whether an article is in a professional journal or an academic journal and therefore how you should use it. Look to see when the article was written. The nationality of the author may also be relevant.

- Try and recognize the assumptions underlying what the author is arguing even if these are not made explicit. If the paper is reporting research results, was the research positivist or phenomenological in its approach? Can you relate the image of an organization that the author is using to one of Morgan's types? Can you recognize whether the paper is written from a managerialist perspective, i.e. the objective of the author is to help managers manage better; from a neutral perspective, i.e. the author is trying to explain an aspect of organizational behaviour; or from the subordinate's perspective, i.e. the author is trying to show how operative level staff are exploited by their managers and the organizational system (in Morgan's terms "the organization as an instrument of domination"). All of these perspectives may be valid but it is important to be able to distinguish between them. Look critically for the evidence that the authors are using to back up their arguments.

- Use the abstract and the summary or conclusions at the end of an article to help you grasp the main points. If you are having difficulty understanding certain passages it is better to speed read the paper two or three times rather than to struggle through it slowly. With books, use the contents pages, preface, introduction and conclusions to help you decide which sections to read. An academic book is not like a detective novel; it does not spoil your enjoyment if you look at the last page first and the book does not necessarily have to be read from cover to cover.

- Experiment with diagrams and mind-maps (Buzan 1995) as ways of taking notes showing the main issues and ideas and how they are connected.

Using your reading

The purpose of organizational behaviour is to develop your ability to "read" organizations and ultimately to improve your ability to handle organizational issues. This means challenging the way you currently "read" organizations, looking at alternative "readings" of organizational problems and deciding, on the basis of the evidence, which ones are helpful to you. Merely rote learning a collection of theories and research findings will not meet this purpose. The learning comes through thinking about the models and theories, through relating them to your own experience, through experimenting and testing things out. The activities at the end of each chapter are designed to help you think about and engage with the material in the text.

Summary

- Organizational behaviour is the systematic study of organizational processes using social science approaches and methodologies.

- Everyone who works in an organization needs to become skilled in "reading" the situations that they have to manage. "Reading" organizations is a skill; some people do it better than others but everyone can improve.

- We can learn to "read" organizations in a number of ways: naturally through our experience in organizations; learning from fictional and documentary accounts of organizational life; picking up tips from popular management gurus; and through the study of organizational behaviour.

- Organizational specialists differ in their basic assumptions about organizations. Morgan (1986) identified a number of different "images" of organization that are used by different organizational theorists. These different "images" can lead to very different advice being given about how to cope with situations in organizations.

- Organization theorists also differ in their approaches to doing research in organizations. "Positivists" use quantitative studies using research methods modelled on those in the natural sciences. "Phenomenologists" are interested in the meanings behind actions and tend to use qualitative studies.

- All organizational theorists are seriously attempting to study organizations. They recognise that organizations are complex and that there are often no easy answers to organizational issues. In this respect they differ from popular management theorists who tend to simplify complex situations and suggest that there can be a "happy ending" if their advice is followed.

- When learning about organizational behaviour we need to take our own learning style into account. According to Kolb, (Kolb *et al.* 1995) learning follows a four-stage process of experience, reflection, theorizing and experimentation. Some people prefer an *activist* approach to learning; they like to learn by doing. Others prefer a *reflector* style; they like to learn by reflecting on past experiences. Some people are natural *theorists*; they are excited by abstract concepts and models. Finally, others prefer a *pragmatist* style; learning by solving practical problems. We need both to build on our learning strengths but also to recognize the value of other styles. So, for example, if you are a natural pragmatist you need to learn that theories can also be useful. If you are natural theorist you need to learn that it is also important to consider how to take action based on your theory. There is nothing as practical as a good theory!

- To study organizational behaviour successfully involves developing good reading skills; knowing what to read and being aware of the authors' assumptions and biases. It involves trying to relate your reading to your own organizational experiences.

The next stage

Experience

The key task in relation to this chapter is to experience different ways of learning about organizations. Even if you have never worked you will have some experience of organizational life, through college and school. But if you work, or have ever worked, in whatever capacity, in a hospitality organization, you will be able to make use of that experience. Watch the staff at work when you are next a customer in a hotel or restaurant; even as customers it is possible to put together a picture of the way in which an organization operates, especially if everything is not working as it should (and it is a way of salvaging something positive from a bad meal or bad stay).

Look for films, documentaries, television plays, novels and reminiscences about the hospitality industry.

There are no hospitality management gurus but look at the work of one of the management gurus. For example, look for something by Tom Peters or a book like *The One-Minute Manager*.

Finally, read at least one article in a professional hospitality journal and one article in an academic hospitality journal. Ideally find articles on the same subject.

Reflection

From your own experience of work in a hospitality organization, write your own case study describing a difficult organizational problem – similar to the case studies at the beginning of the chapter. (If you have never worked in a hospitality organization base your case on a different organization; school or college is fine). Also generate case studies from any films, television programmes, fictional books or biographies that you have found.

Draw a picture of any organization that you are familiar with in any way that portrays to you what it is like. See this as an exercise in creativity so there are no rules. This is best done on a large sheet of paper and lack of artistic ability does not matter. Alternatively take a stack of magazines, tear out any images that are relevant and do a collage of the organization.

Refer back to Box 2.2, "Metaphors for understanding organizations". Which of these metaphors do you instinctively prefer? Which of the sets of advice to Lamin do you support? Which of the metaphors do you instinctively dislike – where you think the advice given to Lamin is wrong? This will help reveal your own theories of organization.

Theorizing

Refer to the "Metaphors for understanding organizations" (Box 2.2). What advice would be offered to Marie (Case 2 Box 2.1) and to Eileen (Case 3 Box 2.1) by organizational theorists using these different metaphors? If you have developed your own case, relate the different metaphors to that as well.

Look at your picture of an organization. What metaphor of organization underlies that? For example, if you have drawn a formal organization chart you are seeing the organization as a machine; if you have drawn a battle between warring factions you are seeing the organization as a political system. Think about any other source material you have acquired – films, books, television programmes etc. What images of organization are portrayed in each of these? Think about any academic articles you have read: what assumptions about organizations do these employ?

In practice

What advice would you give to Lamin, Marie and Eileen and to the protagonists in the case studies that you have written? Why? Does this advice match any one of the metaphors of organization?

What practical benefits do you hope to gain from studying organizational behaviour?

Further reading

There are many good and comprehensive textbooks on organizational behaviour that cover most of the topics in this book and all include an introduction to the subject area. These include Robbins (1998), Vecchio (1995), Ivancevich and Matteson (1993), Buchanan and Huczynski (1997). These are all general textbooks: they are not specifically related to the hospitality industry. For a slightly different approach with more emphasis on what it feels like to work in an organization try Sims *et al.* (1993).

Experiencing Organizations (Fineman and Gabriel 1996) is a book of stories by undergraduate placement students illuminating various aspects of organizational life. None of the stories relate to the hospitality industry but anyone relatively new to organizational life, and even old hands, will find much that they can identify with.

Morgan (1986) is very readable and well worth a look. Although I have referred to the first edition in this chapter, there is a second edition of this book (Morgan 1997). Pugh and Hickson's book *Writers on Organizations* (1996) summarizes the way in which key thinkers on organizations have attempted to understand organizations – this includes a chapter on the management gurus, Peters and Waterman.

Easterby-Smith *et al.* (1991) provide a good introduction to the different philosophies of doing research in organizations. Pedler *et al.* (1996) (Activities 44 to 46), Kolb *et al.* (1995) and Honey and Mumford (1992) provide further insights into the ways in which you can learn from your experience in organizations. If you have doubts about your study skills, try Northedge (1990) and Buzan (1995).

References to further reading

Buchanan, D. and Huczynski, A. (1997) *Organizational Behaviour: an Introductory Text* (Third edition), Hemel Hempstead: Prentice Hall.

Buzan, T. (1995) *Use Your Head* (Revised edition), London: BBC Books.

Easterby-Smith, M., Thorpe, R. and Lowe, A. (1991) *Management Research*, London: Sage.

Fineman, S. and Gabriel, Y. (1996) *Experiencing Organizations*, London: Sage.

Honey, P. and Mumford, A. (1992) *The Manual of Learning Styles* (Third edition), Peter Honey: Maidenhead.

Ivancevich, J. and Matteson, M. (1993) *Organizational Behavior and Management* (Third edition), Homewood Ill.: Irwin.

Kolb, D., Osland, J. and Rubin, I. (1995) *Organizational Psychology: an Experiential Approach* (Sixth edition), Englewood Cliffs, New Jersey: Prentice Hall.

Morgan, G. (1997) *Images of Organization* (Second edition), California and London: Sage.

Northedge, A. (1990) *The Good Study Guide*, Milton Keynes: Open University.

Pedler, M., Burgoyne, J. and Boydell, T. (1996) *A Manager's Guide to Self-Development* (Third edition), London: McGraw Hill.

Pugh, D. and Hickson, D. (1996) *Writers on Organizations* (Fifth edition), London: Penguin.

Robbins, S. (1998) *Organizational Behaviour* (Eighth edition), New Jersey: Prentice Hall.

Sims, D., Fineman, S. and Gabriel, Y. (1993) *Organizing and Organizations: an Introduction*, London: Sage.

Vecchio, R. (1991) *Organizational Behaviour* (Second edition), Orlando: Dryden.

Ways of seeing hospitality organizations

3

Introduction

The hospitality industry is a diverse industry which comprises hotels, restaurants, licensed bars, guesthouses, holiday homes/self-catering establishments, catering (in public sector organizations like hospitals, schools and prisons as well as for the private sector): indeed any organization that serves food and/or drinks and/or provides accommodation for people away from home. It is an important industry to the world economy. It was estimated by the World Tourism Organization that 229 million people, or 10% of the global workforce, worked in the hospitality and tourism industry in 1996 and by 2006, the World Travel and Tourism Council estimates that the number of jobs will have increased to 365 million (BHA 1998).

Most organizations in the worldwide hospitality industry are small – family-run guesthouses and restaurants – but the industry also contains some well-known global names such as McDonald's, Holiday Inns, Hilton and Best Western, as well as national or regional companies. Box 3.1 indicates what impact the hospitality industry can have on a national economy by providing some information about the industry in Britain.

> **Box 3.1 Surprising facts about Britain's fastest growing industry**
>
> SIZE: Hospitality is one of the UK's largest industries, with over 260 000 hotels, restaurants and cafes, pubs and clubs, conference venues and other commercial establishments, and an estimated 100 000 catering outlets.

STRUCTURE: The industry comprises a small number of very large hotel and catering groups – some of these operating on a worldwide scale – and a very large number of small independent businesses.

NATIONWIDE: Hospitality is the country's most geographically widespread industry offering employment in every part of the countryside. Hospitality touches everyone, everywhere in Britain.

CAREERS: . . . Employing 10% of the total UK workforce, hospitality gives full-time or flexible employment – and lifelong, skilled careers – to some 2.5m people.

. . . AND FURTHER CAREER OPPORTUNITIES. The industry is currently providing one in five new jobs and the Henley Centre for Forecasting estimates that the industry will generate an additional 400 000 jobs by 2006.

(British Hospitality Association Fact Sheet)

Hotels and restaurants are part of the hospitality industry but the hospitality industry is also part of the wider service sector, so is sometimes linked with industries such as retailing. The hospitality industry (or at least some parts of the hospitality industry) is also sometimes defined as part of a wider leisure industry, linking hotels, restaurants, bars, clubs, tourist attractions, museums, galleries, theatre and sports facilities.

This chapter will look at the specific issues that hotels and restaurants face as organizations, by considering them as:

1   organizations that provide commercially the hospitality hosts have always provided for guests
2   service sector businesses similar to retailing
3   leisure products competing for consumer spending.

It will then consider the workforce in the hospitality industry and the factors that tend to make the hospitality industry a "Cinderella" industry with a poorly paid, transient and generally poorly qualified workforce. Finally, it looks at the factors that tend to increase the status and quality of jobs in the hospitality industry.

Being hospitable

> ### Box 3.2   Ancient rules of hospitality
>
> God forbid that you should go to your ship and turn your backs on my house as though it belonged to some threadbare pauper and there weren't plenty of blankets and rugs in place for host and guests to sleep between in comfort! Indeed, I have good bedding for all; and I swear that the son of my friend Odysseus shall not lie down to sleep on his ship's deck as long as I am alive here or sons survive me here to entertain all visitors that come to my door.
>
> (Nestor to the visiting Telemachus)
>
> The man you see is an unfortunate wanderer who has strayed here and now commands our care, since all strangers and beggars come under the protection of Zeus, and the charity that is a trifle to us can be precious to others. Bestir yourselves, girls, provide our guest with food and drink and bathe him in the river where there's shelter from the wind. (Princess Nausicaa about Odysseus who she finds naked shipwrecked on the shore.)
>
> (Both quotations from the *Odyssey* by Homer, translated Rieu 1946, p. 59)

From the earliest societies, rules and responsibilities have been developed in terms of the ways in which hosts should provide hospitality to guests, as the quotations from the *Odyssey* written in the eighth century BC indicate.

Telfer (1996) defines hospitality as "the giving of food, drink and sometimes accommodation to people who are not regular members of the household". The following categories of guests require hospitality according to Telfer:

- Those who are "in one's circle" and to whom there is a duty of hospitality (as in the first quotation in Box 3.2).
- Those who seem to be in need of hospitality and therefore invoke a "good Samaritan" response (as in the second quotation in Box 3.2).
- Our friends who are provided with hospitality on the basis of the affection which we feel for them.

As the quotations from the *Odyssey* (Box 3.2) indicate, in many cultures it is regarded as the responsibility of noble households to provide hospitality. The provision of hospitality is an exchange designed to enhance the well-being of both the host and the guest. In the case of natural hospitality, such as described in the *Odyssey*, the host benefits through enhanced prestige and respect within the community for having performed a social duty and, at the same time, is able to keep an eye on a stranger who may otherwise be dangerous ". . . one protects the stranger in order to be protected from him" (Mühlmann 1932 quoted in Wood 1994, p. 73). The guest, of course, is fed, has somewhere to sleep, is entertained and, above all, is safe.

What insights can be gained from studying natural processes of hospitality that are relevant to modern commercial hospitality organizations?

- **Hospitality is about providing basic human needs, for food, drink and somewhere to sleep to people who are not regular members of the family.**   Food, drink and somewhere safe to sleep are central to our well-being as human beings; at the most fundamental level we need them for our survival and to entrust strangers to provide these for us is potentially risky. Will the food be safe to eat? Will we be robbed or murdered in our sleep? For hosts too there are potential risks if we welcome strangers literally into our homes. In an extreme example, some of these issues can be seen in the case of providing hospitality services within prisons (see Box 3.3) It is not surprising that there are cultural rules and norms defining the interactions between hosts and guests. Even the old notion that the provision of hospitality allows hosts to watch and control the behaviour of the potentially dangerous guest has its parallels in certain modern hospitality organizations. In hotels in the old communist block, western guests were seen as dangerous imperialists and hotel workers, who were permanently exposed to imperialist influences, had to be careful in their behaviour and manner of interaction with westerners (Kassova 1995): an attitude which hardly predisposed them to provide friendly and helpful service.

Box 3.3   Hospitality in prison

In a remand prison (where inmates are held awaiting trial) in the UK prisoners spent around 23 out of 24 hours locked in their cells. "You have to understand how important food is to us" explained one of the inmates. "Everyone is tense waiting for news of their trials. Apart from the post, meals are the only things that break up our days."

Meals were served from trollies and taken back to the cells to be eaten. Prison officers looked on as the inmates queued almost in silence. The prison catering officer was always conscious that, in such a highly charged atmosphere, a poor meal might trigger a riot.

- **Hosts are rewarded by enhanced prestige in the community if they provide lavish hospitality to guests.** Indeed, as has been seen, it is expected of community leaders that they should entertain guests with some style. Even now prestigious hotels or restaurants are sometimes bought by the rich and famous as symbols of prestige and as a place for them to entertain regardless of whether the operation is profitable as a business. Similarly people of more modest means dream of owning their own small hotel or restaurant as a lifestyle choice, not only as a means of making a living. The vestiges of the old rites and rituals of noble hospitality can still be seen in more traditional hotels and restaurants today. The grand hotels that grew up in the nineteenth and early twentieth centuries modelled themselves on the old aristocratic great houses and adopted the same styles of service (for example French *haute cuisine*).

- **Hospitality is an exchange for the mutual benefit of host and guest.** There are rules and responsibilities for guests as well as for hosts. The guest in a traditional silver-service restaurant is expected to dress formally, know how to understand the menu, how to order wine, how to tip the waiter and can be made to feel very inadequate if he or she does not know what is expected. Traditional hospitality tends to be defined by the host. Hosts, of course, want to please guests but they define what hospitality the guest should receive and there is a sense in which, if the guest is not satisfied, it is he or she who is unworthy to appreciate what is offered, not the host who is at fault. The London restaurateur, Nico Landenis, was notorious for expelling customers from his restaurants who dared to ask for salt to add to their meals on the grounds that he, not they, was the best judge of whether the meal was properly seasoned. If they dared to question his judgement they were not worthy to eat in his restaurant. This type of approach to hospitality is not confined to high class establishments as the example, in Box 3.4, of the American writer, Bill Bryson's encounter with the proprietress of an English seaside guesthouse in the early 1970s indicates.

Box 3.4   1970s Guesthouse hospitality

I well recall the proprietress, a formidable creature in late middle years called Mrs Smegma, who showed me a room, then gave me a tour of the facilities and outlined the many complicated rules for residing there – when breakfast was served, how to turn on the heater for the bath, which hours of the day I would have to vacate the premises and during which brief period a bath was permitted (these seemed, oddly, to coincide), how much notice I should give if I intended to receive a phone call or remain out after 10pm, how to flush the loo and use the loo brush, which materials were permitted in the bathroom wastebasket and which had to be carefully conveyed to the outside dustbin, where and how to wipe my feet at each point of entry, how to operate the three-bar fire in my bedroom and when that would be permitted (essentially during an Ice Age). This was all bewilderingly new to me. Where I came from, you got a room in a motel, spent ten hours making a lavish and possibly irredeemable mess of it and left early the next morning.

(Bryson, B. 1995, *Notes from a Small Island*, p. 15)

According to Telfer (1996), people *have a duty of hospitality to those who are "in one's circle"*. Thus, traditionally, hotels, restaurants and bars have tended to provide hospitality for a particular group of guests and potential guests who could afford a service but who, because of their class, ethnicity or gender are not "in one's circle", are excluded or made to feel uncomfortable. Thus an affluent working class person may feel that a five-star hotel or a traditional high-class restaurant is "not for people like us" (see Wood 1994 for a full discussion of this); a tourist may shy away from a bar obviously for locals, while a local may feel uncomfortable using restaurants and hotels clearly aimed at foreign tourists and business people; a woman may feel unwelcome in a bar where all the other guests are male or an older person in a club where none of the other guests are older than 25. The rules and rituals associated with hospitality in a particular setting, which are known and familiar to the insiders, can be so obscure to outsiders that they cannot access the service. (Try buying a drink in a traditional English pub, a coffee at the counter in a traditional French café or a meal at a Chinese hawker stall if you have not been brought up to it.)

Natural hospitality involves welcoming guests into one's home. But guests are not members of the household and so there need to be some restrictions about where guests are allowed. *All hospitality operations have a front-of-house area where hosts are on their best behaviour for the benefit of the guest and a private back-of-house area where the "household" can behave in their natural way.* As the classic examples drawn from George Orwell's experiences of hotel work in Paris in the 1930s and Goffman's observations of a Scottish guesthouse in the 1950s illustrate (Box 3.5), guests might be shocked if they knew what was happening behind the scenes. (These, of course, are old examples and hygiene regulations mean, it is hoped, that they are more extreme than anything that would be found today.)

Box 3.5   What the guest does not see

. . . some of the standards of hotel service that were shown or implied in the guests' regions were not fully adhered to in the kitchen. In the scullery wing of the kitchen region, mould would sometimes form on a soup yet to be used. Over the kitchen stove, wet socks would be dried on the steaming kettle – a standard practice on the island. Tea, when guests had asked for it to be newly infused, would be brewed in a pot encrusted at the bottom with tea leaves that were weeks old. Fresh herrings would be cleaned by splitting them and then scraping out the innards with newspaper. . . . Rich puddings, too good for kitchen consumption would be sampled aggressively by the fingerful before distribution to the guests.

(Goffman, E. 1959, p. 120)

It was amusing to look round the filthy little scullery and think that only a double door was between us and the dining-room. There sat the customers in all their splendour – spotless tablecloths, bowls of flowers, mirrors and gilt cornices and painted cherubim; and here, just a few feet away, we in our disgusting filth. For it really was disgusting filth. There was no time to sweep the floor till evening, and we slithered about in a compound of soapy water, lettuce-leaves, torn paper and trampled food. A dozen waiters with their coats off, showing their sweaty armpits, sat at the table mixing salads and sticking their thumbs into the cream pots. The room had a dirty mixed smell of food and sweat. Everywhere in the cupboards, behind the piles of crockery, were squalid stores of food that the waiters had stolen. There were only two sinks, and no washing basin, and it was not unusual for a waiter to wash his face in the water in which the clean crockery was rinsing. But the customers saw nothing of this.

(Orwell, G. 1933)

Selling a service

The previous examples have illustrated some of the ways that a knowledge of the conventions and history of natural hospitality can inform our understanding of modern hospitality organizations. But this book is about hotels and restaurants now. It is interesting that hotel and restaurant companies do not always consider themselves to be in the hospitality business. McDonald's, for example, refer to their "stores" not their "restaurants" and, according to the chief executive of the UK division, consider themselves a retailer. Similarly the managing director of a brewery-owned chain of restaurants defined his operation as leisure *retailing* (see Gilbert and Guerrier 1997).

Shops, hotels and restaurants are all service operations. There are two issues that need to be addressed in relation to the way in which hospitality organizations can be understood as service operations: first, the ways in which managing a service poses distinctive organizational problems compared with managing a production process, and second, the ways in which modern thinking about management encourages all organizations, whether service or manufacturing, to be customer-driven rather than product-driven.

What are the distinctive features of a service organization?

Compare the process of controlling the quality of what is delivered to the customer if one's business is manufacturing cars to the same process if one's business is providing hotel rooms. In both cases quality is important but in the case of the car manufacturer all the quality checks can be completed in the factory under the direct control of the managers. In the case of a hotel, clearly the quality of the fittings and fixtures are tangible and can be controlled in advance but the customer's assessment of the quality of the hotel will also be determined by how well these fixtures are cleaned and maintained – it would be no use having a beautifully decorated and furnished hotel room if it were never cleaned – and by intangible features such as the quality of the welcome he or she receives from the hotel staff. This cannot be directly controlled. A receptionist greets a guest out of the direct sight of a supervisor; even if she or he is given instructions about exactly what to say (and such scripting may not be appropriate), the way that he or she says it, with a smile or not, cannot be controlled. (These issues are explored in depth in Chapter 9.) Furthermore, because the quality of a greeting is intangible, it is difficult to assess what a customer expects. Indeed, a greeting which may be seen as charming and friendly by one guest may be regarded as over-familiar and intrusive by another guest. (Obviously, even if one is in the business of selling cars, customers may be influenced by the quality of the service in the showroom and by the after sales service as well as by the quality of the vehicle. There is a product and a service element in many businesses.)

So hospitality companies, like other service companies, have to control both the *tangible* quality of the product that they provide and the *intangible* quality of the service. A further distinctive feature of services is that they need to be delivered where and when customers need them. A car for sale in one country can be manufactured anywhere in the world; and indeed globally there is a trend towards moving manufacturing facilities into countries where labour is cheap and plentiful. But one cannot site a hotel, for the use of visitors to Paris, in India or Indonesia. Generally, services need to be situated near to the customer. This means that as service organizations grow they tend to grow as multi-unit geographically dispersed organizations. A retail operation will have branches around the country or even the world as a restaurant operation, like McDonald's, or a hotel chain, like Hilton, has units around the world.

Services also need to be delivered when customers want them. One cannot persuade someone to eat dinner at three o'clock in the afternoon just because that is convenient for the restaurant. This means that service operations have to cope with peaks and troughs of demand over the year (some seasons may be quieter than others), over the week (a business hotel may be busy Monday to Friday and deserted on a Sunday night) and during the day (a hotel reception will be rushed in the early morning as many guests are checking out and quiet late morning). A car manufacturer may also cope with peaks and troughs of demand but cars can be stockpiled to be sold when the demand is there. Most services are *perishable*: if a hotel room is not sold one night that sale is lost forever. Thus hospitality operations need to be staffed in ways that can accommodate these peaks and troughs and cope with the fact that customers often demand services outside normal working hours so staff need to be found who are prepared to work "unsocial" hours. Again, in these respects, the hospitality organization faces similar problems to the retailer.

Being close to the customer

Service companies need to deliver what the customers want in a context when they are being told that modern customers are increasingly demanding and sophisticated (Du Gay and Salaman 1992); they will no longer put up with the type of restrictions that Bill Bryson experienced in a 1970s English guesthouse (Box 3.4). Modern managers are also told that the key to the success of any enterprise is to be "close to the customer" and to deliver what he or she wants rather than what the service provider thinks that he or she should have. In this sense the modern service operation works in a very different way from the traditional rules of giving hospitality. Even using the word "customer" has different connotations to using the word "guest". Customers have choice and are engaged in a purely financial exchange: they can choose not to buy our service. Guests accept our hospitality: we want to look after them but we as hosts define what is best for them and expect some show of gratitude, as well as payment, in return. Where traditional hospitality may be shrouded in arcane rituals which put off potential guests who are not part of the circle, the modern service organization tries to make it as easy as possible for new customers to use the service as the example in Box 3.6 indicates.

Box 3.6   Managing new members

A UK hotel company that operates casinos discovered that many new members (in the UK you have to be a member in order to use a casino) either never visited a casino or visited once and never returned. Further investigation suggested that this might have something to do with the attitude of staff. The "technical" term for a new member amongst casino staff was a w. . .er. New members did not know how to play the tables when they first visited, were made to feel uncomfortable and never returned. A new scheme was instituted whereby a new member was identified on a first visit, greeted by a hostess who showed them all the facilities and taken to play at a practice table first of all. This is an example of the way in which service organizations need to train new customers to use the service.

Innovation in service organizations

Service organizations, like all organizations, try to offer customers something distinctive to gain competitive advantage. Although it is true that, in all countries, the hospitality industry is composed of a large number of small independent operations and a smaller number of large companies with chains of outlets, the industry is becoming more concentrated, i.e. more dependent on the big chains. A large company can develop a brand: a hotel, restaurant, bar or café concept which is easily recognizable and where the customer knows what to expect: Holiday Inn, Marriott, McDonald's, Hard Rock Cafe, TGI Friday's, Delice de France are some examples of hospitality brands. Major companies often own a family of brands, different types of outlet aimed at different market segments, in much the same way as a car manufacturer will produce different models of car aimed at different market segments. However, it is one problem to ensure that one VW Polo that rolls off an assembly line is identical to the next VW Polo that rolls off the line. It is a rather different problem to ensure that the McDonald's in Bucharest is identical to the McDonald's in Flagstaff Arizona and the McDonald's in the Champs Elysées in Paris. Leaving aside the issue about whether it is desirable that all units are absolutely identical (which is essentially a marketing problem and outside the scope of this book), there are issues about how the company is organized, controlled and its staff motivated if the aim is to provide a consistent image between different units in the company. Refer back to Case 3 in Box 2.1 for an example of the problems that can arise.

Service companies can also compete through the use of new technology. Whilst service companies are typically thought of as being labour-intensive organizations, it has been seen in other sectors how machines can replace human beings. Many people are now accustomed to drawing cash from automatic machines rather than from a bank cashier; a change which has revolutionized work patterns in the retail banking sector. In the same way it may become more acceptable to pay for a hotel room by swiping a card rather than by queuing to make the transaction with a cashier. (This facility is already available in many hotels.) In the budget market, customers are often prepared to substitute their own labour for the labour of service staff if it means that they can buy the service cheaper. Thus people are prepared to serve themselves food and clear plates in fast food restaurants, carry their own bags in budget hotels etc. Indeed there is some evidence that customers, even those not on a budget, sometimes prefer to be provided with "product" rather than "service". Four- and five-star hotels originally resisted providing tea and coffee making facilities in rooms on the grounds that guests had 24 hour room service available, until they found that guests demanded them. Many hotels provide irons and ironing-boards in rooms even though a laundry service may be available. New technology in the kitchen may also provide hospitality operations with ways of increasing productivity. Cook-chill systems, for example, allow meals to be prepared in advance and only to require reheating and presenting to be served to the customer.

Thus if hospitality organizations are to become part of the modern service sector they need to be seen as organizations that innovate, in terms of the service they provide, the product offered and the technology used, in order to stay close to the customer and gain competitive advantage. On the one hand, this leads to an increased diversity in the concepts offered as companies try to devise brands that offer something different. On the other hand, branded products increasingly dominate the market. In all these ways, the hospitality industry has much in common with the retail sector with which its senior managers compare themselves.

Hotels and restaurants as leisure products

Box 3.7   London restaurants and hotels as style statements

Teatro, arguably chic new restaurant and private club in the heart of Soho designed by United Designers (Vong, Nobu, Met Bar etc). Don't visit wearing Red or Dead – it's the uniform for staff . . . Live, eat and stay in Conran technicolour now the maestro has opened the Feng Shui-ed myhotel in Bloomsbury. It professes to be 'an oasis of calm where visitors can retreat and find a place of inner tranquillity.'

(*Elle Decoration* 1998, p. 44)

If the Metropolitan were a film star it would be Tom Cruise in *Top Gun* – young, good-looking, smart, cool and so damned cocky you'd just love someone to smack it in the mouth. . . . Its owner is Christina Ong, the Singaporean billionairess who also controls the Sydney Hilton, the Inn on the Park and (since 1991) the Halkin, an award-winning 41-room boutique hotel in Belgravia where the staff wear uniforms designed by Georgio Armani. They are dressed in black Donna Karen outfits at the Metropolitan, a modern block on Hyde Park Corner. . . . You might get a glimpse of one of the young film or pop stars, supermodels or designers that hang out here. Even if you don't, the staff are all beautiful enough to model and to make you feel ugly.

(*Independent on Sunday Review*, 22 March 1998, p. 9)

When we think of hotels and restaurants as providers of hospitality, we are focusing on historical continuity: on the ways in which people throughout history and in all parts of the world have always provided food and/or accommodation for people away from home. But undeniably life in the late twentieth and early twenty-first centuries is very different from life even 50 years ago. Thinking about hotels and restaurants as leisure products encourages us to think about change and discontinuity; about the ways in which life in increasingly urban, developed societies is very different from life in the past.

A major feature in modern developed societies is the amount of surplus income that people across all strata and social classes have to spend on items other than the basic necessities of life. Taking Britain as an example, at the beginning of the century, working class consumers spent around a half to two-thirds of their income on food (Burnett 1966/ 1979 quoted in Gabriel and Lang 1995). At the end of the twentieth century, household expenditure on food is nearer one-tenth (MAFF 1994 quoted in Gabriel and Lang 1995). Connected with the growth in disposable income is a growth in the choice available to consumers in terms of the products and services that the income can be spent on and, with the development of laboursaving household devices, on the time available to pursue these choices. Thus Gabriel and Lang (1995) argue that consumption in late twentieth century developed societies has "moved from a means to an end – living – to being an end in its own right. Living life to the full (has) became synonymous with consumption" (p. 7).

For the majority of the population in the developed world, buying a meal out or staying in a hotel represents just one choice about how to spend our money. A meal in a restaurant competes for our spending with buying a new CD or video, buying some new clothes, buying something for our home. People increasingly have access to the full range of hospitality services: not just to a limited range of hotels and restaurants designed for people like them. So, in the course of a week, a person may stay in a four-star city hotel on business, but eat at the local Indian restaurant with colleagues in the evening, have lunch in the cafeteria of a motorway service area, stop for a drink with work colleagues at the local bar, have a pizza with friends in the evening, go out for a special meal with a partner on Saturday night, have lunch with the family at a bistro on Sunday.

What do hotels and restaurants as leisure products have to offer the consumer in contemporary society? They offer us the opportunity to experiment with different identities. So an English couple can travel to France and play at French country life, staying in local hotels and eating in local cafés and restaurants, whilst conversely a French couple can come to England and experiment with English style, eating afternoon tea, fish and chips and drinking in local pubs. Hotels and restaurants provide us with an opportunity to explore the exotic and the different in a society where this is glamourized. In many large cities, there is a search for ever new and different cuisines or for ever new and different decors and experiences to excite consumers as hotels and restaurants become, increasingly, style statements (see Box 3.7). A review of the leisure industry in the UK argues that:

> . . . restaurant operators are seeing an overwhelming demand for themed dining, which they interpret as a public demand for more from a meal out than just the food. When people go out, their argument runs, they want to be entertained, they want something special. Hence the latest industry buzz-word, entertainment. And there is no reason to suggest that this desire for specialness will continue to be the sole preserve of the restaurant customer.
>
> (Nutley 1997, p. 7)

Furthermore people are prepared to pay for a quality product:

> Those in employment, although they are in the relatively highly paid positions, are having to work harder than ever, as a result they are cash-rich but time-poor. The notion of value for money is becoming less

important. In its place is a new concept, value for time. Operators are already reporting that their customers are prepared to pay a premium price for high quality products because they want to make the most of their precious leisure time . . . maximum bangs from the leisure hour.

(Nutley 1997, p. 7)

The negative face of consumption

In many respects these developments may be seen as positive; offering, as they do, the opportunity for many people in modern society to exercise their choice and experience a wide range of products and services that might previously have been accessible only to a few. But consumption also has some less desirable consequences; indeed as Gabriel and Lang (1995) point out "since the fourteenth century, the verb 'to consume' in English has had negative connotations, meaning 'to destroy, to use up, to waste, to exhaust'".

Consumption changes the nature of what is consumed. If an English tea-shop is full of French tourists it ceases to be an English tea-shop. Similarly, a French café full of English tourists ceases to be a French café. The development of leisure products, new hotels and restaurants, changes the character of an area. This is most obviously apparent when considering new tourist resorts in developing countries with pre-dominantly rural economies; examples such as the Greek islands and southern Spain in Europe; Bali, Phuket and Goa in Asia; the Caribbean islands, the Gambia in Africa. An issue here is that while, in the developed world, the majority of the population may have the spending power to access the new leisure products, in the developing world, most people could never afford a meal in a tourist restaurant, let alone a stay in a tourist hotel.

Even in urban environments and in more developed economies a segment of society is 'time-rich and cash-poor' and unable to access the new leisure products. This may cause resentment and problems, as Box 3.8 illustrates.

Box 3.8   The local community and upmarket leisure developments

In many cities around the world, historic dock areas, once the scene of bustling harbour activity but more recently obsolete and neglected, have become transformed into centres for leisure consumption with hotels, restaurants, shops and tourist attractions. In Cape Town, in South Africa, the Victoria and Alfred Basins have been transformed in this way and the V&A Waterfront is now an established destination on the South African tourist trail as well as attracting older, wealthy South Africans and the younger socially mobile Capetonians. The V&A Waterfront as a safe, clean and easily accessible environment has "stolen" customers who might have otherwise gone to eat or shop in the Central Business District or Atlantic Seaboard. These districts, plagued by problems such as litter, crime, prostitution and street children, have been hard pressed to compete. However, questions of racial and class exclusivity have plagued the development from the start. The local press have criticized the development for being sanitized, middle-class and a rip-off. Factions of the Muslim community have expressed anti-Waterfront sentiment. An anonymous flier, signed "a few decent, unapologetic Muslims", was distributed to a number of Cape Town households claiming:

> Many people who live in townships like Khyalitsha, Manenberg, Guguletu etc., never have the time nor the money to visit the Waterfront, and/or they are too preoccupied with bread and butter issues i.e. they work their backs off so that they can provide sustenance to their hungry children. The so-called demise of Apartheid and the promise of a land of milk and honey has unfortunately not reached them yet.

(Adapted from Dodson and Kilian 1998)

The result, according to some commentators, is that new leisure developments are increasingly sanitized versions of local culture; designed to excite moneyed consumers whilst at the same time offering an environment which is safe and secure. At the same time, the amenities for locals and the reflection of their authentic culture are squeezed out; the poorer sections of society are excluded. This fuels their resentment and means that more effort has to be put into keeping desirable consumers safe and protected from "undesirable" elements.

For the study of organizational behaviour, what are the implications of seeing hotels and restaurants as leisure products?

- Hotel and restaurant companies need to compete to offer contemporary consumers increasingly exotic and stylish leisure experiences. With the emphasis on theming and image, staff need to look and act the part as well: the employees are part of the image.

- Contemporary consumers want the exotic but they also want to be safe and secure. The "authentic" product on which a themed experience is based is changed to make it acceptable: so a pizzeria bears little resemblance to the Neapolitan original, a branded Irish pub is but a shadow of an authentic Irish pub. As a consequence the authentic products are squeezed out.

- Hotels and restaurants are located within communities and they have an impact on those communities. Some of these impacts may be positive: they can bring in economic benefits and increase local amenity and choice. But consumption also "eats up": it can deplete natural resources and local culture.

- In any society, the poorest section of the population will be excluded from experiencing the new leisure products; they simply cannot afford to eat in the restaurants or stay in the hotels. This can lead to resentment on their part and to the organizations having to "protect" their moneyed consumers from "undesirable elements". So leisure developments can become almost like walled cities, isolated from the local community. This can be seen particularly in tourist resorts in developing countries but may also be the case in urban developments as was shown in Box 3.8. Another motivation for separating leisure developments from the local community may be to protect the community from the influence of the (international) moneyed consumers. Theme parks, like the Disney products, are perhaps the ultimate "walled cities".

These issues about the impact of hotels and restaurants on the community will be discussed in more detail in Chapter 11.

Work in hotels and restaurants

Having looked at some of the characteristics of hospitality organizations, this section will now look at the type of jobs that are provided in hotels and restaurants and at the people who fill these jobs. It is helpful to use the concept of the labour market in this context. A labour market consists of all the buyers of labour, from all industry sectors with their particular skill requirements, and all the sellers of labour, that is everyone who is currently employed plus those currently outside the workforce either because they are unemployed, retired, undergoing training or temporarily unable to work because they are injured or ill. We can talk about the labour market at the local, regional, national or transnational level. Thus the labour market conditions in London will be different from those in Glasgow, those in Britain different from those in Germany, those in the European Union different from those in the ASEAN (Association of South East Asian Nations) bloc.

As Baum (1995) and Riley (1991a) point out, labour markets operate through thousands of independent decisions made by employers and employees as at any one time there are people seeking work or seeking to change their jobs and employers who are looking to recruit new staff. These independent decisions "make up the trends in mobility, the surpluses of or shortages of supply, the excesses or lack of demand" (Riley 1991, p. 7).

What factors affect the demand for labour in the hospitality industry?

- **The hospitality industry is a labour-intensive industry**. As was shown at the beginning of this chapter, it is an industry that employs a large proportion of the global workforce and of the workforce within specific countries. This makes the industry attractive to Governments of developed countries looking to find alternative employment for people in the face of a declining manufacturing sector and to Governments of developing countries faced with the need to provide work for a growing population. However, as will be shown, this causes problems in economies where there is already full employment. Although the demand for labour can be reduced to some extent through the use of technology, it is difficult to see how it can be reduced significantly in the foreseeable future.

- **The hospitality industry particularly requires unskilled and semi-skilled staff**. It has been estimated (Riley 1991b) that about two-thirds of jobs in the hotel, restaurant and catering sectors are unskilled or semi-skilled. This means that the jobs in the industry are accessible to a large proportion of the population, including those with little formal training.

- **Many of the skills required in the industry are "transferable"**. A trained waiter in one hotel would be able to move to a similar job in another hotel relatively easily. Generalized customer service skills are readily transferable to other industries. Thus a trained receptionist could easily move to the retail sector or into retail banking. As Baum (1995) points out, this means that there is generally a large pool of suitably skilled employees who can be drafted into hospitality jobs, but conversely means that hospitality employees can be readily "poached" by other industry sectors.

- **Hotels and restaurants are subject to fluctuating demand**. Therefore they need to be able to increase staff at times of high demand and shed staff at times of low demand. Many of the jobs provided require "unsocial" working hours, others may be seasonal or temporary.

- **The hospitality industry in some sectors and some countries has a reputation for providing lowly paid employment and poor working conditions**. The industry thus has a poor image and finds it difficult to recruit and retain staff.

Who wants to work in the hospitality industry?

> **Box 3.9   Who wants to work in hospitality?**
>
> My father was actually horrified that I was wasting a good education on catering.
>
> My headmistress left me off the list at prizegiving. She talked about everyone who went to teacher training – she did not mention me (going on to do a degree in Hotel Management).
>
> *(Hospitality managers talking about their decision to go into the hospitality industry)*

We have seen above that the hospitality industry provides large numbers of jobs that are relatively low skilled, may be temporary, part-time or require "unsocial hours" and are often poorly paid. In these circumstances it is hardly surprising if the industry suffers from an image problem, with work in the industry, even at the management level, regarded by many as relatively low status and not a career of choice for bright young people.

But skill is a difficult concept. How do we assess objectively how the skills required to be a waiter compare with the skills required to be a plumber or the skills required to be a teacher or to deal on the stock exchange? There is a sense in which our attribution of the skills required in a job follows the status we ascribe to that job. If a job has a low status in society and is done by low status people, it is assumed that it must require few skills. Being a room attendant must be a low skill job because it is a job done by uneducated foreign women for little pay.

There are a number of other factors that tend to decrease the status of jobs in hotels and restaurants:

- **The work is associated with servility.** Work in the hospitality industry grew out of the work of domestic servants, as the first grand hotels were modelled on the aristocratic grand houses. Putting oneself in a subservient role may be seen as decreasing one's status. Studies of working class men, especially, suggest they are particularly keen to find jobs where they are not expected to be subservient (see Leidner 1993).

- **The work is seen as "dirty work".** To the extent that work in the hospitality industry is about cleaning and clearing up after others it is dirty work and has a stigma attached to it (Saunders 1981). Amongst certain communities, there is also a prejudice against work that may involve serving alcohol or where women are required to serve male guests.

- **The work is seen as women's work.** The domestic work of cooking for and cleaning up after the household has traditionally been seen as women's work (Novarra 1980). Thus work in the hospitality industry, even when done by men, is regarded as women's work. As women have a lower status in society than men, work that is seen as women's work is also accorded a lower status. Hospitality work may also be seen as inappropriate for "real" men in that it involves smiling at and being nice to customers. Women smile more than men and men who are especially "masculine" smile the least (DePaulo 1992). A study of chemical workers in the States observed that many did not support Jimmy Carter's presidential candidacy because they "suspected that a man who smiled all the time might be a homosexual" (see Leidner 1993, p. 200). (Similarly it is sometimes assumed that men working in the hospitality industry must be gay.)

A consequence is that hospitality organizations are disproportionately staffed, especially in the lowest level jobs, by people who are disadvantaged in society and find it difficult to get "better" jobs: women, the young, members of ethnic minority groups, migrant workers. It has been argued that hospitality work attracts "misfits", providing a surrogate family for "all sorts of crooks, queers, men on the run, alcoholics" who prefer ephemeral relationships and are happy to work in other people's leisure time (Mars *et al.* 1979, p. 79 quoted in Wood 1992, p. 19 who points out that there is little empirical evidence to support this contention).

If one takes the UK as an example, the hospitality workforce shows the following characteristics:

- **Gender segregation:** The industry employs a high proportion of women (Lucas 1995) but they are "horizontally and vertically segregated into particular jobs, grades and areas of operation" (Purcell 1993, p. 127). Two-thirds of women are employed as counter and kitchen hands and domestic staff whilst there is a greater proportion of males working in craft and semi-skilled occupations. Purcell (1993) argues that women are found in such jobs not so much because of sex-typing but because of "crowding": "they are appropriate employees not because they are women but because they are disadvantaged workers, competing with other disadvantaged groups" (Purcell 1993, p. 128).

- **Ethnic segregation:** It is difficult to find information on the ethnic mix within the hospitality industry but it seems that the industry does employ a high proportion of black workers, again particularly clustered in low-paid and low-graded work, as well as a high proportion of migrant workers (Lucas 1995).

- **Age segregation:** The industry employs a relatively high proportion of young people. These are found particularly in the commercial sector. The industry seems to show a bias towards recruiting the under thirties even at a time when Britain has an "aging" population and there are decreasing numbers of young people entering the workforce (Lucas 1995).

- **High turnover:** One of the key characteristics of the hospitality labour market in the UK is the very high levels of labour turnover experienced, that is the number of employees leaving their jobs within a given period. Turnover is highest amongst the lowest grades of staff and in the hotel, restaurant and club sectors. In 1992, turnover was estimated to have cost the industry £430 million (HCTC 1994 quoted in Lucas 1995).

Is this pattern of an industry staffed at the operative level by "disadvantaged" workers who do not stay long in their jobs unique to the

UK? There are certainly examples of a similar pattern in other parts of the world. In Hong Kong, for example, labour shortages have been regarded as a serious problem in the hospitality industry and in 1993 the hotel industry introduced a labour importation scheme with the intention of training up people from the Philippines and elsewhere in the region (Go and Pine 1995). As in the UK, the industry complains of a lack of interest in jobs in the hospitality industry and high turnover with staff joining other hospitality organizations or leaving the industry altogether.

As Baum (1993) points out, however, these patterns are not universal. There are parts of the world where jobs in the hospitality industry have a relatively higher status, with higher rates of participation by men and where turnover rates are low. In areas where tourism is the main industry and there is little alternative work, such as the Mediterranean resorts and resorts in the Far East, such as Bali, a job, especially in a large international hotel, may be highly prized. In countries such as Switzerland and Germany, the status of jobs in the hospitality industry is increased because there are regulations requiring employees to have certain qualification before they are employed in the industry. Even in these countries, however, there is some evidence to suggest that not all jobs in the hospitality industry are prized. In Germany, for example, there are more jobs than applicants in the industry, despite an unemployment rate of 12% and a quarter of jobs in the sector filled by foreigners (Guerrier *et al.*, 1998).

Industry of last choice

One way of interpreting the picture of labour markets in the hospitality industry painted above is to argue that hospitality is inevitably a "Cinderella" industry, that will always be an industry of last choice rather than an industry of choice. Where hospitality organizations can attract and retain well-qualified staff easily, this will only ever be because there are limited opportunities to work elsewhere. When people have the choice they will usually prefer to work in other sectors. Hospitality organizations will react to the transient and poorly qualified workforce that they can attract by offering the lowest pay and poorest conditions that they can and by neglecting to invest in training and development. Thus the low status and poor image of the industry is perpetuated.

This is a depressingly negative view. Are there any ways in which hospitality organizations can break out of this vicious cycle? Are there any factors which tend to increase the status of jobs in the hospitality industry?

Choosing to work in the hospitality industry

Box 3.10   Rubbing shoulders with the stars

The hotel caters to extremely wealthy individuals. The clientele is international and covers a wide range of society, from diplomats to Rock stars. We have diplomats who have been coming for years so it's an intimate atmosphere and they recognize new staff immediately. Also there is about 60% corporate business coming over from America, mainly in the film industry. You have stars in but because it is such a private place it's not as if there were lots of photographers and I would say "hello" and have a chat with someone and not realize who they were until half an hour later, because of course they check in under pseudonyms.

(Receptionist at an exclusive London hotel)

The hospitality industry can be a glamorous industry to work in. Hospitality employees may have the opportunity to rub shoulders with the rich and famous (see Box 3.10), to work in an attractive and exotic environment, to dress up (see Box 3.7) and to show off. Hospitality workers may not think of themselves as being servile to customers but instead may enjoy stepping into the limelight and putting on a good performance for the customer. The top names in the industry, especially celebrity chefs, are rich and famous themselves.

Of course, not all hospitality organizations are equally glamorous. Go and Pine (1995) comment that low-profile hotels in Hong Kong tend to lose out in the competition for staff to the top-name hotels like the Mandarin and the Regent. But as consumers increasingly expect something special when they eat out or stay in a hotel so the roles of staff, even in hotels and restaurants catering for "ordinary" people, may be more interesting and more fun. (Waiting staff for the American themed restaurant chain TGI Fridays get to juggle, sing and tell jokes, for example.)

As developed economies move from being manufacturing based to service based, the old stigma attached to service sector jobs may decrease. Similarly, as women's participation in the workforce becomes normal and accepted the old stigma associated with women's work may decrease. In the UK, for example, local government in areas where there is high unemployment due to the loss of manufacturing industry now actively encourage the development of new jobs in the service sector where 15 years ago such jobs were dismissed as low-pay, low-skill and a poor substitute for work in manufacturing.

The temporary and flexible nature of work within many hospitality organizations may be increasingly in tune with current expectations of work. Our old notions that work means a full-time job with one employer are becoming obsolete (Handy 1994). Part-time work, work during "unsocial" hours or casual work may be an attractive option to parents trying to balance jobs and child care or indeed to anyone trying to balance work and other activities in their life. Indeed, as we move towards a 24-hour society the old notion that work was something that people generally did between nine and five, five days a week is being superseded.

Some hospitality organizations may not react to the problems that they face in attracting and retaining good staff by further deflating pay and conditions but may look at improving the motivation of staff by attempting to enhance their pay, conditions and status. As Baum (1995) points out, this may seem idealistic and optimistic but there is some evidence, as will be seen in Chapter 5, that some hospitality organizations are following that route.

So the notion that hospitality organizations are inevitably employers of last choice may be unduly pessimistic. Whilst the low pay, low skill and low status image persists in sectors of the industry, current trends in work and employment may improve the prospects for work in hotels and restaurants. These issues will be revisited in other chapters in this book.

Summary

* The hospitality industry is a diverse industry which comprises hotels, restaurants, licensed bars, guest houses, self-catering

establishments and commercial and public sector catering: indeed any organization that serves food and/or drink and/or provides accommodation to those away from home.

- Hospitality organizations provide commercially the hospitality that hosts provide naturally when they welcome guests into their homes. Comparing commercial hospitality with natural hospitality reminds us that:
  - hospitality is about accommodating basic human needs for food, drink and a place to sleep
  - we feel we have a duty to provide hospitality for those in our circle, people who need help and our friends
  - hospitality is an exchange for mutual benefit: both guests and hosts have responsibilities
  - guests are excluded from the back regions of the household where members of the household can relax and behave naturally.

- The hospitality industry can also be seen as a service industry similar in many ways to retailing. Services differ from products in that they are:
  - *intangible*: it is difficult to measure the quality of a greeting
  - *need to be situated near the customer*: a hotel for visitors to Paris has to be in Paris. A car produced for the Parisian market could be made anywhere in the world
  - *perishable*: if a hotel room is not sold one night that sale is lost forever.

- Modern service companies gain competitive advantage by:
  - delivering what their customers want
  - offering customers a distinctive brand
  - making appropriate use of new technology.

- Hotels and restaurants are also leisure products competing for the spending of modern consumers, who want to experience the exotic and the different in a safe and secure environment. Moneyed consumers demand new leisure products which, from a positive perspective, increase choice and increase spending in a community but which may also marginalize the local "authentic" culture and exclude the poorer sections of society.

- The hospitality industry:
  - is labour intensive
  - particularly requires unskilled and semi-skilled staff
  - requires people with skills that can easily be transferred to other industries
  - is subject to fluctuating demand
  - has a reputation in some sectors and countries for providing low pay and poor working conditions.

- The status of jobs in the hospitality industry is decreased because:
  - the work is associated with servility
  - the work is seen as dirty work
  - the work is seen as women's work.

- Thus hospitality organizations are disproportionately staffed by people who are disadvantaged in society and find it difficult to get better jobs.

- However, jobs in the hospitality industry may become jobs of choice:
  - to the extent that they are seen as glamorous and fun
  - with the increased status given to service jobs with a shift to more service-based economies
  - as flexible working patterns become the norm
  - as some organizations attempt to improve the jobs and conditions of their employees and break away from the low pay, low skill image.

The next stage

Experience

Within the limits of your budget and other constraints, try to eat out or drink in places you would not normally go. Aim to visit places you feel are not for you. (If that is not possible try varying the way that you use the places you normally frequent. So if you normally go to a restaurant with a group of friends, try going in on your own.)

Note:

1. How you feel (comfortable/uncomfortable, safe/anxious, interested/disgusted). Why?
2. Who the other customers are. How do they react to you? Are you made to feel welcome or an outsider?
3. How the staff treat you. Is it easy to use the service? How much help do you receive if you don't know what to do?

Ask some friends or acquaintances, especially those with no connection with the hospitality industry, for their opinion of employment within hotels and restaurants.

Reflection

Think about your own experiences as a host entertaining friends or as a guest being entertained by friends. What obligations as a host did you feel towards your guests? What obligations as a guest did you feel to your host? What similarities or differences are there with your experience of staying in a hotel or guesthouse or eating in a restaurant?

Can you think of any occasions when you have felt uncomfortable or unwelcome in a hotel or restaurant? Why did you feel that way?

Can you think of any occasions when you, as a customer, have been trained or helped to use a service with which you were unfamiliar?

To what extent do you behave as a post-modern consumer looking for an experience rather than just a meal when you eat out? What do you choose to spend any of your disposable income on rather than having a meal out? Why?

Pick four or five jobs in the hospitality industry, for example, the general manager of a five-star hotel, a room attendant in the same hotel, a waiter in the local pizzeria. What would your image be of the person doing that job? What would be their age, gender, ethnic background and educational background? Why would they be doing that job? Why do you have that image?

Theorizing

Think about a particular hospitality organization, a hotel, bar, restaurant or café that you know quite well – somewhere where you work or have worked or somewhere you visit regularly as a customer. What insights can you gain into the way that organization functions by thinking about it:

1. as an organization that provides hospitality commercially to guests, following some of the rules and rituals of natural hospitality
2. as a service sector business
3. as a leisure product.

What type of labour market does that organization work within? Consider its demand for labour: how many staff does it need and with what types of skills; how does the demand for staff fluctuate over the year, at different times of the week and the day; what pay and conditions are offered to staff?

Do you see any evidence of age, gender or ethnic segregation in jobs? What are turnover levels like? What other job opportunities would be open to people working in this organization? How difficult or easy is it to recruit and retain staff? What factors tend to decrease and what factors tend to increase the status of jobs within that organization?

In practice

How would you attempt to persuade Mrs Smegma (Box 3.3) that she should change her way of managing her guesthouse?

How do you manage back-of-house areas so that staff have somewhere to relax and be "off stage" but where they do not engage in practices that would horrify or endanger customers (see Box 3.5)?

Can and should leisure areas like the V&A Waterfront (Box 3.8) do anything to benefit the poorer sections of the local community who may feel excluded?

If you were managing the hospitality organization discussed in the previous section, how would you improve its capacity to attract and retain good staff?

Design an advertisement aiming to improve the image of work within the hospitality industry within your country.

Further reading

For an introduction to industry structure in the hospitality industry you should refer to books such as Knowles (1998), Powers (1995), Medlik (1994) in relation to the hotel sector, and Jones and Pizam (1993) for an international perspective. If you are studying on a hotel or hospitality course, you are probably familiar with these books anyway.

There is not much written as yet about hotels and restaurants and traditional hospitality. The most comprehensive review is in Wood (1994). Read Orwell (1933) for an entertaining insight into the way hotels and restaurants used to function.

Conversely there is extensive material which considers hotels and restaurants as service organizations. A good introduction is Baum (1995) Chapter 5. Davis and Lockwood (1994) contains a number of chapters which consider food and beverage management and operations within a broader service context – see particularly Connell (Chapter 4), Houghton and Lennon (Chapter 6), Jones (Chapter 10), Lockwood (Chapter 13), Alexander (Chapter 21). For a broader consideration of why services and production are different consult Gummesson (1992) and Heskett (1986).

For further reading on hotel and restaurants as leisure products and the negative effects of consumption Urry (1990) is a good starting point. Gabriel and Lang (1995) is a good introduction to the new consumer and consumerism generally.

For a general discussion of labour markets in the hospitality industry refer to Baum (1995) Chapter 4, Riley (1991), Lucas (1995) Chapter 3 and Wood (1992). Apart from Baum, these accounts tend to be UK focused.

References to further reading

Baum, T. (1995) *Managing Human Resources in the European Tourism and Hospitality Industry*, London: Chapman and Hall.

Davis, B. and Lockwood, A. (eds) (1994) *Food and Beverage Management*, Oxford: Butterworth-Heinemann.

Gabriel, Y. and Lang, T. (1995) *The Unmanageable Consumer*, London: Sage.

Gummesson, E. (1992) *Quality Management in Service Organizations*, New York: SQA.

Heskett, J. (1986) *Managing in the Service Economy*, Boston: Harvard Business School Press.

Jones, P. and Pizam, A. (eds) (1993) *The International Hospitality Industry: Organizational and Operational Issues*, London: Pitman.

Knowles, T. (1998) *Hospitality Management: an Introduction* (Second edition), Harlow: Longman.

Lucas, R. (1995) *Managing Employee Relations in the Hotel and Catering Industry*, London: Cassell.

Medlik, S. (1994) *The Business of Hotels* (Third edition), Oxford: Butterworth-Heinemann.

Orwell, G. (1933) *Down and Out in Paris and London*, London: Penguin.

Powers, T. (1995) *Introduction to the Hospitality Industry* (Third edition), New York: Wiley.

Riley, M. (1991) *Human Resource Management: A Guide to Personnel Practice in the Hotel and Catering Industries*, Oxford: Butterworth-Heinemann.

Urry, J. (1990) *The Tourist Gaze*, London: Sage.

Wood, R. (1994) Hospitality culture and social control, *Annals of Tourism Research*, **21**, 65–80.

4 The many faces of culture

Box 4.1 The management meeting

Imagine that you are a newly appointed junior manager working in a large city centre four-star hotel. The hotel has a multinational management team. You are about to attend the first meeting of the management team to be chaired by the new general manager, who is Australian.

The new manager calls the meeting to order five minutes after it was scheduled to start. He takes his jacket off and loosens his tie. "By the way, I want everyone to call me Mike" he says. (The previous general manager who was Austrian was never seen without a jacket and was always called Mr . . . .) "Does anyone know where Eduardo's got to?"

How do you feel?
a. *Pleased that there has been a shift from the stuffy formality of the previous manager.*
b. *Shocked to see a general manager so careless of his formal status.*

Eduardo, the Spanish food and beverage manager, arrives 20 minutes late. He sits down without apology. Jan, the Dutch rooms division manager, looks at his watch with obvious irritation. As Eduardo sits down his mobile phone rings. He answers the call, gets up again and walks to the corner of the room, where he continues speaking for a further five minutes.

How do you feel?
a. *Appalled and ashamed by his behaviour. He should not have arrived at the meeting so late and if he did he should have apologized profusely. And he should have switched off his mobile phone.*
b. *That his behaviour is perfectly normal. It is quite acceptable to be 20 minutes late to a meeting and if he has other business to attend to he can perfectly well look after this while the meeting is going on.*

The meeting embarks on a discussion of a new performance-related pay scheme which Mike, the general manager, is enthusiastic to adopt. Mike notices that Helen, the housekeeper, who is from Thailand, has not expressed her view on this proposal. You know that Helen is very unhappy about it. However, when asked to give her view to the meeting, she simply says "Of course, Mr Carter, if you want to implement this scheme, I will support you."

How do you feel?
a. *That Helen was cowardly and unprofessional not to argue her case at the meeting.*
b. *That Helen was right not to undermine the authority of her boss in such a public forum but that Mike should never have brought the proposal to the meeting without ensuring that his management team broadly supported it first.*

The discussion on the performance-related pay system continues and, if Helen is not prepared to argue her case, Eduardo is. The discussion becomes quite heated as Eduardo very forcibly puts forward an alternative proposal. Clearly exasperated, Jan, the Dutch rooms division manager, says "Switch off the histrionics, Eduardo. Your proposal is insane."

Eduardo completely loses his temper. "What you mean insane" he screams, "I have never been so insulted in all my life." And he storms out of the meeting.

How do you feel?
a. *Shocked by Eduardo's behaviour. No-one should ever lose their temper to that extent at a work meeting. It is a sign of weakness.*
b. *Sympathetic to Eduardo. He could not let such an insult go unchallenged and his behaviour made it clear to Jan that he should not be treated in this way.*

Introduction

Should the boss be "human"? Is it acceptable to openly disagree with your manager? Is it acceptable to lose your temper with your colleagues? Is it important to be punctual? The example in Box 4.1 shows how these issues about how people *should* behave at work are played out.

All the managers in the boxed example, Mike, Eduardo, Jan and Helen, are trying to do "the right thing"; they are behaving in the way they believe they should. So Mike believes that a manager should be informal and not stand on ceremony. Helen believes that one should not openly disagree with your manager and should always treat him with respect. Eduardo believes that it is perfectly normal to arrive late at a meeting and leave your mobile phone switched on. Jan believes that it is right to tell a colleague that he is being an idiot if he is. But why are their assumptions about what is and is not acceptable behaviour so different? One explanation is that their personalities and personal styles are different. But another possible explanation is the difference in their cultures: they have learned to believe that different ways of behaving are appropriate.

This chapter is about the way in which *culture* affects behaviour at work. It will first explore the nature of culture and the way in which culture manifests itself. It will then look at the many faces of culture; the way in which people's behaviour at work can be affected by their *national culture*, and the *organizational culture* of the company that they work for.

What is culture?

Culture may be thought of as: "The way in which a group of people solves problems and reconciles dilemmas" (Schein 1985) or "The collective programming of the mind which distinguishes the members of one group or category of people from another" (Hofstede 1991).

The distinguishing features of culture are that it is:

- **learned**. No-one is born knowing whether it is all right to turn up late to meetings or argue with one's boss! We learn the "right" way to behave from our parents, our community, at school and from our work experience. Culture is, therefore, in Hofstede's (1991) terms, the "software" of the mind: the way our brains have been "programmed" through our experience to respond to situations;

- **shared by one group or category of people**. So the view that it is desirable to be punctual at meetings is not unique to Jan. It is a view that he shares with other people who have had a similar upbringing and background. Thus cultural assumptions can be distinguished from *personality*. An individual's personality is what makes him or her unique. Jan's personality makes him uniquely Jan. His cultural assumptions come from his being a middle class, university-educated, Dutch hotel manager and he would be likely to share those with other middle-class, university-educated Dutch hotel managers;

- **not universally identical**. Not everyone holds the same view about whether it is important to be punctual or not, as can be seen by Eduardo's behaviour. Cultural assumptions are, by their nature, not universally accepted as true. Whilst one group of people may be convinced that one should never ever lose one's temper in a business meeting, another cultural group can be equally convinced that it is important to stress how strongly you feel.

We acquire our cultural assumptions from our family, our community, school and work experiences and, increasingly, through the media. Those cultural assumptions become so much a part of the way in which we think about the world that it is often only when we are confronted with someone who thinks and behaves in a different way that we recognise that they are cultural assumptions.

But, as Hofstede (1991) points out, everybody is part of a number of groups and categories of people from which culture is acquired. Our cultural assumptions are drawn from our:

- **nationality** (or nationalities). So Helen's views about how to treat her manager may be partly explained by her Thai upbringing. Similarly the fact that Mike is Australian may partially account for his view that managers should be unstuffy and informal;

- **regional or ethnic background**. Within countries, there are frequently regional and ethnic differences. So Mike would have been subject to different cultural influences as a white Australian than if he had been an ethnically-Chinese Australian, for example;

- **gender and generation**. Girls tend to be socialized to behave differently from boys in most societies. Similarly, young people will have been subject to different cultural influences from their parents and grandparents;

- **social class and education**. University-educated people may have different cultural assumptions from people from the same ethnic and regional backgrounds who left full-time education as soon as allowed;

- **occupation and organization**. People from the same occupation or professional group may share certain "mental programmes" as may people who work for the same organization. Organizational culture is discussed later in this chapter.

Uncovering culture

Box 4.2   Explicit culture

Some years ago I ran some short courses for hotel managers at a hotel training school in Bali, Indonesia. I was used to running similar short courses in the UK where the programmes would have been run in an informal and low-key way with flexible seating arrangements and the expectation that the group would be active participants in the course. I was surprised by the following differences in Bali.

The teaching room was elaborately decorated with beautiful floral arrangements and a banner with the name of the course. The course was preceded by a lengthy opening ceremony with several speeches and prayers. The participants were arranged according to a formal seating plan and I was provided with a podium to speak from (although it was a relatively small group of about 25 participants) as it was not assumed that I would do anything other than deliver formal lectures. The course ended with a closing ceremony and the exchange of certificates of attendance and presents.

This example is not about right or wrong ways of running training courses, nor is it an illustration of the way training courses are always run in Indonesia. Some of the Indonesian participants, who worked for international companies and were used to "western" style training courses, were also surprised by the elaborate preparations for the course. It illustrates the way that *artifacts*, the way the room was laid out and decorated, the rituals of the opening and closing ceremonies, were the first and most obvious manifestations of the differences between Balinese and UK management culture.

The first and most obvious manifestations of culture lie in artifacts. If I travel to an unfamiliar place, I recognize cultural differences first in aspects such as:

- **physical objects**. The architecture of buildings, the layout and decoration of offices and work space, the way people dress. As a British person travelling in Scandinavia, for example, I will probably be struck by the relative informality of dress codes;

- **language**. How do people address each other? (As a non-native French speaker I could spend years trying to work out when to use the formal (*vous*) mode of address and when to use the familiar (*tu*) form.) What do people talk about? What jokes and stories do they tell?

- **behaviour patterns**. Rites, rituals and ceremonies. I may notice such things as different eating patterns: for example, long lunch breaks and late dinners in Spain;

- **rules and systems**. What rules do people conform to? A first-time visitor to Britain may be struck by the orderly nature of queues. A first-time visitor to Germany may notice the way that no-one crosses a road against a red light, even if no traffic is coming.

But artifacts are only the most superficial manifestation of culture. As one becomes more familiar with a culture so the distinctive shared *norms* and *values* become apparent.

Norms: are the rules the group has about what is appropriate or inappropriate behaviour. For example, there may be a norm about whether it is or is not appropriate to show one's emotions openly at work. Trompenaars and Hampden-Turner (1997) asked managers from different countries whether, if they were upset about something, they would express their feelings openly. Less than a fifth of the respondents from Spain, Egypt and Cuba said that they would not express their feelings. However, three-quarters of the Japanese said they would not show their emotions openly. Therefore one might expect that it would be a norm in Spanish companies for people to show how they feel, but the same behaviour is likely to be perceived as transgressing a norm in Japan.

Values: are our beliefs about what is good or bad or right or wrong. They are the ideals that we strive towards whereas norms are the ways that we think we should behave. For example, Trompenaars and Hampden-Turner (1997) asked managers from different countries whether they agreed with the statement "It is obvious that if individuals have as much freedom as possible and the maximum opportunity to develop themselves, the quality of their life will improve as a result" or whether they preferred the statement "If individuals are continuously taking care of their fellow human beings the quality of life will improve for everyone, even if it obstructs individual freedom and individual development". Those preferring the first statement might be described as placing a high value on individualism whereas those who prefer the second statement value what might be described as communitarianism beyond individualism. Of their respondents, the Israelis, Romanians, Nigerians, Americans and Canadians were most likely to be individualist: over two-thirds supported the first statement. The Egyptians, Nepalese, Mexicans, Indians and Japanese were most likely to be communitarian: over 60% agreed with the second statement.

At the deepest level of culture are *basic assumptions*. These are the taken-for-granted, deeply rooted assumptions that a group shares. They are never explicitly questioned because they are, as far as the group is concerned, obvious. Trompenaars and Hampden-Turner (1997) describe them as follows:

> The best way to test if something is a basic assumption is when the question provokes confusion or irritation. You might, for example, observe that some Japanese bow deeper than others. Again, if you ask why they do it, the answer might be that they don't know but that the other person does it too (norm), or that they want to show respect for authority (value). A typical Dutch question that might follow is: "Why do you respect authority?" The most likely Japanese reaction would be either puzzlement or a smile (which might be hiding their irritation). When you question basic assumptions you are asking questions that have never been asked before.   (p. 23)

Whether culture is being considered at the national, the industry or the organizational level, it can be described in terms of (1) artifacts, (2) norms and values and (3) basic assumptions.

National cultures

> ### Box 4.3   How others see us
>
> English managers are very polite, tenacious, resourceful, reserved and self-disciplined . . . but at the same time, they have generally ethno-centric attitudes towards their foreign counterparts, and can hardly speak a foreign language – it doesn't matter, they all speak English anyway!
>
> (Tayeb 1997, p. 34)
>
> Israeli management is active, interventionist and energetic. The Israeli manager is always happier doing something than thinking about what might be done. The Israeli manager is best in situations where something has to be done quickly, to save the day.
>
> (Lawrence 1997, p. 202)
>
> American time and consciousness are fixed in the present. Americans don't want to wait; they want results now. They move at a rapid pace; everything about their business lives is hurried. Wanting quick answers and quick solutions, they are not used to waiting long periods of time for decisions and become anxious when decisions are not made quickly.
>
> (Hall and Hall 1997, p. 56)

In the boxed example at the beginning of this chapter, I suggested that the behaviour of the participants at the management meeting might be at least partially explained by their nationality. Yet many people feel instinctively unhappy about trying to measure or describe national cultural differences. Can we really generalize about national characteristics to the extent shown in Box 4.3? Are there really no rude, multilingual English managers, no introspective Israeli managers and no unhurried American managers?

In any one nationality, there will, of course, be a range of different values, attitudes and behaviour. All one can attempt to do, in studying national culture, is to pinpoint the average, or most predictable, behaviour. So whilst there may be individualistic Egyptians and communitarian Americans, it still may be useful to say that *in general* American culture is more individualistic than Egyptian culture. Studies of national cultural characteristics, as Hofstede (1991) points out, are not designed to describe individuals from that country but to describe the social systems that they are likely to have built.

"Mr Suzuki is Japanese, therefore he holds collectivist values; Ms Smith is American, therefore she holds individualist values." These are stereotypes and they are unwarranted. . . . If we want to find out about Mr Suzuki and Ms Smith we had better make our judgement after meeting and getting to know them.

(Hofstede 1991, p. 253)

A second question is whether the nation is an appropriate level to study cultural differences. Within most national boundaries, there are significant regional and ethnic differences. Would someone from Milan believe that he or she shared a cultural identity with someone from Sicily, even though they are both Italian? Does a black American have the same culture as an Hispanic American? Nation states are relatively recent political units and even today national boundaries can change (as has been seen with the break up of the old Soviet Union). In some parts of the world, particularly in Africa, national boundaries are a relic of colonial times that have little to do with the cultural divisions in the population.

The argument for studying culture at the national level is, according to Hofstede (1991), partially expedience. It is usually possible to collect information which compares people from one country with those from another but it may be more difficult, from a practical point of view, to break this information down by sub-cultures or regions. There are also, undeniably, factors which link everyone in a nation together: a dominant national language, common mass media, common educational and political systems, for example.

The main case for attempting to study national culture, however imperfectly, is the consequence of ignoring national culture. Until the early 1980s, organization and management theorists rarely discussed and studied national cultural differences. This did not mean that the research and theories produced were free from cultural bias. Most writers on organizations were from the Anglo-Saxon world (from the USA or the UK) and they unwittingly reflected their basic cultural assumptions in their theories. By looking at the differences between national cultures, we can start asking questions about whether the management practices and styles of organization that work in one country can be successfully transferred into another. Referring back to Box 4.1, because Mike's informal style of management was appropriate in Australia, would it work equally well with a group of staff from very different and very diverse cultural backgrounds?

Hofstede's study of national cultural differences

One of the first, and the most well-known, studies of national cultural differences was conducted by Geert Hofstede. Hofstede surveyed over 116 000 employees of the multinational computer company IBM, between 1968 and 1972. His respondents were drawn from 53 different subsidiaries and worked in 30 different occupations within the company. Hofstede used a questionnaire survey to collect his data, asking questions on such topics as what people looked for in a good job and what type of manager they preferred to work for. His data were analysed to provide four dimensions against which national culture could be measured. After subsequent research a fifth dimension was added. The dimensions are: power distance, individualism/collectivism, masculinity/femininity, uncertainty avoidance and Confucian dynamism.

Power distance

Power distance is a measure of the way in which people in different countries deal with the fact that people are unequal. In the work context, it is particularly relevant to the way that people at different levels in the organizational hierarchy relate to each other. In low power distance countries, inequalities between people will tend to be minimized. So bosses are expected to mix with their subordinates, not to flaunt any privileges or status symbols and to consult their subordinates. In high power distance cultures, inequalities among people are considered normal and desirable. The boss is expected to "play the boss" and subordinates expect to be told what to do.

- **High power distance countries** (Hofstede's top ten from 1–10): Malaysia, Panama, Guatemala, Philippines, Venezuela, Arab countries, Indonesia, Ecuador, West Africa and India (tied tenth).

- **Low power distance countries** (Hofstede's bottom ten from 53–43): Austria, Israel, Denmark, New Zealand, Ireland, Sweden, Norway, Finland, Switzerland, Great Britain/Germany/Costa Rica (tied 42–44).

Generally in Hofstede's study, Latin American, Latin European (like France with 15th highest power distance), Asian, Arab and African countries were high power distance. Non-Latin European and countries influenced by Anglo-Saxon culture tended to be low power distance. The USA is relatively low power distance.

> **Box 4.4   Low power distance values encountering high power distance values**
>
> Two British consultants were discussing ways of improving the quality of staff service with some Greek Cypriot hotel managers. "How much do your staff actually know about the services in your hotel?" asked one of the consultants. "For example, have your room attendants ever eaten in your restaurant?" The hotel managers were shocked. "They couldn't possibly eat in the restaurant. What would the other guests think?"

Individualism/collectivism

In individualistic societies, the ties between people are loose. Individuals have a responsibility to look after themselves and their immediate family only. In collectivist societies, people are integrated into strong in-groups which look after them in exchange for their loyalty. In terms of work, in individualistic societies, people look for individual challenge and freedom to express themselves in a job. They expect to be promoted according to their skills, to have time to develop their life outside work and to leave one organization for another if there are better prospects. In collectivist societies, people expect family ties and in-group affiliations to be taken into account in hiring and promotion decisions. They expect their work organization to take care of them and will stay with it in exchange. They prefer rewards to go to the group rather than to the individual, if times are hard they would prefer that everyone had a pay cut rather than a few people being laid off.

- **Individualistic countries** (Hofstede's top ten from 1–10): USA, Australia, Great Britain, Canada, Netherlands, New Zealand, Italy, Belgium, Denmark, Sweden/France (tied tenth place).

- **Collectivist countries** (Hofstede's bottom ten from 53–43): Guatemala, Ecuador, Panama, Venezuela, Columbia, Indonesia, Pakistan, Costa Rica, Peru, Taiwan, South Korea.

Generally, Hofstede found that wealthy, urbanized countries were "individualist" whilst poorer, rural countries had "collectivist" values. Exceptions were some of the newly industrialized countries like Singapore, Korea and Taiwan which had remained collectivist in spite of industrialization.

Box 4.5 Would you paint your boss's house?

Hofstede's collectivist/individualist dimension is associated with what the anthropologist Edward Hall (1976) calls high-context/low-context values and what Trompenaars and Hampden-Turner (1997) call diffuse and specific cultures. In specific cultures (which tend to be more individualist), we separate out the different segments of our life. If a boss meets a subordinate in the supermarket he does not expect to be treated as the boss. His obligations to his subordinates do not stretch outside the workplace and neither do their obligations to him. You do not need to really know someone as a friend in order to do business with them: but this means that any communications between business partners have to be made very explicit (low-context) as people do not know each other well enough to second guess what each might mean.

By contrast in high-context/diffuse cultures, people do not compartmentalize their lives. A subordinate has obligations to his boss even outside work. He would feel pressured to paint his boss's house if asked, even if he didn't want to, because his boss is his boss. But equally bosses have obligations to their subordinates even outside work. A study of the expectations that staff working in a chain of restaurants in Thailand had of their supervisors (Phornprapha 1996) suggested that a good supervisor is someone who treats his or her staff as relatives, using the words and phrases that would only be spoken to a relative, taking care of them when they are ill, finding them somewhere to live and generally showing concern about their personal problems. In a high-context/diffuse culture, you would never do business with someone that you did not know extremely well and you would prefer to do business with members of your in-group; someone in your family or who you went to school with, for example.

So would you paint your boss's house? According to Trompenaars and Hampden-Turner (1997) 68% of the Chinese would, but only 9% of Swedes.

Masculinity/femininity

This dimension looks at the extent to which gender roles in society are distinct. In more masculine cultures, men are expected to be aggressive, tough, competitive and concerned with material success whereas women are expected to be tender and to take care of relationships. In more feminine societies, gender roles overlap and both sexes are expected to be modest, concerned about relationships and about the quality of life. In masculine societies conflicts are resolved by fighting them out whereas in more feminine societies conflicts are resolved through compromise and negotiation. Incidentally, in masculine countries, women are as successful at achieving high positions in work organizations as in feminine countries but those that do tend to have "tough" masculine values (the ex-British Prime Minister, Lady Thatcher, is a good example of this).

- **Masculine countries** (Hofstede's top ten from 1–10): Japan, Austria, Venezuela, Italy, Switzerland, Mexico, Ireland, Jamaica, Great Britain, Germany.

- **Feminine countries** (Hofstede's bottom ten from 53–43): Sweden, Norway, Netherlands, Denmark, Costa Rica, Yugoslavia, Finland, Chile, Portugal, Thailand, Guatemala.

Masculinity/femininity is unrelated to a county's economic development: there are rich and poor masculine and feminine countries. Nor is it clearly related to geographical divide: there are some "masculine" Latin American countries – Venezuela, Mexico, Columbia, Ecuador – as well as some "feminine ones" – Costa Rica, Chile, Guatemala, Uruguay. There are "masculine" European countries – Austria, Great Britain, Italy, Switzerland, Germany – as well as some "feminine ones" – Sweden, Norway, Netherlands, Portugal, Spain.

Uncertainty avoidance

The uncertainty avoidance dimension is about the way in which countries deal with the unpredictable, the uncertain and the ambiguous. In weak uncertainty avoidance countries, people are more tolerant of the deviant and the different. They break rules or circumvent procedures if it seems to be in everyone's best interests to do so. They tend to be less anxious and suffer from less job stress; people in low uncertainty avoidance countries give the impression of being quiet, easy going and controlled. On the other hand, in strong uncertainty avoidance countries, people look for security, they resist novel and deviant ideas, they follow procedure and rules and they tend to be more anxious; they come across as aggressive, fidgety and busy.

- **High uncertainty avoidance countries** (Hofstede's top ten from 1–10): Greece, Portugal, Guatemala, Uruguay, Belgium, Salvador, Japan, Yugoslavia, Peru, France/Chile/Spain/Costa Rica/Panama/ Argentina (tied 10th place).

- **Low uncertainty avoidance countries** (Hofstede's bottom ten from 53–43): Singapore, Jamaica, Denmark, Sweden, Hong Kong, Ireland, Great Britain, Malaysia, India, Philippines, USA.

Latin American, Latin European and Mediterranean countries, as well as Japan and South Korea, score high on uncertainty avoidance. Other Asian countries, African countries and Anglo and Nordic countries score low.

Box 4.6   When to lose one's temper

Different cultures have different norms about the extent to which it is acceptable to express one's emotions. In Thailand, for example, there is a strong norm that people should come across as non-assertive, polite and humble, that they should avoid conflicts and remain calm. So Thai staff value supervisors who do not lose their tempers (Phornprapha 1996).

Trompenaars and Hampden-Turner (1997) tell a story of a British manager in Nigeria who

> . . . found it was very effective to raise his voice for important issues. His Nigerian subordinates saw this unexpected explosion by a normally self-controlled manager as a sign of extra concern. After success in Nigeria he was posted to Malaysia. Shouting there was a sign of loss of face; his colleagues did not take him seriously and he was transferred. (p. 75)

Confucian dynamism

This fifth dimension was added by Hofstede in conjunction with a Canadian social scientist, Michael Bond, who was a long-term resident of East Asia. It addresses what was identified as a western bias in the original questionnaire by adding a set of values which were contributed by Chinese social scientists. The Confucian dynamism dimension compares countries with a long-termist orientation with those with a short-termist orientation. Long-termist countries stress perseverance, thrift in terms of use of resources, the need to accumulate savings for investment, the adaptation of tradition to the modern context and are concerned with "virtue". Short-termists countries have a high respect for tradition, respect social and status obligations regardless of cost, exhibit a social pressure to overspend in order to "keep up with the Joneses", expect quick results and are preoccupied with learning the "truth". In terms of behaviour at work, cultures with a long-termist view would be prepared to wait and persevere in order to achieve results where cultures with a short-termist view would be concerned with seeing results quickly and making a quick return. This dimension has been tested on a much smaller sample of countries (23 in total):

- **Long-termist countries** (Hofstede's top six): China, Hong Kong, Taiwan, Japan, South Korea, Brazil.

- **Short-termist countries** (Hofstede's bottom six): Pakistan, Nigeria, Philippines, Canada, Zimbabwe, Great Britain.

The East Asian countries were the most long-termist. Of the European countries studied, the Netherlands was the most long-termist.

Box 4.7   Sequential and polychronic time

The anthropologist Edward Hall (1959) argues that different cultures view time in different ways. A sequential culture sees time as a straight line. We complete one task and then we move on to another. Sequential cultures are concerned about punctuality: time is scheduled in very thin divisions and it is rude to be even a few minutes late because you would be upsetting someone else's schedule. Once in a meeting, we show someone respect by giving them our full attention and avoiding all interruptions. In a polychronic culture, however, a number of activities run in parallel. Activities do not necessarily have to happen in sequence and it would not be acceptable to use being late for an appointment, for example, as an excuse for not giving time to a friend you happen to meet, so meeting times tend to be approximate. People can do more than one activity at once without insulting those they are with.

A group of British managers were involved in a negotiation with an Egyptian company. "We just couldn't get anywhere" one commented afterwards. "We were in the meeting all day and most of the time they were talking on their mobile phones."

A critique of Hofstede's dimensions

Most researchers agree that Hofstede's work is ground-breaking and that it provides many useful insights into the differences that can be seen in organizations around the world. However, his work is obviously not without its critics.

Some of the criticisms of the research are to do with the methodology used. Firstly, his work was based on a questionnaire survey and some researchers do not believe that surveys can be sufficiently subtle to explore something as complex as culture. Hofstede's response to this is that surveys are not, and should not be, the only way to study national culture but they are a valid way (Hofstede 1998). A survey is perhaps the only way of comparing so many national cultures with each other.

Having decided to use a survey, it is then not easy to design questions that are truly free of cultural bias. We tend to ask those questions that reflect our own culture and may not even consider questions that lie outside it (see Box 4.8). One of the ways that Hofstede tried to avoid that problem was by using a multinational group of researchers to design the questionnaire but as these were all westerners, the original research did not sufficiently reflect the eastern view of the world. Thus the need to add the fifth dimension.

Then there is the issue about the way in which the data are analysed. Are these the only dimensions of culture and are these the right dimensions of culture? Hofstede's are not the only dimensions used to describe culture. Trompenaars and Hampden-Turner (1997) have a rather different list and they criticize Hofstede for "perceiving cultures as static points on a dual axis map" (p. 27).

Hofstede's most controversial dimension is probably the masculinity/femininity dimension. Some people argue that it is misnamed, in that it is essentially about materialism/toughness versus quality of life/tenderness rather than about gender differences and sexism (Pizam *et al.* 1997). Hofstede himself argues that "sexes and sex roles are one of the most profound facts of human existence . . . my choice of terms is based on what *is* in virtually all societies, not on what anyone thinks it should be" (Hofstede 1991, p. 107).

Finally, the sample used in this study has been criticized. Can we really learn anything about cultural differences from a survey of people who all work for the same firm: the American computer giant IBM? Employees of IBM may not have provided a representative sample of the national culture as a whole (Mead 1994).

IBM, at the time of the study, had the reputation of being a company with a strong corporate culture where national differences were minimized. One argument is that if national cultural differences were found in a company such as IBM then they might expect to be seen even more strongly in other parts of the community. The IBM sample was therefore a good one to use to measure differences between national cultures (which is what the research aimed to do).

However, Hofstede's research data is now nearly 30 years old and it may also be suggested that it is now obsolete. Hofstede's (1998) refutation of this point is that he is looking at cultural differences that have roots that are centuries old and there is no evidence of a major shift in the last 30 years.

It is important to remember that Hofstede's dimensions provide only one way of describing national cultures. They do not, and were never intended to, completely categorize any culture and should be seen as a useful starting point in an exploration of cultural differences and not as the final word.

Box 4.8   A personal response to Hofstede's work

I first encountered Hofstede's work at a summer school for management academics in 1979 where Geert Hofstede was one of the tutors. It was an international group drawn from over 20 nationalities and provided him with a good opportunity to test out his research which had not yet been published. He asked us to complete the questionnaire. One question particularly struck me – one of the items for a set of questions on what you looked for in a good job asked "how important is it to do a job where you serve your country?". I would never have thought to include that question in any questionnaire on job satisfaction and I had never seen it in any British questionnaires on this. This reflected my own cultural biases and brought home to me the difficulty of designing a cross-cultural questionnaire.

My second memory is of the resistance Hofstede faced to his model, especially from the British participants. We felt uncomfortable about a theory which appeared to put people into such definite categories and there were long arguments about it. Hofstede would explain our reaction by reference to our cultural background. Indeed writing about this summer school he comments:

> Most British participants . . . despise too much structure. They like open-ended learning situations with vague objectives, broad assignments, and no timetables at all. The suggestion that there is only one correct answer is taboo to them. They expect to be rewarded for originality. Their reactions are typical for countries with weak uncertainty avoidance.
>
> (Hofstede 1991, p. 119)

Organizational culture

In the same way as each nation has its own culture, so each organization may be described as having a culture; its own artifacts, norms and values and basic assumptions. Working for McDonald's is not precisely the same as working for Burger King, even though both are fast food companies. As employees affected by the takeover will have discovered, working for Granada is not exactly the same as working for Forte, even if they are both British hospitality companies. Each organization has its own distinctive way of doing things.

As the culture of a country reveals itself through aspects such as the architecture, how people dress, how they greet each other, what stories they tell, what heroes they revere, so the culture of a company also reveals itself through the physical look of the premises, the way people dress and any uniforms they wear, the way people talk to each other, company logos and mission statements and so forth.

As there are typologies of national culture, so there are typologies of organizational culture. One of the best known of these was developed by Charles Handy (1978), adapted from an earlier typology developed by Roger Harrison.

The Handy/Harrison typology

This divides organizations into four ideal types:

1. The power culture
   Image: The spider's web.
   Example: A small independent hotel run by an energetic and controlling entrepreneur.
   Main characteristics: A single powerful leader controls everything. There are few rules and procedures and formal status means little. You are powerful only if you are well in with the leader.
   Working there: Power cultures can be tough places to work. Only those who are good at playing politics will thrive.
   Strengths: Decisions can be made quickly – as the leader does not need to consult anyone.
   Weaknesses: Dependent on the business skills of the person at the top. If their judgement is sound the business can thrive but if not there will be problems. If the organization grows too big the web will break.

2. The role culture
   Image: The Greek temple.
   Example: Any large well-established bureaucratic company will exhibit some role culture characteristics. A major hotel or restaurant company – e.g. McDonald's.
   Main characteristics: Rules and procedures are everything. The company is divided into separate functions (for example, food and beverage, rooms division) which form the pillars of the temple and a small top management team coordinates everything at the top.
   Working there: Role cultures are safe and comfortable, if rather unexciting, places to work. Employees are expected to do an adequate job and the organization can be slow to reward success.
   Strengths: A good way of controlling a large organization that is operating in a relatively stable environment.

Weaknesses: This type of organization is not good at dealing with change and innovation and is slow moving.

3. The task culture
   Image: The net or lattice.
   Example: A creative organization like an advertising agency. In the hospitality industry, a small and innovative restaurant chain might have this type of culture.
   Main characteristics: Power is based on expertise rather than position. People come together to work on specific projects and use their flexibility and adaptability to make things work. When the project is completed, the team may be dissolved and a different team brought together for the next project.
   Working there: This tends to be a favoured type of organization for junior and middle managers.
   Strengths: This type of organization is flexible and adaptable and good at operating in a competitive environment where constant innovation is needed.
   Weaknesses: This type of organization is very dependent on the skills of its staff and may have problems if people leave. If things go wrong, a task culture can turn into a role or power culture very quickly with a detrimental effect on the morale of most employees.

4. The person culture
   Image: The cluster or galaxy of stars.
   Example: A group of individuals who band together to share office costs, equipment and so forth but who work essentially as individuals, for example, lawyers, architects or doctors. It is difficult to think of an example from the hospitality industry but there are cases of "star" performers who treat the organization where they work as if it is a person culture and only have a loose connection to it, for example some celebrity chefs.
   Main characteristics: People decide how they are going to work themselves. The organization exists for the benefit of the people working within it and no one person has more influence than any other partner. Rules and coordination mechanisms are of relatively minor significance. Any disagreements have to be worked through collectively.
   Working there: Many people would prefer to work in organizations that would provide them with this degree of autonomy but true person cultures are rare.

Strengths: This type of organization makes good use of the talents of the individuals working within it.

Weaknesses: This culture only works in very small, specialized organizations and can easily shift to become a power culture if one person's ambition is too strong, so it rarely lasts long.

Box 4.9   Fun is a serious business

An alternative typology of cultures has been developed by Deal and Kennedy (1982). They also distinguish between four different cultures: the tough guy, macho culture; the work-hard/play-hard culture; the bet-your-company culture (applicable mainly to companies engaged in high risk, long-term research and development, e.g. aerospace or pharmaceuticals); the process culture (similar to Handy's role culture).

The work-hard/play-hard culture may be applicable to many companies in the hospitality industry. No individual decision by a member of front line staff or by a junior manager can severely harm the company – there are too many checks and controls built in. But staff get fairly quick feedback about how they are doing: from customers and from sales figures. Deal and Kennedy argue that this type of company is fairly dynamic and customer focused. People work hard but "fun" elements are built in – games, rallies and competitions – to keep morale up and energy levels high.

Hospitality employees often say that what keeps them in their jobs, in spite of long hours and hard work, is the fun of working with each other and with customers. In work-hard/play-hard cultures, having fun is part of the culture and it has positive benefits in helping people achieve. However, the weakness of this culture is that people can tend to focus too much on the present rather than the future and on quick-fix solutions when things go wrong.

No real organization is going to fit any of Handy's or Deal and Kennedy's (Box 4.9) types exactly. These typologies serve to help one think about the ways in which organizations differ from each other and any real organization is likely to manifest elements of the different types. Also different parts of the organization may manifest different cultures. So, in a restaurant chain, the board of directors may operate like a power culture but individual restaurants may be run as role cultures. The marketing department may run as a task culture and the new product development unit may be a person culture.

Strong and weak cultures

Box 4.10   Working for Disney

Paid employment at Disneyland begins with the much-renowned University of Disneyland whose faculty runs a day-long orientation program (Traditions I). . . . In the classroom . . . newly hired ride operators are given a very thorough introduction to matters of managerial concern and are tested on their absorption of famous Disneyland fact, lore and procedure. Employee demeanour is governed, for example, by three rules:

1.   Practice the friendly smile.
2.   Use only friendly and courteous phrases.
3.   We are not stuffy – the only Misters in Disneyland are Mr Toad and Mr Smee.

. . . Language is also a central feature of "university" life and new employees are schooled in its proper use. Customers at Disneyland are, for instance, never referred to as such, they are "guests". There are no rides at Disneyland, only "attractions". Disneyland itself is a "Park", not an amusement centre. . . . And, of course, there are no accidents at Disneyland, only "incidents".

(Van Maanen 1991, pp. 65–6)

Everyone knows what Disney stands for as an organization. The rules that people who work for Disney have to follow – long hair, facial hair and earrings banned for men, fancy jewellery and heavy make-up banned for women – are legendary. As Box 4.10 demonstrates, Disney goes to great lengths to *socialize* its new staff into the culture of Disney, by training them in the specific language, rules, stories and traditions of the Disney organization. Van Maanen (1991) describes the ways that Disney influences its new recruits, recruiting and selecting them carefully, providing a lengthy classroom-based orientation, using inspirational films and pep talks amongst other methods, using supervisors and foremen to monitor their behaviour carefully once they start work and being ready to harshly discipline and even fire "malcontents", "trouble-makers", "bumblers", "attitude problems" or "jerks".

  Thus Disney may be thought of as having a "strong" culture in the sense that there is a clear set of artifacts (stories, ways of behaving, heroes) which are explicitly taught to new members and with which even people outside Disney can identify. These cultural assumptions are applied throughout the organization.

Deal and Kennedy (1982) argue that companies with strong cultures perform much better than companies with weak cultures. "The impact of a strong culture on productivity" they claim "is amazing. In the extreme, we estimate that a company can gain as much as one or two extra hours of productive work per employee per day" (p. 15). In strong cultures, because everyone aligns him- or herself with the same goals, everyone's energy is channelled in the same direction. People are motivated because they identify with the organization and want it to succeed. Strong cultures have a strong sense of their history and are, therefore, better able to learn from and build on the past.

But is that necessarily true? First, it is important to consider what is meant by a strong culture. Artifacts, as was argued earlier in this chapter, are the most superficial manifestation of culture. So people may comply with the rites and rituals of a culture without buying in to a set of shared basic assumptions. When Disneyland Paris (then called EuroDisney) opened, it fuelled a debate about the extent to which the Disney approach could be transferred to Europe; would French staff respond to Disney training in the same way as Americans? However, as Van Maanen (1991) demonstrates, in Disney in the States as well, employees do not fully "buy in" to all the company's propaganda:

> . . . it is difficult to take seriously an organization that provides its retirees "Golden Ears" instead of golden watches after 20 or more years of service. All newcomers are aware that the label "Disneyland" has both an unserious and artificial connotation and that a full embrace of the Disneyland role would be as deviant as its rejection.   (p. 67)

So even apparently strong cultures may not be quite as consistent and unified as they look from the outside. There are pockets of resistance and whilst people may comply with the behaviour required to operate in the culture they may not totally align themselves with the basic assumptions. This may be healthy. These are work organizations, not religious movements! There are countless examples from history of religious cults or political sects with very "strong cultures" where members have been "brainwashed" to pursue violent ends. A strong culture is not necessarily an ethical culture.

Whilst it may be argued that strong cultures can learn from their history, it can also be argued that strong cultures can become too wrapped up in the past (Brown 1995) and fail to recognize that the old ways of doing things are no longer appropriate, or that the way of managing things that worked in one context might not work in another.

Espoused culture and culture-in-practice

> ### Box 4.11   What we say we do and what we do
>
> Doing research in one hotel company in the UK, I was told by the Head
> Office management team that an important aspect of the company's
> culture was that all employees were valued and there was a supportive
> and participative management style. I subsequently interviewed one of
> the assistant managers working in one of the company's hotels. "What do
> you need to learn in order to be a better manager?" I asked him.
>
> "The first thing I need to learn is how to give a good bollocking. The
> second thing I need to learn is how to take a good bollocking" (bollocking
> is slang for severely reprimanding).
>
> It seemed that the management culture actually operating in the hotels
> was not the same as the culture Head Office claimed was operating.

As the example from Disney showed, even in the strongest organizational culture, not everyone conforms. Senior managers are now
very conscious of the need to present their organization's culture positively to customers and potential employees. The messages about
companies presented in formal documentation (in annual reports,
publicity material and in speeches by senior executives) may be
described as the *espoused* culture. This is what people, especially those
at the top of the organization, want the organization to be like. But this
espoused culture may be very different from the way that the culture
actually operates on the ground; what may be described as the *culture-
in-practice* (Brown 1995 building on Argyris and Schon 1978).

Brown (1995) argues that many people are quite able to tolerate a
high degree of discrepancy between the espoused culture and the
culture-in-practice. People can accept that companies need to present
themselves in the best light and the reality will not always match up.
Höpfl (1993), in a case study on British Airways – another company
with a strong organizational culture – describes how people may try to
deal with these ambiguities. She has one of her British Airways
managers, in the case study, describe his feelings about the differences
between the espoused culture and the culture-in-practice thus:

> We talk about caring but I see bullies who are very successful. We talk
> about risk but you try it. I'd be scared about making a genuine mistake –
> I can't see me taking risks and surviving. We talk about valuing the

individual and recognizing that people have domestic lives but, in honesty, who does? I'm never at home. . . . We know it (the company's projection of its culture and values) is hype – they know it's hype. It's okay. It's reassuring. It makes you feel good. But do I believe it – well that's a totally different question.

(Höpfl 1993, pp. 122–3)

The sources of organizational culture

Box 4.12   Bill Marriott

Bill Marriott (senior) who founded the Marriott company and hotel chain was described by Ronald Reagan as a "living example of the American dream". His biographer confirmed that:

> The corporation was literally his creation – his lifelong poem, his heart's blood masterpiece. His drive and later his dream, his philosophy, the effort he gave and the effort he demanded of others, his concern for people – for nearly half a century these conditioned and vitalized every policy, every decision, every corporate move.
>
> (O'Brien 1977, p. 2)

Marriott's maxim was that "It takes happy employees to make happy customers". Marriott's non-recognition of trade unions in the 1930s and 1940s were justified through the argument that:

> Bill and Allie (his wife) didn't need the American Federation of Labor (AFL) . . . to persuade them to be good to their employees. . . . They were all a big happy family and all in business together. If everyone worked hard, led a good life and stayed loyal to the company, they would be rewarded materially.
>
> (O'Brien 1977, p. 179)

Continuity of influence has been provided by the appointment of Bill Marriott (junior) to the position of President, then Chairman of Marriott International Inc.

(Adapted from Nickson 1997)

The founder of a company obviously has an ideal opportunity to mould it according to his or her vision and ideals. Thus many companies will draw many aspects of their culture from the personality and style of their founders. Founders will also be influenced by their backgrounds and national identity. In the example in Box 4.12, Bill Marriott's Mormon background and middle American values influenced his direction of the company. Kemmons Wilson (founder of Holiday Inn) and Conrad Hilton (founder of Hilton) also made much of their faith in the American dream (Nickson 1997). One of Conrad Hilton's motives in developing hotels outside the USA was to establish "little Americas" which would both be a home-from-home for American travellers and also extend American values and influence around the world.

However, as companies grow and develop and as leadership passes on from the founder, so his or her influence will be moderated by the values and background of the new senior people. Sometimes, as in the Marriott example, the influence of the founder may be perpetuated by the appointment of another family member. But this is not without its problems. Charles Forte who founded the Forte organization (a UK hospitality company) handed over to his son Rocco. However, there were continuing comments in the press about whether Rocco Forte could continue with his father's legacy (especially while his father was still alive) and in 1995 the Forte organization lost its battle against a hostile takeover bid by Granada (see Nickson 1997).

Often, however, founders are replaced by professional managers. Their backgrounds, both their nationalities and their work experience, will influence the organization's culture. Using the Handy/Harrison typology, a company run by a charismatic founder may retain strong elements of a power culture where professional managers may shift it towards a role or task culture. Roper *et al.* (1997) comment that where chief executive officers of international hotel groups have typically come through the ranks of the hotel industry, many companies are now bringing in outsiders who bring with them new perspectives. Some companies develop a preference for senior people with certain functional expertise and this, again, is likely to influence the culture. Bass, for example, has been described as a "control oriented company run by accountants" (Hotels 1996 p. 3 quoted in Roper *et al.* 1997) and, true to form, they have recently appointed a chief executive of Holiday Inns Worldwide (part of the Bass group) who has a strong financial background.

But, as was discussed in the previous section, founders and senior managers are likely to be able to influence the *espoused* culture of the organization. In individual hotels and restaurants the *culture-in-practice* may be very different. In a global hotel company, for example, it is likely that the culture in any individual hotel will be influenced by the culture of the country in which it is situated. But, as the example in Box 4.1 illustrates, one cannot assume that the nationality of the people who work in a hotel will always be of the "host" nation. The hospitality industry tends to be a multi-cultural industry and one of the issues about this is that managers and employees in the same unit may not necessarily share the same cultural assumptions. Further, as Roper *et al.* (1997) point out, the culture of the customers may also influence the culture of the unit. One may ask what are the cultural influences on an American-owned hotel in London which caters mainly for Japanese visitors.

Jones *et al.* (1994) comment that it is better to think of an international organization as a "cultural mosaic" rather than a "cultural melting pot". Corporate culture, even in those companies with strong cultures, does not completely obliterate local cultural identities; subcultures and diverse identities remain. Roper *et al.* (1997) argue that it is even better to think of organizations as "cultural kaleidoscopes" where there are different influences which merge and alter pattern as the organization develops. I shall return to these issues in later chapters of this book.

Summary

- Culture can be described as "the collective programming of the human mind which distinguishes the members of one group or category of people from another" (Hofstede 1980). Our cultural assumptions affect how we view the world, make decisions and solve problems.

- Culture is learned. A person's cultural assumptions will be affected by their nationality, regional or ethnic background, gender, generation, social class, education, occupation and the organization they work for.

- The most superficial manifestation of culture is in artifacts: material objects, stories, rites, rituals, ceremonies, heroes and symbols. At a deeper level, culture affects norms and values: what people believe they should do and how they distinguish between good and bad, right and wrong. At the deepest level, culture affects our basic assumptions about what the world is like and our place within it.

- Many researchers are now studying the ways in which national culture affects behaviour in organizations. The most famous study was conducted by Hofstede (1980, 1991). He identified five dimensions of national culture – power distance, individualism/ collectivism, masculinity/femininity, uncertainty avoidance and Confucian dynamism – and has scored different countries against these dimensions.

- As nationalities may be argued to have cultures, so organizations can be described as having cultures. Handy (1978) distinguishes between four types of organization: the power culture, the role culture, the task culture and the person culture.

- Some organizations have much stronger cultures than others. They make more effort to socialize their employees, through careful selection and training, to conform to the cultural norms and values of the organization. In the hospitality industry, Disney is a good example of a strong culture. Although some writers have claimed that organizations with strong cultures are more effective than those with weak cultures, most researchers would not agree. Organizations with strong cultures may have difficulty adapting to change.

- The espoused culture of an organization is not necessarily the same as its culture-in-practice. The espoused culture is the way the leaders of an organization would like it to be. It can be seen in their mission statements, annual reviews, the speeches made by senior executives. The culture-in-action describes the cultural norms people actually conform to.

- An organization's culture is influenced by the values and attitudes of its founder and senior managers and the national culture in which it is situated. In an international company, the culture of each unit is likely to be affected by the country in which it is based, the range of nationalities of its managers and employees and the nationality of its customers, making up a kaleidoscope of different cultural identities.

The next stage

Experience

When you next have the opportunity to travel to another country, try to identify the features of its national culture. Look particularly for artifacts: buildings, dress, behaviour, symbols, stories, rites and ceremonies that tell you something about the culture.

Try to experience your own national culture as an outsider. What aspects of the culture would strike you if you were a foreigner? You may find this exercise easiest to do on a return from a trip to another country. Alternatively ask a friend from a different national background what aspects of your country's culture strike them. Try to see your home with their eyes.

Try to build up a picture of the culture of any organization you have access to. In particular, look for differences between the espoused culture and the culture-in-practice. You might pick a hotel company, for example, and first collect the public statements that the company makes about itself. What does the annual report or the publicity material that the company issues to prospective employees and to customers say about its culture? Then go into one of the company's hotels. What can you learn about the company's culture by noting decor, dress, and the behaviour of employees? Finally, try to interview someone who works, or has worked, for the company and find out what it is like in practice. Note any discrepancies between these different ways of looking at culture.

Reflection

Refer back to Box 4.1. What is your personal reaction to each of the incidents described? How does your reaction relate to your national identity, i.e. are you reacting as someone conforming with the norms of your national background would be predicted to? Where should you be placed according to Hofstede's dimensions if you conformed to your country's norms? (Refer to Hofstede 1980 or Hofstede 1991 if necessary.) If you do not identify yourself with your country's norms, are there other influences in your background that might account for your distinctiveness?

Can you think of any examples of misunderstandings due to differences in cultural values based in your personal experience? (See for example Box 4.4 and Box 4.6.) Can you relate them to any of the dimensions of cultural difference decribed in this chapter? (If not, can you find an explanation from your further readings?)

Reflect on your experience as a new employee in an organization. How were you socialized into the culture of the organization? Would you describe the organization as a strong or a weak culture? Why? If you have worked for an organization with a strong culture and another with a weak culture, what were the differences in the way you were treated as a new employee?

Refer to the Handy/Harrison typology. Which of these different organizational types would be your "ideal" organization? (There is a self-diagnosis questionnaire in Handy 1978.) Can you relate any organizations that you are familiar with to these types? What happened that would make you describe one organization as a power culture, for example, and another as a role culture?

Theorizing

Hofstede argues that national culture strongly influences organization culture. Take two distinctively different national cultures: for example, you might look at a low power distance, individualist, masculine, low uncertainty avoidance and short-termist culture like Britain and compare it with a high power distance, collectivist, feminine, strong uncertainty avoidance and long-termist culture like Thailand (refer to Hofstede 1980 or Hofstede 1991 for each country's ranking). How would you expect typical UK organizational culture to differ from typical Thai organizational culture? Can you find any evidence that UK and Thai organizations are like that? (After attempting your own analysis read Hofstede 1991 Section III as a comparison.)

Some international companies try to impose a common corporate culture across all their outlets whilst others seem to accommodate a diversity of sub-cultures. What are the advantages and disadvantages of both approaches?

In practice

If you were Mike in Box 4.1, how would you manage these cultural misunderstandings?

You are the assistant manager of a restaurant and have just welcomed a new unit manager from another country (you decide which). She has never worked in your country before and asks your advice about the do's and don'ts of working here. What advice would you give her?

You have the finance and the premises and you are about to open your own restaurant. You have lunch with your friend who is a management consultant and ask his advice about the next steps. "What type of culture do you want your restaurant to have?" he asks. What is your reply?

Further reading

There are chapters in all the main organizational behaviour textbooks covering the issues in this chapter (see Further Reading Chapter 2). Beyond that, Adler (1991) is a good general textbook which focuses particularly on national cultural differences. Trompenaars and Hampden-Turner (1997) is well worth reading and so, of course, is Hofstede: start with *Cultures and Organizations* (1991). For some research which relates Hofstede's dimensions to the hospitality sector, consult Pizam *et al.* (1997).

As regards organizational culture, a good general text which covers all the issues (it also looks at the relationship between organizational and national culture) is Brown (1995). You can also refer to Handy (1978). Lundberg and Woods (1991) look at organizational culture in a restaurant setting.

To gain more insight into what it feels like to work in a strong culture I would recommend both Van Maanen (1991) on Disney and Höpfl (1993) on British Airways. For a discussion of the way in which founders affect organizational culture within the hospitality industry refer to Nickson (1997) and Roper *et al.* (1997).

References for further reading

Adler, N. (1991) *International Dimensions of Organizational Behavior* (Second edition), Boston, Mass: PWS-Kent.

Brown, A. (1995) *Organisational Culture*, London: Pitman.

Handy, C. (1978) *The Gods of Management*, London: Penguin.

Hofstede, G. (1991) *Cultures and Organizations*, London: McGraw Hill (paperback version HarperCollins Business 1994).

Höpfl, H. (1993) Culture and Commitment: British Airways, in Gowler, D., Legge, K. and Clegg, C. (eds) *Cases in Organizational Behaviour and Human Resource Management*, London: Paul Chapman.

Lundberg, C. and Woods, R. (1991) Modifying restaurant culture: managers as cultural leaders, *International Journal of Contemporary Hospitality Management*, **2** 2: 4–12.

Nickson, D. (1997) 'Colorful stories' or historical insight? – a review of the auto/biographies of Charles Forte, Conrad Hillton, J.W. Marriott and Kemmons Wilson, *Journal of Hospitality and Tourism Research*, **21**, 1: 179–192.

Pizam, A., Pine, R., Mok, C. and Shin, J.Y. (1997) National vs industry cultures: which has the greatest effect on managerial behavior, *International Journal of Hospitality Management*, **15**, 347–362.

Roper, A., Brookes, M. and Hampton, A. (1997) The multi-cultural management of international hotel groups, *International Journal of Hospitality Management*, **16**, 2: 147–159.

Trompenaars, F. and Hampden-Turner, C. (1997) *Riding the Waves of Culture* (Second edition), London: Nicholas Brealey.

Van Maanen, J. (1991) The Smile Factory: Work at Disneyland, in Frost, P., Moore, L., Reis Louis, M., Lundberg, C., Martin, J. (eds) *Reframing Organizational Culture*, California: Sage, 58–76.

5

Motivation, job performance and job satisfaction

Box 5.1 Employee of the month awards

Employee of the month and employee of the year awards are commonly introduced as a method of motivating operative level staff in hotels. These awards have been introduced into some hotels in Bali, Indonesia by some of the international chains operating there. At a management development course, some of the Balinese managers complained about these schemes. "My staff come to me" they said, "and say, 'please don't make me employee of the month because if you do all my friends will be jealous and I won't be able to enjoy my work.'"

What do people want from work?

From a broader discussion of the nature of hospitality organizations, this chapter now moves on to explore the issue of how people behave in organizations. What motivates people to want to put effort into their work? This has been one of the most debated topics in management. People who have only a slight knowledge of management theory have often heard of the Hawthorne experiments, of Maslow's hierarchy of needs and of Herzberg's motivators and hygiene factors. Managers have good reason to be interested in motivation theory. Surely, if people want to work, if they are motivated to work, they will work better than if they are not motivated. In fact, the connection between motivation and job performance is not quite as straightforward as it may seem at first (this will be discussed in more detail below). Nevertheless, the issue of how we manage people so they want to do what we want them to do is a central one. Anyone who has tried to manage a group of staff or even organize a group of fellow students to complete a project or a group of friends to organize a social event will testify that it is not easy to sustain motivation.

Early theories about motivation usually claimed to be universal theories. The implication was that they would be equally relevant when motivating a waiter from Italy or a hotel manager from Singapore or a room attendant from Bulgaria. However, most of the early theories of motivation were, as Adler (1991) affirms, "developed in the United States by Americans and about Americans". As has been shown in the previous chapter, cultural differences do affect behaviour at work.

Box 5.1 suggests that a method of encouraging staff to work hard, an Employee of the Month scheme, that may be an appropriate reward in the United States may be seen as a punishment in other cultures, in this case Bali. However, this example is not clear cut. Perhaps some Balinese employees would respond positively to an Employee of the Month scheme, whereas some employees in the States may think being made Employee of the Month will affect their working relationships.

This chapter will explore the following issues:

- **What is motivation?** I will review the theories of motivation that have been developed, from the earliest theories of Taylor and Mayo to more recent ideas such as expectancy theory and equity theory. In particular, the chapter will consider whether any of these theories describe psychological principles which can be applied to people everywhere.

- **How is motivation related to job performance and job satisfaction?** Are people who put effort into their work necessarily the best workers? If you put effort into your work do you necessarily enjoy your work?

- **How does money motivate?** What are the limitations of using money as a motivator? How does tipping (a practice widespread in the hospitality industry) affect the behaviour of staff?

Motivation at work is about a person's willingness to work. Wright (1991) defines it as "the willingness to expend effort on a particular task in order to attain an incentive or incentive of a certain type" (p. 77).

A distinction is usually made between two types of theory about motivation:

1. **Content theories**: these focus on understanding *what* people want, need or desire.
2. **Process theories**: these theories focus on *how* people's wants, needs and desires affect their behaviour.

The earliest theories of motivation tend to be content theories.

Content theories of motivation

Box 5.2   Taylorism

All of us are grown up children, and it is . . . true that the average workman will work with the greatest satisfaction, when he is given each day a definite task which he is to perform in a given time, and which constitutes a proper day's work for a good workman. . . . It is impossible, through any long period of time, to get workmen to work much harder than the average men around them, unless they are assured a large and permanent increase in their pay . . . however, . . . plenty of workmen can be found who are willing to work at their best speed providing they are given this liberal increase in wages.

(Taylor, 1911, p. 120)

. . . Taylor's workers were expected to be as reliable, predictable and efficient as the robots that are now replacing them.

(Morgan, 1986, p. 33)

Taylor and Taylorism

F.W. Taylor pioneered what is now described as "Scientific Management" and was one of the first management theorists to concern himself with motivation. Taylor was an American engineer whose major studies were completed in the 1890s. He advocated rational scientific study of human behaviour in the same way as one might use scientific method to investigate an engineering problem. "Laws (of motivation), which apply to a large majority of men, unquestionably exist and when clearly defined are of great value as a guide in dealing with men" (Taylor 1911).

The underpinning principle behind Taylor's thinking about management was the "separation of conception from execution" (Braverman 1974). Managers should "think" and workers should "work". Managers should scientifically discover the best way of performing a particular task, teach workers to perform it in precisely that way, and reward them for doing it correctly. The implications of Taylorism for job design and organizational design are discussed in more detail in Chapter 7. Here the focus is on the way Taylor thought that people could be motivated to put effort into their work. His belief was that people had a relatively simple set of needs at work and could be encouraged to work through the provision of relatively simple rewards, particularly money.

In the 1950s, Douglas McGregor described the beliefs about human nature that underpinned Taylorism in what he called the "Theory X" view of management:

1. The average man is by nature indolent – he works as little as possible.
2. He lacks ambition, dislikes responsibility and prefers to be led.
3. He is inherently self-centred, indifferent to organizational needs.
4. He is by nature resistant to change.
5. He is gullible, not very bright, the ready dupe of the charlatan and the demagogue (McGregor 1960).

McGregor's focus here was on the way managers think their staff are motivated. He is definitely not arguing that most people conform to these Theory X views but he is arguing that many managers act *as if* their staff are Theory X. Of course, the implicit assumption in Taylorism is that managers are different. Workers may be an indolent rabble but there are some people, the managers, who have more self-discipline and intelligence and can be put in charge. The only way they can exercise control is through coercion and bribery.

The reason that Taylor's ideas, although they were developed a hundred years ago, are still relevant to discuss today is that these ideas still permeate management thinking. Taylorist ideas were developed by Henry Ford (1863–1947) into a system of car manufacturing in which individual jobs were highly specialized and individual workers highly directed. These same Fordist approaches can still be seen in, for example, fast food chains such as McDonald's. McDonald's, like Ford, routinizes the work of its crews so that jobs become almost "idiot proof" (Leidner 1993).

Taylor's assumptions about motivation are subject to criticism on several grounds. Of course, it can be argued that Taylor oversimplified and distorted human nature and motivation. People may, as McGregor (1960) argues, "live for bread alone when there is little bread". Taylor failed to recognize the other social and psychological needs that people seek to meet at work, and jobs designed according to "scientific management" principles may pay the rent or the mortgage but may feel boring, alienating and soul destroying. From a management perspective too, Taylorism has its drawbacks. If managers treat workers like idiots they tend to find them behaving like idiots, rigidly applying the rules without thought or doing what they need to in order to be rewarded or avoid punishments even if that is not in the best interests of the company.

Box 5.3   How to create a Theory X worker

A student took a summer job in a factory and was given the task of minding a machine. Being a mechanically minded person he studied the way that the machine worked and when it went wrong he could see immediately what the problem was. But two men in white coats descended on the machine, pushed him to one side and refused to listen to his advice about how to fix it. The next time the machine went wrong, the student did not even attempt to offer advice to the engineers. He went off for a coffee break, hoping that the engineers would take some time to solve the problem.

The human side of organization: Mayo, Maslow, McGregor and Herzberg

"Human relations" and "neo-human relations" thinkers reacted against Taylor's assumption that people could be treated like robots and argued that in order to understand organizations, we need to understand the nature of human beings, their feelings, wants and aspirations. Such thinkers also tended to be optimistic about the extent to which organizations can provide opportunities for their employees to achieve personal growth and fulfilment through their work.

Elton Mayo's famous "Hawthorne Studies" were conducted in the Hawthorne Works of the Western Electric Company in Chicago in the 1920s and 1930s. At the outset of these studies, Mayo was interested in the effects of rest pauses on fatigue, accidents and labour turnover. As the research progressed and Mayo discovered that the productivity of his experimental group increased when he increased the number of rest pauses *and* when he decreased them, the research team changed its focus and its explanation of how people at work are motivated. Mayo's study highlighted how relationships within the work group and the relationship between the supervisor and the work group affect behaviour at work. Employees, according to Mayo, are motivated by "the logic of sentiment", whilst managers are driven by "the logic of cost and efficiency"; employees care about how they are treated at work, whether they get on with their co-workers and supervisor, how they are valued, not whether the firm is making a profit or not.

In the 1950s and 1960s, several American organizational psychologists, particularly Douglas McGregor, Frederick Herzberg and Chris Argyris, tried to take Mayo's ideas further. They were particularly interested in the ways in which operative level jobs could be modified or "enriched" to be more challenging and fulfilling and they were strongly influenced by Abraham Maslow's Theory of Motivation.

Maslow described himself as a humanistic psychologist who was interested in human potential and the type of society, and work organization, that allows human beings to reach their full potential. Maslow identified a hierarchy of five basic needs that he argues are shared by all human beings:

1. *Physiological needs*: the basic physical needs that all animals need to satisfy: hunger, thirst and sleep.
2. *Safety needs*: to live in a secure and predictable world. To be protected from danger and accident. To have a safe home and a secure income.
3. *Social and love needs*: to have family and friends. To feel that they have a place in a group and that they are liked and valued by others.
4. *Esteem needs*: to be respected by others and to have a high evaluation of themselves.
5. *Self-actualization*: to fulfil one's potential whatever that may be, to do what one is fitted for. In Maslow's words "what a man [sic] *can* be, he *must* be" (Maslow 1943).

According to Maslow, people are not motivated by satisfied needs. If a human being is starving, she will be driven to satisfy that basic physiological need, i.e. to find food, and will not care about esteem or self-actualization. However, as soon as the basic physiological needs are broadly satisfied, the next level of need in the hierarchy becomes important, i.e. the safety needs, and one ceases to be concerned about the physiological needs. If you know you have enough to eat and will have enough to eat, you do not waste your time worrying about where your next meal is coming from. A fortunate person living in modern society may have the lower needs in the hierarchy broadly satisfied. She may have a home, a steady job, family and friends and be respected by others. For that person, according to Maslow, the need for self-actualization will be the need which drives her behaviour and this is the one need that cannot be satisfied. The more one self-actualizes the more one needs to self-actualize.

Relating Maslow's hierarchy to the work situation, there are a number of ways in which organizations can attempt to satisfy the different needs in the hierarchy:

- **Physiological**:   Basic wages/salary
                            Working conditions, such as the correct
                            temperature etc.
                            Adequate rest breaks and meal breaks

- **Safety**:   Safe working environment
                            Job security
                            Pension and health care packages

- **Social**:   Compatible work group
                            Friendly supervisor
                            Opportunities to socialize
                            Sports and social facilities
                            Parties and outings

- **Esteem**:   Impressive job title, office, company car
                            Feedback and praise for good work
                            Work that is important and challenging
                            Rewards linked to achievement: employee of
                            the month, merit pay etc.

- **Self-actualization**:   Challenging and interesting work that
                            becomes a way of expressing who you are
                            and is a major part of your life.

Box 5.4   Self-actualization

Michel Roux and Nico Ladenis both own Michelin-starred restaurants and so clearly love and gain fulfilment from their work that they may be regarded as "self-actualizing" in Maslow's terms. The following description by Michel Roux of Nico gives some indication of the way his work is his life.

"I met Nico in the late seventies . . . I knew about him and his restaurant, Chez Nico, in Dulwich. At the time he had a reputation for upsetting some of his customers, especially those who dared to question what he had cooked. . . . It was obvious that he loved what he was doing. Unusually he was completely self-taught. . . . I asked him if he had thought of going to work with one of the great chefs in a three-star Michelin restaurant. . . . That week in France changed Nico's professional life. For him, Vergé was God, so the opportunity to get involved in one of the greatest kitchens in Europe was a turning point for him.

("How we met", *Independent on Sunday Review*, 20 October 1996, p. 91)

Maslow's work remains influential because:

- it is a useful way of classifying the different needs that people try to fulfil through work;

- it drew attention to the "higher-level" needs of esteem and self-actualization and therefore influenced writers such as Herzberg, McGregor and Argyris to claim that the way to motivate people at work was to give them challenging and demanding tasks rather than, as Taylor had advocated, simple ones.

However, the model also has its limitations:

- Research evidence does not support Maslow's five-stage hierarchy. It is probably safe to claim that there is a two-stage hierarchy and that people need to have their lower order needs (the existence and security needs) broadly satisfied before the higher level needs will influence their behaviour.

- Human motivation is considerably more complex and diverse than is recognized in this type of general theory. Maslow underestimated the effects of social and cultural factors on motivation, i.e. he assumes that what will motivate a group of waiters in France will equally motivate a group of receptionists in Malaysia. Even the needs and wants of one person may not remain the same; what motivates me today may not motivate me next year or even next week. It has been argued (Hofstede 1980) that Maslow was unwittingly influenced by his own cultural background as an American when he argues that individual self-actualization is what human existence should be about. People from other cultural backgrounds may view life in less individualistic terms.

In summary, Maslow's hierarchy is helpful if one wants to know what categories of motives one should think about when designing a motivation system for a workforce. It is of little help if the problem is: "How do I motivate this particular room attendant (or group of room attendants)?" The process theories of motivation can offer more useful advice to the manager with the latter problem.

Maslow's ideas were popularized for managers by Douglas McGregor (1960). His Theory Y assumptions about the way human beings are motivated, which is based heavily on Maslow's ideas, contrast with Theory X assumptions, which were based on Taylorism and have been discussed above.

The Theory Y view of management is that:

1. the expenditure of physical and mental effort in work is as natural as play or rest. Human beings do not inherently dislike work;
2. external control and the threat of punishment are not the only means of bringing about effort toward organizational objectives. People will exercise self-direction and self-control if they are committed to what they are doing;
3. commitment to objectives is a function of the rewards associated with their achievement. Self-actualization can be a reward for work;
4. the average human being learns over time not only to accept responsibility but to seek it;
5. the capacity to exercise a relatively high degree of imagination, ingenuity and creativity in the solution of organizational problems is widely, not narrowly, distributed in the population;
6. in modern organizational life, the potential of the average human being is underutilized (McGregor 1960).

Theory Y takes an optimistic view of human capabilities. Given the right work environment, according to McGregor, human beings are capable of much more creativity and ingenuity than we give them credit for. People are not naturally lazy, stupid or self-centred: if they behave that way that is because of the way they are treated (see Box 5.3).

There is one final early writer about motivation who needs to be discussed: Frederick Herzberg. Herzberg, like Maslow, makes a broad distinction between lower level needs and higher level needs. His Motivator–Hygiene theory, unlike Maslow's Hierarchy of Needs, was based on *empirical* research: a study of 200 engineers and accountants in Pittsburgh in the late 1950s. Herzberg argued that the factors that cause someone to be satisfied with their job are not the same as those that cause them to be dissatisfied with their job. Positive satisfaction requires the presence of *motivators* – achievement, recognition, interesting work, responsibility and advancement – that is, Maslow's higher level needs for esteem and self-actualization. Dissatisfaction is associated with *hygiene factors* – company policy, supervision, salary, interpersonal relations and working conditions. If the hygiene factors are good, according to Herzberg, people will not be dissatisfied with their jobs but they will not be positively satisfied either. Managers should therefore focus on providing staff with interesting and challenging jobs: on enriching jobs rather than simplifying them.

Researchers who have attempted to replicate Herzberg's study have not discovered the same neat division between the factors that cause job satisfaction and those that cause job dissatisfaction. The original two-factor theory is therefore largely discredited. However, Herzberg's work has contributed the following to our knowledge of motivation.

- The factors motivating people at work can usefully be divided into *intrinsic* and *extrinsic* factors.
  - Intrinsic factors are the characteristics of the work itself – how interesting the work is, how demanding it is.
  - Extrinsic factors relate to the context of the work – the physical environment, whether one likes one's colleagues and supervisor, salary and perks.

- One can improve motivation by improving the intrinsic interest of the job. However, contrary to Herzberg's original claims, this is not the only way to improve motivation and it will not work with all employees or all of the time.

Box 5.5 demonstrates how Herzberg saw intrinsic and extrinsic factors and how he thought that doing interesting work would help individuals to grow psychologically and motivate them. Note the similarity with

Maslow's ideas about human beings and the contrast with Taylor's theories of motivation.

Box 5.5   Herzberg and motivation

Why do the motivators affect motivation in a positive direction? An analogy drawn from a familiar example of psychological growth in children may be useful. When a child learns to ride a bicycle, he is becoming more competent, increasing the repertory of his behavior, expanding his skills – psychologically growing. In the process of the child's learning to master a bicycle, the parents can love him with all the zeal and compassion of the most devoted mother and father. They can safeguard the child from injury by providing the safest and most hygienic area in which to practice; they can provide all kinds of incentives and rewards, and they can provide the most expert instructions. But the child will never, never learn to ride a bicycle – unless he is given a bicycle! The hygiene factors are not a valid contributor to psychological growth. The substance of a task is required to achieve growth goals. Similarly, you cannot love an engineer into creativity, although by this approach you can avoid the dissatisfactions with the way you treat him. Creativity will require a potentially creative task to do.

(Herzberg 1966)

Process theories of motivation

Expectancy theory

An expectancy theory of motivation was originally formulated by Tolman and Lewin in the 1930s, was first applied to the work situation by Vroom in the 1960s, and was further developed and elaborated by Porter and Lawler in the late 1960s. Expectancy Theory first attempts to answer the question: "What makes someone put effort into their work?"

What makes someone put effort into their work?

The obvious answer to that is that people put effort into their work because they expect certain desirable outcomes from working hard.

These outcomes may be intrinsic – I will feel satisfied because I have solved a difficult problem – or extrinsic – my boss will recommend me for promotion, the customer will give me a bigger tip, I will be made "Employee of the Month". Effort is, therefore, influenced by our *expectancies* about the outcomes of working hard.

Stop

Think about a task that you have to do. It may be a task at work (handling a project) or at college (writing an assignment) or associated with a leisure activity (taking part in a sports match). Write down about six outcomes that you expect if you work hard at this task.

If you have attempted the above task honestly, you will realize that people do not always believe that they will be rewarded for working hard. You may have some positive outcomes in your list: if I work hard other people will respect me, if I work hard I will get a better mark for my assignment etc. However, you may also have thought of some disadvantages of working hard: "if I work hard I will be too tired to enjoy going out with my friends in the evening", " if I work hard and my boss/lecturer/coach praises me, my friends may get jealous". (Refer back to the boxed example at the beginning of the chapter.) There may be outcomes that you would like to happen but that you do not believe are associated with working hard at the task. You might like to get a good mark for an assignment but believe that, however hard you work, this will never happen because you are not clever enough or because your lecturer does not like you.

According to expectancy theory (Porter *et al.* 1975), the amount of effort that a person puts into a task can be calculated by listing the main outcomes that the person expects from working hard at the task and for each of these outcomes calculating:

- **The expectancy**: the perceived probability that the outcome will occur if the person works hard (on a scale of 0 – outcome will not happen; to 1 – outcome will definitely happen);

multiplied by

- **the valence or value of the outcome**: how desirable or undesirable the outcome is (on a scale of +3 – very desirable; to –3 – very undesirable).

An illustration of the calculation is given in the box below. If you are mathematically minded, you may like to try to calculate the motivational force that you will put into a task in the same way.

Box 5.6   Motivational force for a waiter one lunchtime

Outcome 1: "If I work hard I will earn more money"
Expectancy: 0.1 (Salary is fixed and not dependent on how hard I work. Tips go into a central pot so are determined by how hard the team works, not just me)
Valence: +3 (I am broke and would really like to earn more money)
E × V: $0.1 \times 3 = 0.3$

Outcome 2: "If I work hard I will be tired at the end of the day"

Expectancy: 1.0 (Yes, the harder I work the more tired I will be)
Valence: −1 (I want to go out after the shift and would prefer not to be too tired)
E × V: $1 \times -1 = -1.0$

Outcome 3: "If I work hard my supervisor will notice and praise me"

Expectancy: 0.1 (The supervisor never notices how hard anyone works and rarely praises or criticizes anyone)
Valence: 0 (And I don't care what she thinks of me anyway)
E × V: $0.1 \times 0 = 0$

Outcome 4: "If I work hard the customers will be nicer and easier to serve"

Expectancy: 0.4 (However, sometimes even if I work hard, because of problems in the kitchen things go wrong and the customers are not happy)
Valence: 2 (On the whole it is easier to deal with satisfied customers)
E × V: $0.4 \times 2 = 0.8$

Outcome 5: "If I work hard I will enhance my career prospects"

Expectancy: −0.1 (I don't want a career in the hotel or restaurant industry. Working as a waiter might even be a disadvantage long term)
Valence: 3 (I am really interested in my career)
E × V: $-0.1 \times 3 = -0.3$

Outcome 6: "If I work hard it will be harder to chat to my workmates"

Expectancy: −0.5 (Customers can really get in the way of a good gossip)
Valence: 3 (Chatting to my mates is the best part of this job)
E × V: $-0.5 \times 3 = -1.5$

Motivational force (or effort put into job)

$0.3 - 1.0 + 0 + 0.8 - 0.3 - 1.5 = -1.7$

As the total is a negative number the theory predicts that this waiter would not put effort into his task.

Of course, it would be a very unusual waiter who actually decided how hard he was going to work based on this calculation! But expectancy theory does assume that human beings are calculating creatures, who do consider the likely outcomes of their actions and weigh up the attractiveness to them of alternative options. Expectancy theory merely provides a model through which researchers can replicate these decision processes. Note that the waiter in the situation above is behaving perfectly rationally in his terms. In a different job or even in a different situation in this job, he might work very hard. But on this occasion, there is no advantage for him to bother.

There are several clear messages for managers trying to motivate staff:

- You cannot motivate someone by offering them a reward that they do not value. And you cannot necessarily assume that all your staff will value the same reward in the same way. For some people being made "Employee of the Month" would be wonderful. Other people might see it in a less positive light.

- People will only be motivated by a reward if they believe that there is a strong link between working hard and gaining the reward. I may want to be a millionnaire but it is clear to me that working harder at my present job is unlikely to help me achieve that goal!

- It is the individual's *perceptions* of the link between their effort and the reward that matters. I may believe that my boss has no influence over whether I am promoted or not. I may be totally wrong; my boss may have a lot of influence over that decision. However, my actions will be determined by my beliefs about the situation, not what the situation actually is.

The expectancy model does not merely attempt to explain why people may or may not put effort into their work. It goes on to explore the relationship between effort, work performance and job satisfaction.

Working hard, working well and feeling good about it

We are all familiar with the story of the student who dashed off an assignment in an hour the night before it was due in and received a better mark for it than the student who spent most of the last month struggling to complete the same piece of work. Effort is not always rewarded and lack of effort does not always mean we cannot do our work adequately. The customers served by the waiter in the example in Box 5.6 might not have been aware of his lack of motivation.

Stop

What other factors, apart from effort, affect work performance? Why do some people work hard but do not work well while others produce satisfactory work with no effort at all?

The other factors, apart from effort, that affect work performance include:

* **Ability**. Do you have the knowledge and skills needed for the task? Ability may relate to aptitude, training or practice and experience.
* **Resources**. Do you have the equipment, materials and support to perform the task?
* **Goal clarity**. Do you understand what is expected of you? The student who writes a bad assignment, for example, may not have understood what the lecturer wanted and how the assignment would be evaluated.

Job satisfaction

In expectancy theory, job satisfaction is the end result. When we have completed a task, handed in an assignment for example, there are certain outcomes from this. These outcomes may be *intrinsic* (a feeling of pride for having done a good piece of work, of relief for having handed it in on time) or *extrinsic* (a mark and comments from the lecturer). Our level of satisfaction reflects our feelings about these outcomes. Locke (1976, p. 1300) defines job satisfaction "as a pleasurable or positive emotional state resulting from the appraisal of one's job or job experiences". A common way of thinking about job satisfaction is in terms of the degree of "fit" between what an organization requires of its employees and provides for its employees and what the employees are seeking from the firm (Mumford 1972). Employees are looking for a "fit" against a number of dimensions; intrinsic work interest, pay and rewards, social relationships, level and type of control and so forth, so job satisfaction becomes a multidimensional rather than a global concept, where employees can be satisfied with their colleagues, for example, but dissatisfied with the nature of the work itself.

Box 5.7   Job satisfaction amongst Finnish hotel receptionists

Many hotels have difficulty recruiting suitably trained staff for operative level positions. But what happens when the opposite is true; recruitment is easy and staff tend to be overqualified for their jobs? In Finland, a high proportion of young people continue into higher education (over 70% in 1990); a growing number of these study courses aiming to prepare them for supervisory and management roles in the hospitality industry. In the early 1990s, Finland was hit by a deep recession and a sharp growth in unemployment. Many of these students discovered, on graduation, that at best they could find operative level jobs in the hotel industry; jobs for which they were overqualified.

A study of hotel receptionists in quality hotels in the Helsinki area aimed to see whether these overqualified receptionists were less satisfied with their jobs than normally qualified receptionists. The receptionists were asked to complete a standard questionnaire called the Job Descriptive Instrument (designed by Smith *et al.* 1969), which measures satisfaction with five elements of a job: the work itself, pay, supervision, promotion opportunities and co-workers. They were also asked some questions designed to test whether they thought their skills were underemployed in their current job and questions about their educational qualifications. Responses were received from 91 receptionists of whom 31 had a degree or diploma in hotel management and 60 had other qualifications. The results showed that indeed the overeducated were, on average, less satisfied with all five elements of their work than the normally educated receptionists, particularly with the nature of the work itself, pay and promotion opportunities.

(Adapted from Kokko and Guerrier 1994)

There are several reasons why it is to an organization's advantage to have a workforce who enjoy their jobs. Turnover and absenteeism tend to be lower if job satisfaction is high; it is self-evident that you are less likely to leave and more likely to turn up for work if you enjoy what you do. However, will you necessarily work harder? Research studies have indicated a relatively low correlation between work performance and job satisfaction. In other words, the best workers are not necessarily the most satisfied with their jobs and poor workers can enjoy their jobs. There are several reasons why:

- **The rewards from work are not always linked to work performance**. Suppose I come into work one morning and stop to have a chat over coffee with some of my colleagues. We chat on for about an hour and then I think that I should go into my office and get on with some work. The telephone rings and it is a friend and we gossip for a while. Then someone pops in and asks me if I want to go for lunch. I may have really enjoyed the morning although I have done no work at all. And if I am paid a monthly salary I will be paid the same for that morning's "work" as I would have been if I had been toiling all morning with no break for a coffee or a chat.

- **People do not always know how good their work is**. A waiter may believe he is really good at dealing with customers since they never complain (not knowing what they are saying about him behind his back). Conversely, some people can be insecure and rate their own work skills much lower than their manager rates them. Our feelings of satisfaction are linked with our beliefs about our work performance, not the actuality, and we cannot always rely on good quality feedback from managers and colleagues to confirm how well we are doing.

- **People may not feel they are being fairly rewarded for the effort they are putting into their work**. Suppose that there is a waitress working alongside the demotivated waiter in the example above (Box 5.6) and she works extremely hard and is very good at her job. What happens when she compares herself with the demotivated waiter who is doing the minimum? She earns the same as he does in terms of her basic wages and share of the tips but as she works much harder for the same reward she may paradoxically feel less satisfied. (He after all, gives little to the job and expects little from it so his expectations may be met.) Surprisingly often organizations reward poor performers and punish good performers; for example by giving less work to poor performers (as they cannot be trusted to do it properly) and giving more work to good performers (who will manage it) (see Wright 1991). Equity theory attempts to describe the way perceptions of fairness affect motivation and job satisfaction.

Equity theory

Adams' (1963, 1965) equity theory suggests that people are concerned about the relative level of their rewards compared with others. Returning to the waitress and waiter example, the hardworking waitress will compare:

*   **her rewards**: pay and tips, praise from supervisors, promotion opportunities and the sense of achievement and enjoyment she gains from her job

relative to

*   **her inputs**: both the effort that she puts into her work and the investments she brings to it (her qualifications, the length of time that she has been with the company, the experience she brings from other jobs)

with

*   **the waiter's rewards**: both intrinsic and extrinsic

relative to

*   **his inputs**: both in terms of effort and investments.

The waitress may feel that she is treated fairly compared to the waiter. She may calculate that although she works harder than him for the same basic pay and tips, she enjoys her job more, is highly regarded in the firm and has better long-term opportunities. These factors help to balance the equation. However, she may look at how hard she works compared with how little he puts into his work and feel that she is being under-rewarded. According to Adams, she will be motivated to try to restore the balance. She may do this by trying to affect the waiter's rewards (complaining to the managers about him) or inputs (berating him to work harder) or by trying to affect her own rewards (pushing the managers to promote her or give her a raise). But the easiest factor that she can influence is her own effort; she can simply work less hard herself to restore the equilibrium.

Our perceptions of equity thus affect both our satisfaction with our work (if we feel fairly rewarded in terms of what we put into our work we are satisfied) and the effort we put into it. Adams' theory predicts that people are motivated to correct both their perceptions that they are under-rewarded and their perceptions that they over-rewarded. However, people may not always react to the guilt of feeling overpaid by working harder; they may find more convenient ways of correcting the balance such as changing their perceptions of their inputs or comparing themselves with other, better paid, people.

The implications for managers of the process theories

Expectancy and equity theories do provide some useful guidelines about what managers should do in order to motivate their staff. The ultimate goal is to ensure that employees are motivated to put *effort* into their work, that effort can be transformed into good *work performance* and that performance leads to valued and equitable rewards and thus *job satisfaction*.

To encourage employees to put effort into their work, managers need to:

1. check that employees are being offered rewards they value
2. check that they perceive a link between working hard and receiving more of the rewards that they value.

To ensure that effort is translated into good work performance, managers need to:

3. check that employees understand what they are expected to achieve
4. check that they have the skills, training, resources and support that will enable them to work well
5. ensure that employees have feedback on their performance.

To ensure that work performance results in job satisfaction, managers need to:

6. check that employees are rewarded for good work
7. check that employees feel they are fairly rewarded.

This seems like a simple list but it involves assessing a whole range of human resource practices from payment systems to the design of jobs, to the selection and training of staff, to appraisal and evaluation of performance. Indeed the expectancy model is such a useful theoretical framework because it shows how all these different organizational processes interact with each other.

Are the process theories universal?

As the process theories make no assumptions about *what* motivates people but merely focus on *how* our needs and wants affect our behaviour, they are normally thought to be more universally applicable than the content theories. Mendonca and Kanungo (1994, p. 286), for example, claim that "the employee's job performance in *any* culture will improve through the practices of goal setting, performance feedback and valued rewards. The underlying psychological principles of work motivation incorporated in these practices are universally valid and, therefore, have pan-cultural applicability". However, they go on to argue that the way these principles are implemented will need to vary from culture to culture: you may be able to give feedback in a more direct and confrontational way to an employee in the United States, for example, than to one in India.

Adler (1991), on the other hand, claims that even expectancy theory is culturally dependent as it assumes that human beings are calculating creatures who, consciously or unconsciously, assess their preferences in a rational way and then decide how much effort to put into their work. This can be seen as a limitation of the theory generally. As Locke (1975) points out, much human behaviour is impulsive, habitual or emotional rather than rational. However, employees may be more likely to think of work in this calculating way if they live in cultures where they are encouraged to think of work in terms of what they as individuals can get out of it (i.e. with individualistic values) rather than in cultures where a moral commitment is made towards work (i.e. cultures with collectivist values).

Money and motivation

> ### Box 5.8   Motivating tour guides
>
> A small company in Bali, Indonesia organized day and half-day coach tours of the island. Balinese people have particular obligations to their home village and are expected to participate in important religious ceremonies there. However, since many of them now have paid jobs which make it difficult to take time off, they are allowed to pay a fine to the village rather than attend the ceremony. The owner of the company complained that when his tour guides had a ceremony which they were required to attend, if they were due to take a group of Europeans on a tour, they would happily pay the fine as they expected to receive good tips. However, if the group was Australian, who do not normally tip tour guides, they would claim that they had to attend the ceremony.

At the beginning of this section, F.W. Taylor's ideas that linking pay to performance was the best way to motivate people to work hard were dismissed as being naive and simplistic. But equally, in modern society it would be naive to suggest that behaviour is not affected by the promise of money, as Box 5.8 indicates. The difficulty is that there are often negative consequences as well as positive ones from using money as an incentive.

People value money not just because it enables them to buy the necessities of life. Relating monetary rewards to Maslow's hierarchy, money is not just a way of satisfying lower level needs. It may also, for example, help to satisfy esteem needs. What we earn can be seen as a mark of our worth and status. For certain entrepreneurs making money may be the way in which they self-actualize.

Using the expectancy theory model, money may be one of the rewards that staff place a value on. But whether they would work harder if their pay were linked with performance would depend on the other outcomes that they expected in return for hard work. Returning to Box 5.1 at the beginning of the chapter, the Balinese staff who asked not to be made employee of the month may have valued any monetary award that was associated with this, but for them the negative outcomes, in terms of the way it would disrupt their relationships with their colleagues, outweighed the benefits.

There are also practical problems associated with linking pay and performance in that it is difficult to design a financial incentive that is truly linked with all aspects of job performance. Performance-related pay can distort behaviour in that people are motivated to engage in those behaviours that will gain them the extra financial reward at the expense of other aspects of their work. The waiter focuses on those guests who he expects to be good tippers at the expense of other guests, for example. The salesperson oversells to maximize commission. As Box 5.9 shows, people can be very creative about finding ways of gaining desired rewards and they do not always do this in the way that the people who designed the reward systems intended.

Box 5.9   Not what was intended

A hotel chain wanted to encourage its managers to support staff training. Unit managers were set targets for the number of hours' training to be undertaken by staff in the hotel over a year and the amount of training undertaken was one of the factors against which a manager's performance was evaluated and the level of his or her annual bonus defined. Staff in one hotel complained that the manager's definition of what constituted training was rather broad. Staff who were setting the room up for a training session were logged as undertaking training!

Summary

- Theories of motivation can be divided into two types. The older theories of motivation are *content* theories, that attempt to define what motivates people. Newer theories of motivation tend to be *process* theories, focusing on how our motives affect our behaviour.

- One of the best known of the content theories is Maslow's Hierarchy of Needs. Maslow claimed that people have both lower level needs (food and safety) and higher level needs (to be loved, respected and to self-actualize). Maslow's ideas were used by other neo-human relations theorists to support their claims that employees could be motivated by providing them with intrinsically interesting and challenging work. Whilst Maslow's model is now regarded as an oversimplification and there is no evidence that human needs are arranged in the five-stage hierarchy he proposed, it remains a useful way of classifying the different needs that people try to fulfil through their work.

- Expectancy theory claims that people will put effort into their work if they believe that, by doing so, they will gain valued rewards. Organizations need to ensure that an employee's effort will be translated into good work performance by providing appropriate resources, training and feedback.

- If there is a good fit between the rewards people gain from work and those they expect to gain, they will be satisfied with their jobs. Satisfied workers are not necessarily more productive workers but they are more likely to stay with the company and have lower levels of absenteeism.

- Equity theory suggests that people are concerned about the fairness of the way they are rewarded compared with others. If they feel under- or over-rewarded they will be motivated to reduce the imbalance. People may respond to feeling that they are under-rewarded by reducing the amount of effort that they put into their work.

- Money remains an important motivator for many people at work but attempts to link pay and performance may have negative consequences as well as positive ones.

The next stage

Experience

We all have experience of what it is like to be motivated or not motivated. If you do not have any work experience, then you will have experience of how motivated you have felt to study or engage in hobbies.

Experience of unskilled and repetitive jobs will give you some sense of what it feels like to do this type of work. Look for opportunities to work in front-of-house and back-of-house jobs, in jobs where you are paid a flat wage or where you get tips or are paid by performance. Obviously, any opportunities you have to work in a supervisory or management capacity will give you some sense of the problems of trying to motivate other people.

Reflection

Think about an occasion when you felt very motivated at work or studying something. What were the factors that made you feel this way?

Think about an occasion when you felt demotivated at work or when trying to study something. What were the factors that made you feel that way? What does this tell you about how you are motivated?

Have you ever worked in a job where you gained tips or your pay was in some way linked to your performance? How did this affect your behaviour? Collect examples from friends of their experience of pay and results systems.

Can you think of any examples from your own experience of situations where people are rewarded for being poor performers at work and punished for being good performers? How did this affect the motivation of staff in that situation?

Have you ever felt under-rewarded compared to others? Why (think about your inputs and rewards compared with your perception of their inputs and rewards in line with equity theory)? How did you react? Have you ever felt over-rewarded? How did you react? Who do you compare yourself with when deciding whether you are under- or over-rewarded, and why?

Theorizing

What theory would you use to explain why the overqualified Finnish receptionists (Box 5.7) were less satisfied than their normally qualified colleagues?

Does it matter if the overqualified receptionists are dissatisfied with their jobs? In what ways would you expect their dissatisfaction to affect their behaviour (given that with high unemployment they may not express their dissatisfaction by changing job)?

In Box 5.4, it was proposed that Michel Roux and Nico Lademis might meet their needs for self-actualization through their work. Could a kitchen porter or a room attendant equally meet their needs for self-actualization at work? How useful is Maslow's concept of self-actualization?

In practice

1. A human resources manager in a hotel tells you that he discriminates against applicants with supervisory or management qualifications who apply for operative level jobs. Do you agree with this approach? What are the arguments against it?

   How could you motivate overqualified people stuck in jobs that do not make use of their skills?
2. You are the manager of a hotel restaurant in the States where tips are an important component of staff pay. You discover that European guests are not treated as well as American guests because they are not seen as being good tippers. What do you do?

   How would you motivate managers to invest in the training of their staff (see Box 5.9)?

Further reading

All of the main Organizational Behaviour textbooks (see Further Reading Chapter 2) contain chapters on motivation at work. In addition, Wright (1991) provides an excellent review of the main theories. For more detail on the earlier theorists, try Pugh and Hickson (1996). Adler (1991) includes a section on cultural differences and motivation and Kanungo and Mendonca (1994) look specifically at motivation at work in developing countries (with a specific emphasis on India). Wiley (1997) looks at the way in which motivation at work is changing over time.

There is not much research specifically using the motivational models described in this chapter in relation to the hospitality industry. You can refer to Gabriel (1988) and Kokko and Guerrier (1994), however. In relation to tipping, try Lynn and Graves (1996), for a positivist treatment of the topic, and Shamir (1983), for a more phenomenological approach.

References for further reading

Adler, N. (1991) *International Dimensions of Organizational Behavior* (Second edition), Boston, Mass: PWS-Kent.

Gabriel, Y. (1988) *Working Lives in Catering*, London: Routledge and Kegan Paul.

Kanungo, R. and Mendonca, M. (eds) (1994) *Work Motivation*, New Delhi: Sage.

Kokko, J. and Guerrier, Y. (1994) Overeducation, underemployment and job satisfaction: a study of Finnish hotel receptionists, *International Journal of Hospitality Management*, **13**, 375–386.

Lynn, M. and Graves, J. (1996) Tipping: an incentive/reward for service, *Hospitality Research Journal*, **20**, 1: 1–14.

Pugh, D. and Hickson, D. (1996) *Writers on Organizations* (Fifth edition), London: Penguin.

Shamir, B. (1983) A note on tipping and employee perceptions and attitudes, *Journal of Occupational Psychology*, **56**, 255–259.

Wiley, C. (1997) What motivates employees according to over 40 years of motivation surveys, *International Journal of Manpower*, **18**, 3: 263–280.

Wright, P. (1991) Motivation in Organizations in M. Smith (ed.), *Analysing Organisational Behaviour*, Basingstoke: Macmillan.

6 Groups and leading groups

Box 6.1 Us against them

The food and beverage manager of a four-star hotel was unpopular with his staff. They felt that he was always checking up on them and trying to catch them making a mistake. The hotel had an open-plan public area so it was possible to see right through from reception to the bar and restaurant areas. Whenever the waiting staff saw this manager start to walk in their direction, one of them would organize for him to be paged to another part of the hotel.

Working with others

The previous chapter looked at motivation at work primarily from the perspective of the individual employee. But we do not generally work totally independently of others. The behaviour of those we work with impinges on what we do. (This was recognized in the case quoted in Box 5.1 of the Balinese employee who did not want to be made Employee of the Month because her work colleagues would be jealous and torment her.)

An effective work team is a powerful asset to any organization. However, as the example in Box 6.1 illustrates, work teams are not inevitably on the side of the managers. Work groups that decide, for whatever reason, to make life difficult for their leaders in an organization can be difficult to contain.

This chapter is about groups and the way that they work. It is also about the people who try to lead groups. Are leaders "born" or "made"? Is there one best leadership style? Are different leadership styles required to manage different types of people and different types of task?

How do groups work?

In psychological terms, a group consists of two or more people who interact with each other and who define themselves as a group. Thus a dozen people travelling on the same light aircraft and not talking to each other would not comprise a group. But if the aircraft had an engine failure and the passengers had to work together to save themselves, they would quickly become a group and would always identify themselves as a passenger on that plane. (If you have ever seen a disaster movie you will recognize this scenario.)

Most people belong to both *formal* and *informal* groups at work. Employees will always be part of one formal work group and may be a member of more than one. For example, the supervisor for the bar staff in a restaurant would be both a member of the bar staff group and also a member of the supervisory team: both formal work groups. But she might also identify herself as one of a group of staff who play tennis together or one of a group of staff who have worked in the restaurant for over five years.

- **Formal groups** are set up to help employees achieve particular organizational objectives. Most organizational tasks are too large to be assigned to one person independently; people need to pool resources and expertise in order to get things done. Roles and membership of formal groups tend to be fixed. The formal leader of the group is usually appointed by management whether or not he or she would have been the person chosen by the team. All those who have a particular work role are members of the group whether the other members want them in the group or not.

- **Informal groups** exist because organizations are places where people interact and inevitably forge friendships and alliances. Membership of such groups is voluntary; people are attracted to be part of informal groups where there are others with similar interests, a similar background or similar concerns. Informal groups can be helpful in organizational terms because they can make it easier to solve problems that cross traditional organizational boundaries and because they can add to the satisfaction and enjoyment that people gain from their work. But managers can find informal groups threatening to the extent that they undermine formal structures and make it harder for managers to control (see Box 6.2).

Box 6.2   The informal group versus the formal group

A receptionist at a four-star hotel had worked in all the different functional areas of the hotel so she knew all the room staff and restaurant staff very well. When reception was very quiet late in the evening, using her initiative, she would help out her "friends" with room service if they were particularly busy. But the front office manager was very unhappy about this when he found out. "We look after our problems, not their problems" he told her. Her obligations to her formal work group were in conflict with her obligations to the informal group of her friends.

Individuals who are part of a group often behave differently from the way they would on their own. Refer back to the example in Box 6.1. Would all the restaurant staff have worked against their manager in this way if it were not part of a group game? The group provides individuals with social support for their actions. "It must be okay because everyone else is doing it." Group pressures may encourage some individuals to participate in an activity they privately disagree with because they want to stay "in" with the others: "I don't think we should treat the manager in this way but if I don't go along with the game everyone else will think that I am a spoilsport and have no sense of humour."

Group norms

People who are part of a group feel under pressure to conform to the group's norms. Norms are the, usually unwritten, rules about how members of the group should behave. Group norms have the following characteristics (Porter *et al.* 1975):

- **Norms are structural characteristics of groups, which summarize and simplify group influence processes**. Group norms may be thought of as the group's personality. Norms make group life easier. For example, if a management group develops the norm that the weekly management meeting will start ten minutes after the formal time on the agenda and that everyone will attend it, no member of the group will need to waste time worrying about whether he or she really needs to attend the meeting (they do) and whether it is all right to arrive 20 minutes late (it isn't). Refer back to the management meeting in the case at the beginning of Chapter 4 (Box 4.1) for an example of the problems that arise when the group has no agreed shared norms about how to behave.

- **Norms apply to behaviour – not to private thoughts and feelings**. It is quite possible that one or more of the restaurant staff in the case in Box 6.1 do disagree privately with this treatment of their manager. But they would only be transgressing the norms if they refused to go along with what their colleagues were doing.

- **Norms are generally developed only for behaviours which are viewed as important by most group members**. Work groups, for example, usually develop norms about such matters as how hard members should work, how they should cooperate or not cooperate with their managers and with other groups, about hours of work (Do we leave on the dot at the end of a shift? Do you need to be prepared to work any hours required?). They might be less likely to develop norms about which football team everyone should support. However, behaviour which may seem unimportant to outsiders (like which football team members support) *could* be viewed as highly important within the group. Norms develop where a group *believes* the behaviour is important.

- **Norms usually develop gradually, but norms can be developed quickly if members wish**. For example, if all the members of a management team are frustrated that the weekly management meeting drags on for several hours, someone may say "Can't we agree to call the meeting to a close after an hour, whether we have finished all the business or not?" If everyone agrees, a new norm may have been established for future meetings.

- **Not all norms apply to everyone**. High status group members may be allowed to deviate from the norms. New members are often required to conform closely to all norms.

Where do norms come from?

Groups are continually changing and developing. However, when a new group is formed, it tends to work through a series of recognized stages whilst people establish a way of working together. Tuckman (1965) identified these stages as:

- **Forming**. When the group first comes together, people are concerned about each other's reaction to them. People try to test out what is acceptable and unacceptable behaviour. At the forming stage of the group's life, the group members tend to be scrupulously polite with each other and inhibited about expressing open disagreement.

- **Storming**. At this stage, the group is trying to establish a pecking order of members. The informal group leaders emerge during this stage (although early leaders may be replaced later in the group's life). There are often outright conflicts during this stage between different members of the group and between the group and its formal leader. The group can use humour in a destructive way: joking around as a way of avoiding the task at hand.

- **Norming**. This is the stage at which the group develops its norms. Group members start to identify with the group. It becomes more cohesive and there is a sense of shared responsibility. The tasks of the group and the roles of individual members are clarified.

- **Performing**. Having worked through the previous stages successfully, the group can now concentrate on the task at hand. Conflict within the group is at a minimum.

Not all groups work through this sequence in a fixed way. Stages may overlap and some stages (particularly "storming") may not be apparent in some groups. Groups can become stuck in one of the stages and never manage to function successfully. Or groups can regress to earlier stages. If the membership of the group changes significantly or there are major changes in the way the group functions (for example, a reorganization of work tasks), the group may need to work through the stages again.

Box 6.3   Group stages in a tour group

Whilst this discussion has been primarily about groups of people at work, these group processes apply to other types of group. A group of people on a tour holiday together will tend to work through the same stages of development. The tour guide, as the formal leader of the group, plays a major role in ensuring the group's successful development. Bowen (1998) conducted a participant observation study of a soft adventure tour in Malaysia. He describes the way in which the holidaymakers on this tour worked through the stages of group development, from the *forming stage* as everyone tried nervously to identify other members of the tour at the airport, through a *storming stage* as the group criticized and lost faith in the tour guide who did not mix sufficiently with the group and did not appear to be fully familiar with the route, through to a *norming stage* as informal leaders emerged and the group established a way of operating.

The stages of group development are often particularly apparent in the type of situation when people who have not known each other previously have to spend much of their time together for several days or weeks. Other examples are people attending residential training programmes or people working on short-term projects (for instance, opening a new hotel or restaurant).

Group cohesion

As a group of people develop norms and work through these stages of development so the group becomes *cohesive*. Highly cohesive groups are ones where group members are attracted to the group and want to remain part of it. In cohesive groups, as the word suggests, people are stuck together.

Groups tend to become cohesive if:

- **they are homogenous**, i.e. the group members have similar attitudes and a similar background to each other. So it is harder to create group cohesion in a culturally diverse group than in a single culture group (Adler 1991). However, culturally diverse groups may have other advantages over single culture groups (see the section on "groupthink" below);

- **the group is relatively small**. In smaller groups, it is easier for all members to interact with each other;

- **there is frequent interaction between members**. It is harder to build a cohesive group if group members' physical location or hours of work mean that they do not see each other frequently;

- **the group is isolated**. Members have little opportunity to interact with people outside the group. Staff working in an isolated country hotel or staff who always work a night shift, for example, are likely to become a cohesive group;

- **the group is encouraged through reward systems and competition with others to become cohesive**. Management teams can build cohesive groups by having group incentives rather than individual incentives, by encouraging group loyalty and healthy competition with other groups (for example, competition between the different units in a chain).

Box 6.4   TGI Friday's

TGI Friday's is an American restaurant and bar concept which trades under license through Whitbreads Restaurant and Leisure Division in the UK. Employees benefit from an individualized reward system: the better they perform the more they can earn. However, the organization cannot allow individualism to become overly dominant as it could lead to a potentially harmful level of competition between employees. Team briefings are used to encourage team loyalty and ensure that healthy competition does not become harmful conflict.

Team briefings occur immediately before the two key shift periods – morning and evening. Two teams meet in each unit – the restaurant and bar team and the kitchen and back of house team – so all staff are involved. The sessions last 20 to 30 minutes, and are informal. A fun atmosphere is created and jokes are told. Employees are encouraged to identify primarily with the team with whom they work and with the branch.

The following comment is typical of employee views of the benefits of such briefing sessions:

> "From when we start we have a meeting, well all the waiters, they try and give us a little 'pep talk'. At first you think it is a little sad, but it is very good, it sort of motivates you. There are jokes and

everyone is out from the cold, we are all laughing away. You come
in, you are laughing and your friends are around you, making jokes
at the table, just having a good time while you are working."

(Adapted from Lashley 1997, pp. 62–63)

The effects of cohesion

In general, it is positive for both the work organization and for
members of the group if a group is cohesive. This is why organizations
like TGI Friday's try to build cohesive groups (Box 6.4). Members of
cohesive groups enjoy the security and pleasure of working with
people they like. People can "pull together" and coordinate activities
more effectively. However, highly cohesive work groups are not
always more productive than less cohesive groups.

First, it depends on the norms and goals of a group. In the TGI
Friday's case the norms and goals of the work teams were in line with
the norms and goals of the organization as a whole. Therefore, higher
cohesiveness would be likely to lead to higher productivity overall. But
some cohesive groups develop anti-management norms (see Box 6.1).
In this case, the more cohesive the group is, the lower its productivity
may be (as members feel increasingly compelled to comply with low
productivity norms). There is also the issue (see Box 6.5) of the way
that managers should treat cohesive informal groups.

Cohesion can cause other problems even in groups with high productivity norms. Janis (1972) coined the term *"groupthink"* to describe
the behaviour of highly cohesive groups that are so convinced that
they are right that they do not question the actions they are taking and
can lose touch with reality. Janis developed this analysis from studies
of political decision making, such as the Bay of Pigs fiasco in 1961,
when the US government's decision to invade Cuba almost led to a
third world war. Some of President Kennedy's closest advisors, even
though they were opposed to the plans privately, felt unable to argue
their case strongly when everyone else seemed so convinced that what
they were doing was right.

This is an example from politics, but there are equal dangers of
"groupthink" developing in the Boards of Directors of major firms
where the board may be composed of like-minded people with similar
backgrounds. This may be one reason why international hotel

companies are increasingly appointing outsiders to their boards rather than promoting internal candidates who may not question the *status quo* (Roper *et al.* 1997). Adler (1991) argues that culturally diverse groups tend to be less prone to "groupthink" than single culture groups as members bring with them a wider range of perspectives.

Box 6.5   Should managers stop gossip?

In every organization, gossip – informal communication about what members of the organization are up to – is pervasive. Gossip in informal groups helps to build cohesion: it unites the group and keeps out outsiders. People who cannot join in the gossip because they do not know the people and the history of the people who are being discussed find themselves excluded from the group.

Should managers try to stop groups gossiping? The gossip of an informal group can be seen as a challenge to a manager's authority. Gossip can be subversive in the way that humour is (as seen, for example, in the behaviour of the staff in the Box 6.1 case). It can also be viewed as a waste of time. Employees who are gossiping are not working as hard as they should.

But Noon and Delbridge (1993) argue that it would be futile for managers to attempt to eliminate gossip. Whilst gossip can be disruptive, it can help oil the wheels in organizations. More importantly, gossip is fun. It provides employees with a release from otherwise monotonous and stressful jobs.

Roles in groups

The discussion so far has focused on what group members share and how they behave in similar ways. But in good groups, individual members contribute different skills and insights. If you watch a group of people interacting with each other, for example in a meeting, you will notice that not everyone contributes in the same way. One person may do much of the talking and always be trying to force his or her ideas on the others. Another person may be good at calling the group to order and reminding everyone about what they are trying to achieve and where they have got to. Another person may be good at calming down disagreements or fights.

Belbin (1981, 1993) has studied the way in which people perform different roles in teams and the way in which the personalities of group members influence the roles they play. He identified eight different useful team roles in his first book and subsequently slightly adapted these and added a ninth role.

Belbin's roles

- **The Plant**: is a creative, imaginative person who comes up with unorthodox solutions and helps the group solve difficult problems. The Plant is sometimes too preoccupied with these ideas to effectively communicate them to other members of the team or to think about the detail of how they should be implemented.

- **Resource Investigator**: is an extrovert and an enthusiast who is good at developing contacts and exploring opportunities outside the group. Resource investigators are people who are never in their offices and if they are, they are always on the phone. The Resource Investigator can be over-optimistic and lose interest in a scheme once the initial enthusiasm has passed.

- **Coordinator**: is mature, confident and a good chairperson. The Coordinator clarifies the group's goals, encourages it to take decisions and delegates tasks well. Coordinators can be seen as manipulative and can delegate work they should be doing themselves.

- **The Shaper**: is dynamic and challenging and thrives on pressure. The Shaper pushes the group to achieve and has the drive and courage to overcome obstacles. However, Shapers can be insensitive to the feelings of other members of the group. They can provoke others or hurt their feelings.

- **Monitor Evaluator**: is rational and hard-headed, good at looking at all the options and seeing the difficulties inherent in certain solutions. (A good monitor evaluator can help avoid "groupthink".) But monitor evaluators can be over-critical and are not good at motivating others.

- **Teamworker**: is cooperative and diplomatic. The teamworker helps to avert conflicts in the group and helps to build on group members' skills. Teamworkers can be easily influenced and indecisive in crunch situations.

- **Implementer**: is disciplined, reliable and efficient. The implementer is good at turning ideas into action. Implementers can be inflexible and slow to respond to new ideas.

- **Completer**: is painstaking and conscientious. Completers are good at checking and seeking out errors and at delivering on time. They can tend to worry unduly and to be over-concerned about detail.

- **Specialist**: is single-minded and dedicated. The specialist provides knowledge and skills that may be in rare supply. Specialists can tend to contribute only in a narrow field (their specialism) and be poor at seeing the "big picture".

Belbin argues that a good team requires a balance of different roles. A team composed entirely of shapers or of plants would be disastrous. Our personalities fit us better for some roles than others. An extreme introvert would not be a natural resource investigator, for example. However, with experience and in the right circumstances, we can learn to contribute to groups in different ways.

Belbin's work reminds us that the effectiveness of a team is not just the responsibility of the team leader. Everyone can contribute something to good team work, even if they have no specific task related expertise to bring, for example in the role of teamworker or completer.

Box 6.6   The top management group

I was asked to run a training course for the senior directors of a firm who recognized that they had difficulty functioning as a team. I asked them to complete a questionnaire analysing the role they played in the group against the Belbin types. Six out of the seven were extreme "shapers". This made for a very argumentative group.

Leading the group

Whilst Belbin's research indicates how all members of a group influence what happens within that group it would be naive to suggest that all members of the group have equal influence over the group. Adapting the memorable phrase from George Orwell's book *Animal Farm*, even in the most democratic of groups "all group members are equal but some are more equal than others".

Leadership is about influencing people. The leader is the person who can influence people to do things they otherwise would not, who can inspire the group and change attitudes. The leader of the group is not necessarily the formal supervisor or manager of the group. Work groups can have powerful informal leaders who influence the group although they have no formal role of authority. But a person in a formal role of authority, a supervisor or manager, is usually expected to take a leadership role. Leadership can be studied not just at the very top of the organization but also in the middle and at the lower levels of an organization.

History books are full of accounts of great leaders, kings and queens, generals, politicians, captains of industry, and people have looked for certain characteristics in their personalities and make-up that differentiate a Napoleon or Alexander the Great or Lincoln from ordinary men and women. In the same way, the earliest psychological theories looked for particular attributes of an individual, psychological, social or physical, that would distinguish the good leader from the bad leader. Are good leaders, this research asked, stronger (even physically bigger), more dominant, more confident, more intelligent than bad leaders? This approach is termed the *trait approach* as it assumes that the qualities that make a good leader are inherent in the person: the leader is "born" and not "made". However, hundreds of studies attempting to search for the traits of a good leader have failed to reach any conclusive results. Some traits seem to be loosely associated with leadership skills but it is not possible to define the traits of the "ideal" leader across all situations.

From the 1940s onwards another approach to leadership emerged. The assumption was that it was not who the leader was that was important but what he or she did. This approach is termed the *behavioural style* approach. Researchers investigated, for example, whether a democratic leadership style was more effective than an autocratic style of leadership. One of the most influential sets of studies using this perspective were the Ohio State studies (Fleishmann 1973). These studies argued that there were two major dimensions of leadership style:

1. *Consideration*: This is the extent to which leaders are considerate to their subordinates i.e. show warmth, are willing to trust them, are willing to explain their actions and are willing to listen to them.

2. *Initiation of structure*: The extent to which a leader organizes and structures the work of subordinates and determines who does what.

The Ohio studies assumed that these dimensions were generally independent of each other. So a leader could be high in consideration and low in initiating structure, low in consideration and high in initiating structure, low in both dimensions or high in both dimensions. It was hypothesized that the effective leader would be one that is high in both consideration and initiating structure. Unfortunately, the results of the Ohio studies were also inconclusive. Employee morale seemed to be slightly higher and there were lower rates of turnover when a leader used a considerate style but no one style was consistently associated with higher group performance.

Thus a third approach towards leadership emerged: the *contingency approach*. This argued that we need to take into account the context in which the leader operated, for example the type of people they were leading and the type of task that needed to be handled. The appropriate style of leadership would depend on these contingencies. Theories include Fiedler's (1967) Contingency Model and House's Path–Goal Theory.

Fiedler's Contingency Model

Fiedler used a rather unusual and controversial method of measuring leadership style, based on a person's perceptions of his or her least preferred co-worker. He asked people to think about the person that they had greatest difficulty working with and then to rate that person on a rating scale on such dimensions as whether they are pleasant or unpleasant, warm or cold etc. Fiedler inferred that a person who has a relatively favourable view of the least preferred co-worker has a relationship-oriented, whilst someone with an unfavourable view of the least preferred co-worker has a task-oriented, leadership style.

Fiedler argues that whether it is better to have a task-oriented or a relationship-oriented leader depends on the "favourableness" of the situation. Fiedler identified three elements to this:

- **Leader–member relations** or whether the leader was generally accepted by his or her subordinates

- **Task structure** or the extent to which the task is clearly specified, goals are clear and everyone knows what they are doing

- **Position power** or the extent to which the leader could reward or punish subordinates.

There are eight different ways in which these elements may be combined:

1. Good relations, structured task, strong position power
2. Good relations, structured task, weak position power
3. Good relations, unstructured task, strong position power
4. Good relations, unstructured task, weak position power
5. Poor relations, structured task, strong position power
6. Poor relations, structured task, weak position power
7. Poor relations, unstructured task, strong position power
8. Poor relations, unstructured task, weak position power

These eight situations run from the most favourable to the most difficult. Thus a leader in situation number one, for example a popular owner-manager of a simple-service style restaurant, would have everything in his or her favour. Conversely, a leader in situation eight, for example an unpopular person asked to chair a committee of his or her peers to produce a report on a hotel's likely future information technology needs would have everything stacked against them.

> ## *Stop*
>
> *In which of the situations 1–8 would a task-oriented low-LPC (least preferred co-worker) leader be more effective? In which of the situations would a relationship-oriented high-LPC leader be more effective?*

Fiedler's research findings suggest that the low-LPC, task-oriented leader was more effective in situations 1, 2, 7 and 8, that is in both highly favourable and highly unfavourable situations. The high-LPC, relationship-oriented leader (who saw someone's advantages and strengths even though he or she disliked them) was better at handling the middle range situations 3, 4, 5 and 6.

Fiedler's research raised two important questions about leadership:

1. One-best leadership style? Fiedler contradicts the notion that there is one best leadership style. He argues that one type of leader may be best in some situations, but another type of leader may have more success in other situations.

2. Choose the leader to fit the situation? Fiedler argues that one's leadership style is a part of one's personal style that is difficult to change. Once a task-oriented leader, always a task-oriented leader. It is better to choose a leader to fit the situation or alter the situation to fit the natural style of the leader than to ask the leader to change his or her approach.

Fiedler's model has been criticized on the following grounds:

*   There is no satisfactory answer to the question about why high-LPC leaders are successful in moderately favourable situations and low-LPC leaders in highly favourable or highly unfavourable situations (Vecchio 1995). One suggestion is that relationship-oriented (high-LPC) leaders are more complex thinkers who can cope with the situations with some favourable and some unfavourable elements. In very favourable and very unfavourable situations, it does not help to think too much: just focus on the task and get on with it.

*   The results when other researchers have tried to replicate Fiedler's findings have been inconclusive (Smith and Peterson 1988, Smith 1991).

*   The least-preferred co-worker dimension does not seem to measure an underlying personality dimension, as Fiedler argued, after all (Smith and Peterson 1988). The same people repeating this test at different times can have widely different results – one year they are high-LPC relationship oriented leaders, the next year they are low-LPC task-oriented leaders.

Path–goal theory

Path–goal theory argues that subordinates will do what leaders want if leaders help them achieve what they want. Leaders must ensure that subordinates know how to achieve the leader's goals. They must also ensure that subordinates achieve their personal goals at the same time (House 1971). Path–goal theory complements expectancy theory (see Chapter 5).

Leaders need to fit their leadership style to the characteristics of the subordinates and the task environment in order to ensure that subordinates are fully motivated to achieve the organization's goals. Four possible leadership styles are described (House and Mitchell 1974) and, unlike Fiedler, the contention is that any one leader can vary his or her approach and adopt any of these styles:

- **Directive leadership**. Involves letting subordinates know exactly what should be done and how it should be done and in asking them to follow standard rules. In terms of the Ohio studies, the style is high in initiation of structure.

- **Supportive leadership**. Means treating subordinates like equals, being friendly and approachable and sensitive to their needs. In terms of the Ohio studies, high in consideration.

- **Participative leadership**. Means consulting subordinates before making decisions, asking for suggestions and advice over specific decisions, and taking that advice into account.

- **Achievement-oriented leadership**. Means setting challenging goals, having confidence in those who perform well and emphasizing excellence.

According to this theory, leaders should vary their approach according to, for example, how closed-minded and rigid their subordinates are. More authoritarian subordinates will prefer more directive leadership. They should vary it according to whether subordinates are "internals" (Rotter 1966), i.e. feel in control of their own destiny, or "externals" who feel their life is controlled by fate. Internals respond to participative leadership. They should also vary their approach according to the task. For example, a supportive approach will be helpful when the task is boring, repetitive and unsatisfying (in those circumstances a directive approach is counter-productive). A directive approach will help reduce anxiety if the group has to deal with an ambiguous situation.

Path–goal theory demonstrates how leaders need to be responsive to the needs of their subordinates if they are to lead a group. However, as Smith (1991) points out, if all leaders do is respond to their followers, in what sense are they actually leading anyone? Once again empirical studies based on this theory have often failed to support it (Smith and Peterson 1988, Vecchio 1995, Smith 1991).

Contingency theories reviewed

Mainstream research into leadership has, in summary, yielded rather disappointing results. Smith (1991) comments that "looking back on half a century of research into leadership is quite depressing. What it amounts to is a seemingly endless succession of theories which hold sway for a few years and then fall because of lack of empirical support" (p. 225). Knights and Wilmott (1992) comment that "there has been considerable dissatisfaction with the progress and achievements of (orthodox) leadership research. . . . Studies are criticized for their tendency to pursue 'artificial rigour' in preference to the generation of 'startling insights'" (p. 761). About the only definitive results the research has yielded are negative ones: there is no one 'ideal' leadership personality, there is no one best way of leading people and there appear to be no simple contingency relationships whereby one style always works in one situation.

So, is there anything useful that can be said about leadership?

Power and influence

Leadership is about getting people to do things that they might not necessarily want to do. Leadership is, therefore, in some sense about the exercise of power. A classic analysis of power was provided by French and Raven (1960). They distinguished between five bases of power:

1. **Reward power**. This is the power to provide or withhold valued rewards, such as bonuses or tips, pay rises, promotion, desirable job assignments. People in formal positions of authority, supervisors and managers, usually have some degree of reward power although they will not always have power to determine pay rises or promotions.

2. **Coercive power**. This is the power to punish, for example by withholding bonuses, by disciplinary actions and by, in the last

resort, dismissal. Coercive power is used quite extensively even in the most progressive organizations to get people to do things. Refer back to Chapter 4 for an illustration of the way in which Disney backs up its positive reinforcement of desirable behaviour with coercive sanctions against perceived "troublemakers". Informal leaders, too, can use coercive power, for example by denying their friendship to recalcitrants. However, one problem with coercive power is that subordinates may be inclined to respond to what they see as a heavy-handed approach with some tactics of their own (see Box 6.7).

Box 6.7   Sabotage in the Merchant Navy

On the ship, on which we had no running water for washing, sometimes the buckets would disappear without any apparent cause; quite obviously some enraged individual was throwing them over the side. It was not unusual for members of the catering staff (who were subjected to a stream of "do this, do that, do this, do that" orders from obnoxious second stewards) to feel so fed up they would heave a whole pile of dirty dishes through an open porthole instead of washing them. Stewards who do personal laundry are quite capable of "making a mistake" and burning through a shirt with an iron.

(Ramsay 1966)

---

3. **Legitimate power**. This is power based on having designated authority. So a waiter does what his supervisor tells him not because of potential rewards and punishments but because the supervisor is a supervisor and the waiter accepts her right to tell him what to do. Legitimate power is the same as Fiedler's position power and can also be termed *authority*.

4. **Expert power**. This power is based on a person's perceived knowledge or technical skill. Thus we do what a doctor tells us to because we think that he or she knows more about medicine than we do. People at lower levels in organizations sometimes have expert power over their managers. A chef, for example, may use his technical expertise to influence the general manager. (Is this why many hospitality managers feel they need kitchen skills – see Chapter 10?)

5. **Referent power**. This is power based on a person's attractive personality or special qualities which make other people feel they identify with him or her and want to be like him or her. This is power based on charisma.

Box 6.8   The charismatic leader

In the military, Curtis Samuels (a US hotel general manager) would be said to have what's called "command presence". Tall and trim, Samuels strides through his hotel with an undeniable confidence and mission. Samuels has set up a system to measure the performance of each department based on guest satisfaction. Much of what happens in his hotel revolves around the magic 92% guest rating which is Curtis's vision of "what is good". . . . One executive said, "Curtis taught us direction; 'what is good'". A number used the word vision, one saying, "He gave a sense of vision to the hotel by focusing people towards goals, especially related to guest service". A third felt Samuels had "galvanized" the hotel to be the best. One senior EOC member said that his major challenge was to "keep the faith" with Curtis Samuels. The best description, however, of this attribute of Curtis's leadership skills was given by his long-term friend and director of marketing who called him a "together person".

(From Nebel 1991, p. 286)

Different leaders use these bases of power in different combinations. Some researchers distinguish between *transformational* and *transactional* leadership (Burns 1978, Bass 1985).

- **The transformational leader** uses his or her charisma. Followers are prepared to trust them. They give followers their personal attention when necessary, show them how to think about problems in new ways and inspire them with a vision of what lies ahead. The transformational leader motivates others by transforming their individual self-interest into the goals of the organization. Curtis Samuels, as described in Box 6.8 above, would appear to be a transformational leader.

- **The transactional leader** exchanges rewards and punishments for performance. He or she makes rewards contingent on good work, but otherwise intervenes only when a subordinate's work is below standard.

A study by Rosener (1990) compared male and female managers and argued that they tended to use power differently. Men were more likely to make use of the power that came with their organization position and authority and to use "transactional leadership" styles. Women were more likely to ascribe their power to interpersonal skills, charisma and hard work and to adopt a "transformational style". Women tried to share power and encourage participation.

Does this make women better leaders than men? Having earlier dismissed the notion that there is one best leadership style, it would be simplistic to argue that the transformational manager is better than the transactional manager. A transformational manager may be most effective at the top of the organization and in conditions of instability and change (Sinha 1995). Even then a transformational leader could be dangerous if he or she lacks the judgement or ethical values to lead the organization in the right direction.

The leader/follower relationship

It is meaningless to talk about the leader without talking about the follower. Leadership is a relationship between the leader and the follower. As the various contingency theories demonstrate, it is a different matter trying to lead a group of people who dislike you and think you should not be in charge to trying to lead a group of people who think you are marvellous. It is a different matter trying to lead a group of poorly skilled and compliant subordinates to a group of self-confident and self-opinionated experts (like herding cats, as is sometimes said about managing academics). Followers give their leaders their power. I only have legitimate power over you to the extent that you believe I should be able to tell you what to do; I only have expert power to the extent that you believe I am an expert; I only have charisma if you believe I have charisma; I even only have coercive power if you are afraid of the sanctions I possess (and you believe I will exercise them).

Most leadership theories tend to be based around a notion that there is the leader and there is the group and that the leader adopts very much the same approach with everyone in the group of followers. However, Graen and his colleagues (Dansereau, Graen and Haga 1975, Graen and Scandura 1987) have developed a theory called the *vertical dyad linkage model*. They argue that leaders have a series of one-to-one relationships (dyads) with each of their subordinates, and that, being human beings, leaders prefer some subordinates to others. The favoured subordinates become an in-group: are given more important tasks, invited to share in decision-making and "mentored" by the leader. The non-favoured subordinates, the out-group, are treated in a more formal and distant way and given less important tasks. Not surprisingly, research indicates that members of the in-group are likely to be more satisfied with and committed to their work than members of the out-group.

Box 6.9   Does it matter what your boss thinks of you?

Research into the perceptions of the operative staff working for a restaurant chain in Bangkok (see also Box 6.10) suggested that one of the characteristics of a poor supervisor for them was someone who was biased or prejudiced (who took sides when there was a conflict between staff). On the other hand, they valued supervisors who were not biased or prejudiced.

So what do followers think about leaders who have favourites? Does it depend on whether you are one of the favoured or not?

How do subordinates become a member of the in-group or the out-group? This is not altogether clear but it seems to be based on the leader's initial impression of the subordinate's competency. The way a leader understands a subordinate's behaviour is, therefore, crucial. It is possible to see the same behaviour exhibited by two different people and interpret it in different ways.

Suppose that I have two subordinates, Bob and John. Bob is definitely one of the out-group. I do not think he is competent or committed and I assign him only trivial tasks. On the other hand, John is one of the in-group and I view him as a trusted assistant. Suppose that I have asked each of them to produce a report and they both hand it in late. It is likely that I will attribute Bob's lateness to his idleness and incompetence: his poor performance reinforces my poor opinion of him. But the same behaviour will appear out of character for John. I am likely to be more sympathetic towards him. Perhaps I will take the view that I am pushing him too hard or that I have been unreasonable in my demands.

So a leader's behaviour to a follower is not just based on what the follower does but on the leader's *attributions* about the cause of their behaviour and, of course, those attributions may be wrong. At the same time, the follower is trying to make sense of the leader's behaviour. This may provide some explanation of the research quoted above (Rosener 1990) which suggested that women and men exhibit different leadership styles. Culturally women are expected to be supportive and cooperative and their subordinates may respond positively to them when they are. Conversely, tough and aggressive behaviour may meet more resistance when coming from a woman than from a man (see Wilson 1995 for a fuller discussion of leadership and gender).

Cultural differences

> ### Box 6.10   Thai subordinates and their supervisors
>
> Interviews were conducted with 125 waiting and kitchen staff working for a chain of restaurants in Bangkok. They were asked about "the best thing that your supervisor did that you liked the most" and about "the worst thing that your supervisor did that you liked the least". The 300 incidents from these interviews were classified as follows:
>
> - **Expertise**: 136 out of 327 incidents related to the supervisor's competence. A good supervisor had technical expertise, took their work seriously, was friendly and nice to deal with, a good teacher and coach when mistakes were made.
>
> - **Power and mismanagement of emotions**: 66 out of 327 incidents (largely negative ones) related to how the supervisor used their power. Supervisors were criticized if they were unreasonable, inconsistent and not caring about staff, if they did not give staff a second chance if a mistake was made, and if they lost their temper at work.
>
> - **"Sacrifice" oneself for one's staff**: 53 out of 327 incidents related to the supervisor's willingness to sacrifice himself for his staff, by taking the blame for staff's mistakes, helping staff deal with personal problems, taking care of them when they were ill and representing them to management.
>
> - **Bias or prejudice**: 41 out of 327 incidents related to selfishness and prejudice. Supervisors were disliked for looking after their own interests first, bringing their personal problems to work and taking sides when there was a conflict between staff.
>
> (From Phornprapha 1996)

Referring to Box 6.10, one may ask whether the characteristics that these Thai employees looked for in their supervisor would be the same as those that a group of Canadian or Scandinavian restaurant staff would also look for in a good supervisor. Competence might be valued everywhere but the emphasis that the Thai employees place on the supervisor looking after them even at his own expense, may be a particular feature of a high-context, diffuse culture (Box 4.6). By contrast a study of car workers in the UK found that the most frequently-cited reason for getting on with one's supervisor was that he left one alone (Goldthorpe *et al.* 1968, see Smith and Peterson 1988, p. 99).

Some research in developing countries suggests that the most effective style of leadership in these countries is a "nurturant-task leadership style". Sinha (1995) argues that subordinates in India (where he comes from) tend to be dependency-prone and that it is the role of leaders to help them become more independent. But in high power-distance cultures, participative styles of leadership are difficult for staff to handle. Nurturant-task leaders care for their subordinates, help them grow and cultivate an emotional and personalized relationship with them but provide that nurturance only when subordinates have performed agreed tasks.

Once again, the message is that leaders need to be sensitive to the needs and perceptions of their staff. Rushing round to help someone who is ill may be highly valued in some cultures (and work cultures) but regarded as inappropriate interference in others. Acting as a "father-figure" may be valued in some places but regarded as unacceptably paternalistic in others

Do groups need leaders?

The assumption behind leadership theories is that groups need to be led and that they are generally led by one person. A further assumption is that what the leader does is important: that leadership skills matter and leaders do make a difference.

Are these assumptions necessarily valid? First, it may be argued that leaders, at least formal leaders, are not always necessary because a skilled and motivated group of people can effectively manage themselves, by rotating different leadership functions between them. There is an increasing amount of interest in the use of *autonomous working groups* within organizations and the way in which such groups operate within hospitality organizations will be discussed in Chapter 7.

Second, it can be argued that leaders are unimportant because there is sometimes very little that they can do to make a difference. A supervisor working in a popular branded restaurant is working within a tightly defined set of rules and procedures, may have little direct control over the rewards and sanctions and, therefore, may have little influence, whatever they do, over the success or failure of the group.

How can group working and leadership skills be improved?

What does all this research teach about how to improve our skills at working within a group and leading groups? There are no "quick fix" solutions but there are a number of general lessons to be drawn.

*   People who hardly know each other cannot function effectively as a group immediately. A group needs time and opportunities for interaction in order to develop. Organizations are beginning to recognize this by building in specific "team-building activities" (see Box 6.4) or by thinking about how they schedule staff (see Box 6.11). Obviously, there are particular problems in building teams in those sectors of the hospitality industry where there is very high turnover of staff or where large numbers of casual staff are employed. These issues will be discussed in Chapter 7.

> **Box 6.11   Scheduling staff in teams**
>
> Motorway service areas are open 24 hours a day and pose problems for the scheduling of staff. One company has experimented with systems of scheduling staff as teams with their own supervisor, rather than as individuals. This is similar to the approach used in organizations such as the fire service where good teamwork is obviously essential and when "red watch" come off duty "blue watch" comes on duty (see Guerrier and Pye 1994).

- For a group to function for the benefit of the organization, it is essential that positive group norms are developed. It is easier to influence the group's norms at an early stage in its life, which reinforces the value of putting by some time and space for team-building activities when a new group is formed.

- As individuals, we can all contribute to the success of a group even when we are not leading that group and even if we feel we have little specific expertise to offer. It is helpful to be aware of the role or roles that we are comfortable with playing within a group. Am I a natural *plant*, or a natural *implementer*? Do I know that I will always be a useless *completer*? But it is also helpful to try to extend one's repertoire of roles. If I usually try to play the *shaper* role in a group, could I be a useful *resource investigator* instead if the group already has enough shapers?

- In a similar way, it can be helpful to be aware of one's natural leadership style. Do I tend to be a task-oriented or a relationship-oriented leader? Do I tend to be directive, or supportive, participative or achievement-oriented? Can I learn to extend my repertoire of leadership approaches?

- The key skill is to learn when one particular approach to leadership is likely to work as a way of achieving one's intentions and when another approach can work better. As the discussion about contingency theories demonstrated, there are no easy rules-of-thumb. But effective leadership is about fitting one's approach to the needs of the people one is leading, the nature of the task they are doing and the organizational context, whilst being aware of the power that one has to influence them.

Summary

- Everyone at work is a member of at least one group. Groups may be formal and informal.

- Groups develop norms; or rules about the ways in which group members should behave. Although norms can develop at any time in a group's life, they often develop early in the group's existence.

New groups often work through the stages of *forming*, *storming* and *norming* before they can perform effectively.

- Some groups are more cohesive than others, i.e. group members are more strongly attracted to being part of the group. Group cohesion can be positive for organizations but only if the group has high productivity norms. Cohesive groups can be affected by "groupthink".

- Individual members contribute differently to the success of a group. Belbin (1981, 1993) has identified nine useful roles that individuals can play in groups. Our personalities make it easier for us to play some roles rather than others. A unbalanced group, made up of people trying to play the same role, is less effective than a balanced group.

- Historically, models for understanding leadership have progressed from "trait" approaches, which tried to identify the characteristics of a good leader, to "behavioural" approaches which tried to identify what a good leader would do, to "contingency" approaches which tried to work out when one leadership style would work and when another would be more effective. The notion that there is one best leadership style has been refuted but it seems that neither are there any simple sets of contingencies that define when one leadership style works better than others.

- Leaders can make use of different sources of power to influence their team. *Transactional* leaders rely on rewards and punishments in exchange for good performance whilst *transformational* leaders use their charisma to inspire the group.

- Leadership is a relationship between the leader and the follower. Leaders treat some members of their team (the in-group) differently from other members (the out-group), according to vertical dyad linkage theory. The leaders' treatment of individual members of the group is based on their *attributions* about the causes of that person's behaviour. Equally, followers have expectations about what is appropriate leadership behaviour and attempt to influence the leader.

- There are cultural differences about what is expected from a leader. Some researchers suggest that whereas a participative style of leadership may be appropriate in developed countries with low power-distance values, a nurturant-task style works better in many developing countries.

- It could be that traditional leadership theories overstate the importance of the single leader and that many work groups can manage themselves, rotating leadership roles within the group. Such autonomous work groups will be discussed in Chapter 7.

- People can improve their skills of working in a group and leadership skills by analysing their own style of interaction and trying to increase their repertoire of styles.

The next stage

Experience

We all have plenty of experience of working within groups: either at work, or at college (working on group assignments), or in our social lives (membership of a club or a sports team, for example). Try to pick up aspects of group process in any group that you are a member of. What are the norms of the group? How do you feel about conforming to the norms? How cohesive is the group? What roles do individual members of the group play? What role do you play? How do you feel about being a member of the group? Do you behave inside the group in the same way as you do when you are outside the group? Do you feel a different person when you are with one group of people compared with when you are with another?

If you have an opportunity to join a new work group, try experimenting with a different role. If you are normally a "shaper", try taking a less assertive role. If you are normally a supportive teamworker, try focusing on the task rather than how people are getting on with each other. You might also try varying your approach in an ongoing group. If you are normally a quiet member of the group, be more assertive. If you normally take a leadership role, try taking a back seat. How do other members of the group react?

Try to initiate a discussion about group process in any group you are a member of. If possible try to get all group members to assess themselves against Belbin's roles. (A self-perception questionnaire that can be used for this can be found in Belbin 1981.)

Try to find opportunities to lead a group. Note how you feel about taking a leadership role. What is easy and what is difficult about being a leader? Do you interact differently with different members of the team? If you cannot lead a group yourself, think how it feels to be led. Try to interview someone who you would identify as a good leader about their approach to leadership.

Reflection

Identify two groups that you have been part of at some stage: one very successful group and another group that was a disaster. Try to analyse the characteristics of these groups. What happened at the early stages of the groups' development? What were the norms of the groups? How cohesive were the groups? What roles did individual members play and what impact did this have on the success or failure of the group? Was there anything that could have been done to make the unsuccessful group a success? (If you can think of any examples of an unsuccessful group which later worked very well, or a good group which fell apart, these may be particularly revealing.) What general principles can you infer from these examples about what comprises a good group and what comprises a poor group?

Identify two leaders of groups you have been part of: someone you would identify as a good leader and another that you would identify as a poor leader. How would you define their leadership styles: task- or relationship-oriented, directive, supportive, participative or achievement-oriented, transformational or transactional? How did they use their power? What were the characteristics of the situation in which they were operating: the nature of their followers, the nature of the task that was being handled, the organizational context? Why do you think one leader was successful and another was not? How much of a difference did the situation make? Did all members of the group have the same opinion of the leader as you did? Why?

Theorizing

It has been argued that a cohesive group is not necessarily a productive group. What are the relationships between group cohesion and group productivity?

Why do individual group members conform to group norms? How can one guard against "groupthink", when members of the group are over-conforming?

The "trait" approach to leadership, which argues that there are a set of personal characteristics which determine whether someone will be a good leader or not, has been largely discredited. But is there a relationship between a person's leadership style and their personal characteristics?

To what extent do the characteristics of followers influence a leader's behaviour?

In practice

You are working as a tour guide for a small group of holidaymakers on a "soft" adventure holiday. What can you do to mould them into a successful group?

You are a supervisor managing a group of casual staff providing the catering for a sports event. How can you build them into a successful team?

What should the food and beverage manager in Box 6.1 do to win over his team?

Further reading

Most general textbooks on organizational behaviour provide full summaries of theories about group behaviour and leadership, including descriptions of some theories not included in this chapter, for example, refer to Vecchio (1995), Ivancevich and Matteson (1993), Smith (1991). For a slightly different approach to leadership which focuses on the way leaders manage meanings refer to Sims *et al.* (1993).

Adler (1991) includes a useful chapter which looks specifically at the way in which multicultural teams function. Both books by Belbin (1981, 1993) are readable and interesting although they just focus on the Belbin roles.

Wilson (1995) includes a chapter which specifically examines gender differences in leadership. Smith and Peterson (1988) is an excellent academic review of leadership theories but is heavy going for students. Similarly, Sinha (1995) explores leadership within developing countries but the book is written for those who are generally familiar with academic theories in this area.

There are few recent studies which specifically look at leadership and group processes in the hospitality industry. Lashley (1997) includes some discussion and hospitality case study examples related to team building and work groups. Nebel (1991) is worth reading for his discussion of the leadership style amongst hotel general managers.

If you are specifically interested in developing your skills in working within groups and leading groups, several management skills books look specifically at this; for example, Evenden and Anderson (1992) or Pedler *et al.* (1996).

References for further reading

Adler, N. (1991) *International Dimensions of Organizational Behavior* (Second edition), Boston, Mass: PWS-Kent.

Belbin, R.M. (1981) *Management Teams*, Oxford: Butterworth-Heinemann.

Belbin, R.M. (1993) *Team Roles at Work*, Oxford: Butterworth-Heinemann.

Evenden, R. and Anderson, G. (1992) *Making the Most of People*, Wokingham: Addison-Wesley.

Ivancevich, J. and Matteson, M. (1993) *Organizational Behavior and Management* (Third edition), Homewood Ill.: Irwin.

Lashley, C. (1997) *Empowering Service Excellence*, London: Cassell.

Nebel, E. (1991) *Managing Hotels Effectively: Lessons from Outstanding General Managers*, New York: Van Nostrand.

Pedler, M., Burgoyne, J. and Boydell, T. (1996) *A Manager's Guide to Self-Development* (Third edition), London: McGraw Hill.

Sims, D., Fineman, S. and Gabriel, Y. (1993) *Organizing and Organizations: an Introduction*, London: Sage.

Sinha, J. (1995) *The Cultural Context of Leadership and Power*, New Delhi: Sage.

Smith, M. (ed.) (1991) *Analysing Organizational Behaviour*, Basingstoke: Macmillan.

Smith, P. and Peterson, M. (1988) *Leadership, Organizations and Culture*, London: Sage.

Vecchio, R. (1995) *Organizational Behaviour* (Third edition), Orlando: Dryden.

Wilson, F. (1995) *Organizational Behaviour and Gender*, London: McGraw Hill.

7

Designing jobs and organizational structures

Box 7.1 The way things were

It was much more gracious – slower living. There would be many more staff because staff were cheaper. The manager – who would be formally dressed, probably in tails – would come round and talk at every table. A maid would come round and do the valeting. There would be no fridges or trouser presses in rooms. The manager would have been horrified by the idea of a kettle in the room. Room service would arrive on a tray. Shoes would be left outside the door to be cleaned.

Then a chambermaid was just a chambermaid, a barman was just a barman and a waitress was just a waitress. Now we expect the same person to be all three. In the old days many of the staff in the restaurant stood around doing nothing. A head waiter never actually waited – he just clicked his fingers and pointed at people. In the bigger restaurants he just signalled to a station waiter and he didn't do much either.

(Hotel manager from the Lake District (in north-west England)
recalling Lake District hotel life in the 1970s)

Introduction

How many people are needed to staff a particular organization? What jobs do they do and how much responsibility do they have? How are these jobs coordinated? How many levels are needed in the organizational hierarchy? As the example in Box 7.1 demonstrates, approaches to job design and organizational design that were used in the past are not necessarily applicable now. Over the last 20 years or so, there has been a general trend amongst hospitality organizations to *delayer*, i.e. to reduce the number of levels in the hierarchy, to reduce the number of staff employed in each unit (perhaps by using technology to replace staff or by reducing the services offered) and to require staff to be more flexible. However, this trend is not universal. In certain types of organization, for example in the fast-food sector, operative employees may still do simple and specialized jobs. In certain settings, for example in developing countries where staff are still relatively cheap to employ, staffing levels may be as lavish as they were in the Lake District in the 1970s.

This chapter will explore different approaches towards the design of jobs and for linking these jobs together into organizational structures.

Enrich or simplify?

> **Box 7.2   Routinize or empower?**
>
> McDonald's had routinized the work of the crew so thoroughly that decision making had practically been eliminated from the jobs. As one window worker told me, "They've tried to break it down so that it's almost idiot-proof." Most of the workers agreed that there was little call for them to use their own judgement on the job, since there were rules about everything. If an unusual problem arose, the workers were supposed to turn it over to a manager.
>
> (Leidner 1993, p. 74)
>
> It was more than considerate of the Marriott night porter to trace my lost wallet – it meant he had to re-trace my entire journey through Vienna. All I could remember was that I'd been travelling on a Southern District streetcar. Miraculously, from this tiny piece of information, the night porter from the Marriott hotel managed to trace the route I'd travelled, the particular streetcar I was on, and my wallet. I was astounded that he went out of his way so much to help me. But, as I now know, everyone at Marriott works this way. Personally assuming responsibility for the needs of every guest. It's called *Empowerment*. And thankfully, they never seem to find anything too much trouble.
>
> ("Always in the right place at the right time." Marriott advertisement in the UK – see Lashley 1997, p. 23)

The examples in Box 7.2 represent two opposing approaches to the problem of designing jobs for operative level staff in hotels and restaurants. McDonald's uses what was identified in Chapter 5 as a Taylorist approach. Jobs are simplified and routinized to the extent that they become "idiot-proof". It has been argued (see Chapter 5) that such simple jobs are not motivating for the people who have to do them. However, it can also be argued that this is a sensible approach to designing jobs for the unskilled and transient employees who work in the fast-food sector (see Chapter 3).

On the other hand, the approach at Marriott (at least as described in this example) is to expand and develop the jobs of even the most junior staff and to require them to use their initiative and discretion. This approach is also termed *job enrichment* and, as has been shown in Chapter 5, writers like Herzberg and Porter and Lawler argue that enriched jobs, since they provide more opportunities for intrinsic motivation, are likely to result in a more committed and productive workforce.

The characteristics of an enriched job

The most widely-used model looking at ways in which jobs can be redesigned to make them more instrinically interesting is the job characteristics model of Hackman and Oldham (1980). According to this, factors such as employees' motivation, satisfaction and also their willingness to turn up to work, to remain in a job and the quality of the work they do are influenced by three critical psychological states:

1. the extent to which work is experienced as meaningful
2. the extent to which they feel they are responsible for the outcomes of their work
3. their knowledge of the results of their work.

Thus the Marriott night porter in the example in Box 7.2 feels that what he does makes a difference to the experience of the guests, that it is he who is responsible for retrieving the guest's lost wallet and he knows how the guest feels and what the company thinks when he finds the wallet. In contrast, it might be expected that typical McDonald's employees do not feel that their work makes an enormous difference to the success of McDonald's or the well-being of the customer; they are not encouraged to take responsibility for anything that goes wrong but to pass the problem on to the supervisor; and they may not know, at the end of the day, what they have contributed to the company or what the customers thought about the product.

Hackman and Oldham argue that five core job characteristics influence these critical psychological states:

- **Skill variety:** the extent to which the job involves using a number of different skills

- **Task identity:** the extent to which a person completes a whole piece of work from beginning to end

- **Task significance:** the extent to which the job affects the lives of others (or the job holder recognizes that it affects the lives of others)

- **Autonomy:** the extent to which the job holder can plan and schedule his or her own activities

- **Feedback:** the extent to which the job holder has information about the effectiveness of their performance.

I will compare two jobs against these job characteristics: the role of a kitchen hand preparing vegetables as part of a large traditional kitchen brigade and the role of an assistant working in a small sandwich bar and café.

A kitchen hand preparing vegetables experiences little *skill variety*: all he or she works on is the vegetables with no involvement in other parts of the meal. Likewise there is little *task identity* since he or she is not involved in cooking the whole meal. Obviously the task is *significant*, as presumably guests want their vegetables to be well prepared but since the kitchen hand has no direct contact with the guests he or she may not recognize the significance of the work. There is little *autonomy* in that the work of the kitchen hand is scheduled by others. There will be *feedback* from the senior chefs if the work is not done correctly but there is no feedback from the customer. In comparison, the work of an assistant working in a small sandwich bar is likely to involve some *skill variety* in that the assistant has to take orders, prepare the sandwich and the drinks and serve the customer. Likewise there is *task identity* in that the assistant handles the whole process from the beginning to the end. And, in that the assistant has direct contact with the customer, he or she is likely to be more aware of the *significance* of the job. There is direct *feedback* from the customer and the assistant would need to put right any mistakes made. There is some *autonomy* or discretion about how the work is done, particularly in slack periods. It is likely, for example, that the assistant could vary the recipe of the sandwich to meet the needs of the customer whereas a McDonald's employee would not be able to vary the recipe of a McDonald's hamburger. Thus, against the job characteristics model, the job of an assistant in a humble sandwich bar would be "better" than the job of a kitchen hand preparing vegetables for some grand restaurant; that is, it would have, in Hackman and Oldham's terms, more *motivating potential*.

How much scope is there in reality to redesign work at the operative level? Even with a role as apparently tightly defined as that of a hotel room attendant, whose main task is inevitably to clean hotel bedrooms, relatively minor changes in the way in which the job is organized can increase its motivating potential.

The traditional way in which a room attendant's job is organized is that a supervisor is responsible for scheduling the room attendant's work, for checking each room to see that it has been cleaned correctly and for returning the room to reception when it is ready for occupation by another guest. Using the Hackman and Oldham model, the motivating potential of this job can be increased by:

- giving the room attendant responsibility for scheduling his/her own work. This increases *skill variety* and *autonomy*;

- giving the room attendant responsibility for the same rooms all the time so that they effectively become his/her rooms. This increases *task identity*;

- giving the room attendant responsibility for checking his/her work. This increases *task identity*, *skill variety* and *feedback*;

- giving the room attendant responsibility for returning the room to reception. This increases *task identity*, *skill variety* and possibly *task significance*. (The room attendant rather than the supervisor will have direct contact with reception and be conscious of any problems if the room is not returned on time.)

- taking actions to increase the contact between the room attendant and the customer. For example, one might put a picture of the room attendant or a signed note in the room, letting the customer know who was responsible for cleaning the room. This increases *task significance* and encourages *feedback* from the customer;

- encouraging room attendants to greet guests that they encounter and ensuring that they are able to answer questions about hotel facilities. This means ensuring that they have seen other parts of the hotel (the restaurant, the leisure facilities etc.). It may mean providing some language training. These steps increase *skill variety* and *task significance*.

None of the steps outlined above is particularly radical and all have been used in some establishments. But these changes should significantly increase the motivating potential of this role. So why might employees not respond positively to improved jobs and why might hotels choose not to adopt these job redesign practices?

Stop

You have to convince the management team in a hotel where the jobs of the room attendants have been organized in a traditional way to redesign the role along the lines described above. What objections would you expect them to raise? Now you have to "sell" the changes to the room attendants. What objections would you expect them to raise?

Job enrichment: from the perspective of the employee

Do employees always prefer enriched jobs? The assumption behind the Hackman and Oldham model is that job enrichment works for the benefit of employees. Because they are more motivated, the organization gains from their higher levels of satisfaction and performance. However, the Hackman and Oldham model argued that these gains would be mediated by the employees' *growth need strength*. Some employees are just not motivated by interesting work; they are low in growth need strength. All that concerns them is the money they earn. (Refer back to the discussion in Chapter 5 about expectancy theory, which argued that you cannot motivate someone by offering them a reward that does not interest them and that people vary in the rewards they look for from work.)

Research by Lee-Ross and Johns (1995) looked at different groups of staff working in seasonal hotels on the English seaside: those who were all year live-in staff, all year live-out staff, seasonal live-in staff and seasonal live-out staff. Their results seemed to indicate that the all year live-out staff were most likely to be interested in enriched jobs. By contrast, the lives of the seasonal live-in staff tended to revolve around the friends and activities they had outside work and they were less concerned about whether their work was intrinsically interesting.

However, one must be careful not to assume that people who do boring and repetitive work always choose to do so because they are only motivated by money and do not want an intrinsically interesting job. Gabriel (1988) studied employees doing various catering jobs in and around London: in hospital catering, catering for a school/community centre, fast-food, a gentleman's club and independent cafés and restaurants. He argued that although many of these staff were doing jobs that offered little reward apart from a (poor) pay packet at the end of the week, they were not solely motivated by money at work:

> Although most workers depended on their job for their livelihood, not a single group in my sample saw good pay as the most desirable quality of a good job. Interest and variety was seen as more desirable than good pay for all groups except for the ancillary workers at Saint Theresa's (the hospital), for whom job security and good workmates were most important. Those who said that they stayed in their job because they needed the money said so because their jobs had little else to offer, not because they approached work purely as a means towards earning money.
>
> (Gabriel 1988, p. 157)

Box 7.3   The kitchen porter and the leisure centre attendant

Doing some research on job design in a UK hotel, I interviewed some leisure centre attendants about what they liked and disliked about their jobs. These staff had qualifications as fitness instructors and they resented spending much of their time sitting by the pool watching that no-one drowned. They particularly hated mopping up the pool area.

Subsequently, I interviewed one of the kitchen porters who was amazed (and delighted) that anyone should want to talk to him about his work. "Is there any job in the hotel that you would really like to do?" I asked. "Well, I would love to be able to clean the pool" he said.

As Box 7.3 illustrates, a task that may be intrinsically interesting and fulfilling to one employee may be seen as boring and demeaning to another. Similarly, an interesting amount of task variety in a job for one employee may be seen as boring and undemanding to another and stressful and anxiety-provoking to a third. A job which is very import-ant, where the jobholder has full discretion about what he or she does, which requires a wide variety of skills, where the jobholder is respon-sible for following the whole task through from beginning to end and where there is immediate feedback if something goes wrong is, on the one hand, potentially interesting and rewarding but, on the other hand, potentially stressful and difficult to cope with. The need, ideally, is to fit the characteristics of the job with the skills and motivations of the person doing that job.

A further issue in relation to job enrichment from the perspective of the employee is whether employees can end up being exploited by their employers because they are encouraged to take full responsibility for the outcomes of their work. The following example, from a Marriott hotel, was held up as an ideal, demonstrating how a fully committed employee in a well-designed job will give beyond what is expected for the customer and by extension for the company.

> A guest at a hotel asked Marlene Abbott, a guest room attendant, to arrange for items of clothing to be laundered. The timing of the request meant that it would be difficult to fulfil, so rather than telling the guest this, she took the guest's laundry home and did it herself
>   (Hubrecht and Teare 1993, p. iv quoted in Lashley 1997, p. 104)

However, as Lashley (1997) points out, is it really reasonable to expect an operative staff member to spend their own time, electricity and washing powder in this way or should there be limits on the commit-ment expected from staff?

Job enrichment: from the perspective of the employer

If job enrichment really does produce more committed employees, do employers actually adopt these principles? There is currently consider-able interest in *empowerment* initiatives amongst hospitality employers. Empowerment, as Lashley (1997) points out, is a concept with different meanings in different organizations but it generally refers to initiatives designed to give employees more discretion in the way they manage customer requests. Empowerment then essentially affects the employee's *autonomy*, although within very specific boundaries, and thus is in line with job enrichment principles. Thus a waiter's essential job would be very much as it always was and he would not be allowed to suddenly invent his own menu items but he would be expected to use his common sense and initiative to meet reasonable customer requests (such as providing milk rather than cream with coffee). Ivancevich and Matteson (1993) point out that job enrichment initiatives in practice have tended to emphasize the autonomy and feedback dimensions and placed less emphasis on task identity, task significance and variety. It seems to be easier to increase the responsibility that people have for their work (which is what empowerment does) than to change the essential nature of the task itself.

There is also some evidence that jobs in the hospitality industry are changing in ways which increase *task variety* and *identity*. In particular, there has been an increase in the extent to which staff are expected to be *multiskilled*. For example, someone working on reception might be expected to combine the tasks of receptionist, reservationist, cashier and switchboard operator rather than just concentrating on one of these roles. The advantage from the company's point of view is that fewer staff may be needed to perform the same role. The possibility of productivity gains rather than an improvement in quality of working life for the employee may be a major reason for investigating multiskilling.

However, for multiskilling to work, staff not only have to be motivated to increase the skills that they use at work but they also have to be trained to handle a range of skills. Prais *et al.* (1989) compared staffing practices in British and German hotels and argued that because German hotel employees were generally better trained and educated than their British counterparts they could handle a wider range of skills:

> The benefits of the broad scope of receptionists' training courses in Germany were apparent from the way those at reception carried out a variety of tasks that were often in separate hands in Britain: reservations, room allocation, information for guests, carrying luggage to guests' rooms, switchboard operation, supervision of room cleaning, guest accounts, payments and, often, breakfast preparation – all were carried out by the 'receptionist' in German hotels. . . . If two guests arrived simultaneously at a German hotel, and two staff-members were working primarily as cashier and receptionist respectively, then both staff-members turned to work on checking in; in Britain, narrower training and narrower job descriptions would often rule this out. (p.62)

There are also a few examples of hospitality organizations that have adopted some quite radical job redesign approaches. Harvester Restaurants, a chain of UK popular-eating restaurants, re-organized its staffing around *autonomous working groups* (Box 7.4). This approach to job redesign shares many features with the Hackman and Oldham approach but is based around building teams of workers which take responsibility for managing themselves. The approach grew out of work conducted by the Tavistock Institute in London in the 1950s (Trist and Bamforth 1951) and subsequent experiments in Scandinavian car factories (Volvo and Saab).

Box 7.4   Autonomous work groups at Harvester Restaurants

. . . There are now only three layers of personnel between the guest and the Managing Director. Staff within the restaurants are organized into autonomous work teams and are now referred to as team members. Each team has its "team responsibilities" and some team members take on additional duties as *Shift Coordinators* and *Appointed Persons*. Restaurant management consists of just two roles, *Team Manager* and *Team Coach*.

At restaurant level, the Team Manager and Team Coach were no longer "managing" the staff but were responsible for enabling and facilitating staff to be more self-managing and empowered. Each restaurant is organized around three teams which reflect the key operational areas (bars, restaurants, kitchen). Each team has its own *team responsibilities*, that is, those aspects of business performance for which it will be accountable. In the restaurant, for example, the team will be responsible for guest service, guest complaints, sales targets, ordering cutlery and glassware, cashing up after service and team member training. In the more advanced cases, members take part in the selection and recruitment of new team members.

(Lashley 1997, pp. 44–45)

Against job enrichment

However, referring back to Box 7.2, for every Harvester, there are also examples of hospitality companies, like McDonald's, where, far from being enriched, jobs are simplified and specialized and operative staff given little discretion.

The Marxist sociologist, Braverman (1974), argued that top management is always motivated to increase their control over the work process. The main motivation for introducing new technology is that it allows them to do just that: jobs can be simplified, fragmented and ultimately eliminated through complete automation. Far from wanting empowered and committed employees who can take decisions and use their initiative, according to Braverman's hypothesis managers would rather have jobs that are "idiot-proof" and can be done by anyone (preferably by people who do not need to be paid much), or better still, jobs that can be done by robots. Robots do not get tired, argue with the manager or go on strike. Thus Braverman claimed that workers who once had some degree of control and power at work because of the craft skills they possessed were progressively being deskilled.

Braverman (1974) developed his thesis in relation to the manufacturing sector, but it is easy to find examples of the use of technology to deskill or eliminate jobs in the hospitality industry. The word "technology" is being used in a broad sense to include not just computers and machines but also products and "ways of doing things". This process is at its most developed in fast-food companies like McDonald's. Indeed, Ritzler (1993) uses the term "the McDonaldization of society" to describe the process whereby firms organize work processes in increasingly standardized ways to meet society's demand for predictable, quick and convenient products and services.

In a McDonald's outlet, staff do not mince the beef, bake the bread, make the pastry for the apple pies and cut up the potatoes for the french fries. The food prepared for McDonald's arrives at the outlets largely preformed and pre-prepared ready to be cooked or heated and served to the customer. Within the outlet, the process for cooking or heating each of the products is carefully controlled. McDonald's staff do not have to use their judgement to tell when a hamburger is properly cooked: each part of the process is carefully timed. This makes it possible for the food to be served to the customer quickly. (It is *fast* food, after all.) It also makes it easier for the company to standardize the product: so that a McDonald's anywhere in the world will taste very much the same as it is prepared from the same ingredients and in the same way.

But the same processes can be seen in other parts of the hospitality industry. If you return to the example given at the beginning of this chapter (Box 7.1), it can be seen that many of the reductions of staff that have been possible in Lake District hotels have been possible because of the introduction of technology:

- Using different food preparation systems in the kitchen – buying in more prepared or partially prepared food (i.e. pre-prepared potatoes rather than preparing them oneself); using technologies like cook-chill which allow the meals to be prepared in advance and reheated – can reduce the size of the kitchen brigade while maintaining or improving the quality of the food.

- "Product" in bedrooms or corridors, e.g. kettles, coffee makers, minibars, trouser presses, irons, shoe-shining machines, drink vending machines, eliminates the need for room service/valet service.

- Simpler food service systems, plated or buffet service rather than silver service, reduce the need for highly skilled waiting staff.

In a McDonaldized society, where people are looking for quick and convenient services, the above changes which reduce the number of staff required and the skills they need is likely to improve customer satisfaction rather than reduce it.

So there are two apparently contradictory trends at work here. On the one hand, there is the argument that companies should design intrinsically interesting jobs that allow their employees some control and discretion. On the other hand, there is the argument that technology allows companies to de-skill and eliminate jobs and reduces the control and power of employees. Can these contradictory impulses be reconciled?

Firstly, return to Braverman's (1974) contention that technology inevitably leads to deskilling. It is certainly true that technology makes certain skills obsolete. One may question whether these are necessarily high-level craft skills. If buying in pre-prepared (by a machine) vegetables eliminates the need to employ someone to chop carrots, or buying a dishwasher eliminates the need for a pot-washer, are we really eliminating *highly-skilled* jobs?

It may be more realistic to argue that technology leads to reskilling. Returning to the Lake District example (Box 7.1), this included illustrations of the ways in which jobs had been de-skilled and eliminated but also examples of the ways in which they were being enriched through multiskilling. Whilst one may no longer expect a chambermaid to act as a valet, she may now be expected to serve behind the bar. The overall job requires different skills but not necessarily fewer skills.

Perhaps what is happening, then, is not a generalized move towards deskilled operative level jobs but a shift towards a mix of "enriched" and "simplified" jobs. But when is it appropriate to "enrich" and when to "simplify"?

The flexible organization

In Chapter 3, it was argued that one of the key characteristics of hospitality organizations, as service organizations, is that the services they sell are *perishable*. A restaurant table which is not filled one evening cannot be stored: that sale is lost forever. Customers demand services when it is convenient to them, often outside normal working hours. It is not possible to persuade someone to have dinner at 3 o'clock in the afternoon just because that would allow staff to finish at five. Hotels and restaurants are subject to peaks and troughs of demand. Therefore, they particularly require staff who are flexible.

There are two main types of ways in which staff can be flexible: they can be *functionally flexible* or they can be *numerically flexible*.

- **Functional flexibility**. Functionally flexible staff are those who are able and willing to do more than one job. Functional flexibility may operate across different jobs at the same level: the room maid who will serve breakfast or help out in the bar as well as cleaning rooms. It may operate across the same job in different locations: the waiter who works in the coffee shop as well as the formal restaurant of the same hotel. Finally, it may involve moving between jobs at different levels: the supervisor who will stand in for an absent manager or even the manager who will help out in the kitchen or restaurant if needed. Functional flexibility implies the type of job enrichment strategies that have been discussed above.

- **Numerical flexibility**. Numerical flexibility means being able to vary the hours and periods that people work so that these match the busy and the quiet times of the establishment. So it may involve employing waiters part-time for evening and weekend shifts only. It may involve hiring temporary or casual staff to cover major events (for example hiring casual waiting staff to serve at a wedding). It may involve hiring staff on short-term contracts: for example, taking on staff at a resort for the summer season only. It may involve strategies such as not replacing employees who leave (and specifically recruiting people who may not wish to stay very long) or even finding excuses to dismiss staff if business is slow.

Atkinson (1985) has proposed an ideal model of a flexible firm where there is a *core* group of staff who perform the key activities of the company. They have job security and access to career opportunities within the firm but in return they are expected to be functionally flexible.

These core staff are surrounded by a *peripheral* group who perform tasks which are not so central to the organization's success. They have less job security and few career opportunities. They do relatively simple jobs that are not specific to the organization (so they could transfer their skills to another organization) and are not expected to be functionally flexible. But they are numerically flexible.

This is an *ideal* model in that it is not exactly based on any real organization but Atkinson proposes it as a way to design a firm which is fully flexible.

Box 7.5   Flexibility in practice

This case is based on a chain of restaurants operating in the London area. It is a small but expanding chain with six restaurants at present providing south-east Asian food adapted for European tastes. One of the restaurants is situated in a suburb in south-west London. Although open from 12 noon till 12 midnight seven days a week, it is very quiet on weekday lunchtimes and in the afternoons but packed on Friday, Saturday and Sunday evenings.

The restaurant is staffed by a manager, who lives on site, and two assistant managers, one for the restaurant and one for the bar area. There are two chefs. On weekday lunchtimes, these will be the only staff on duty. The assistant managers will double up as waiting and bar staff for those customers there are. They have other work to get on with if the restaurant is empty. The chefs work preparing the *mise en place* for the evening if they have little to prepare for lunch. As all these staff are salaried and not hourly paid staff and would be required to be at work anyway, the company incurs little extra cost from keeping the restaurant open at a quiet period.

Chefs are particularly difficult to recruit as they need to be highly skilled and knowledgeable about Asian cuisine. The menu is quite extensive and dishes are freshly prepared. Although the company recruited fully trained south-east Asian nationals initially – the head chef in this restaurant is Thai – they are keen to develop their own chefs. The assistant chef is Algerian and it is planned that he will become head chef in one of the new restaurants when he is fully trained.

Waiting staff, on the other hand, do not have to be highly skilled. Service is family-style and the restaurant's atmosphere is casual. Although it is helpful if they can give advice about the food, all the dishes are explained in some detail on the menu. Waiting staff are hourly paid and many are students working part-time or are temporary visitors to London. Managers make informal arrangements with waiting staff, sending them home early if the restaurant is quieter than expected but sometimes asking them to come in at short notice if it is unexpectedly busy.

The operations manager (who was responsible for all the restaurants in the chain) commented that: "When I first came I wanted to make sure that everybody was part of the family and that everybody had the same benefits. Then the reality of the bottom line and keeping down the wage–cost percentage hit me. We give an excellent package to our core staff but there really isn't much point in providing expensive benefits to people who are going to leave you anyway. It only pushes up your costs." It is interesting that the operations manager had spent the previous evening cooking in one of the other restaurants in the chain, filling in for a missing chef.

The example in Box 7.5 illustrates how core and peripheral staff can be used in practice to provide flexibility in a hospitality organization. In this case, the core staff comprise the three managers and the chefs. These are staff that it is in the company's interests to look after and retain because their skills make a real difference to the success of the restaurant chain and they need to be trained in the specific requirements of this chain. But in return for being provided with good rewards and career prospects within the company, these core staff are expected to be functionally flexible. In the case of the managers, this often seems to involve being prepared to trade down, that is, to do a job which would normally be carried out by a subordinate.

The waiters are treated as peripheral staff, doing simplified jobs. The job of a waiter is relatively low skilled in this particular restaurant. In order to control labour costs, the company needs to be able to match the number of waiters on duty with the number of customers in the restaurant. Therefore, for this group of staff, numerical flexibility is crucial. The waiters are, in some respects, second-class citizens compared with the other staff, in terms of the benefits provided for them and the career opportunities open to them. It may be argued that this does not matter because they are probably not interested in long-term careers with the company: they want short-term work or part-time work. In fact, it may be in the company's interest to recruit waiters who may not wish to stay with the company very long because they can use job turnover as a way of achieving numerical flexibility – someone who leaves may not be replaced if the restaurant is quiet – and a bright waiter will not stay long enough to become bored and stale.

The converse argument is that it is dangerous to treat the waiters as peripheral staff. They are the staff in front-line contact with the customers so their skills and behaviour do matter to the company. But because the company invests less in peripheral staff, it is harder to gain their commitment and motivation. Further, this strategy may only be possible in a place like London with a large transient population where it is relatively easy to recruit suitable waiting staff.

In Chapter 3, it was argued that some parts of the hospitality industry have a reputation for providing poor pay and low-skilled jobs. The example in Box 7.5 demonstrates how, in an attempt to be cost-effective and productive, hospitality organizations can choose to operate with a relatively small core of staff who have interesting jobs, good prospects and are relatively well paid, surrounded by a larger group of relatively poorly paid and poorly skilled peripheral staff. One consequence of this at a macro-level may be that it is hard to persuade well-qualified people that there *are* interesting and skilled jobs in the core activities of the hospitality industry when their first experience of work in the industry has been in the poorly paid and low-skilled peripheral jobs (see Baum 1995, p. 86).

Distancing strategies

Box 7.6   Contracting out

The expertise of hoteliers lies in managing rooms. Just because someone is a good hotelier doesn't mean they are a good restaurateur. The restaurant

> market is changing so quickly that you need to be a specialist restaurateur to truly understand it. That is why so many hotels are choosing to contract out their restaurants to specialist restaurant companies.
>
> (Restaurant consultant)

There is one other method that organizations can use to increase flexibility: that is to make use of external agencies or contractors. The organization does not employ people directly to do the task themselves, it transfers the responsibility to "distanced" or external groups. These may be sub-contractors, self-employed workers, temporary help agencies or the producers of pre-prepared products.

Examples of "distancing" strategies in use in hotels include:

- sending out laundry rather than having an in-house laundry
- using the local take-away pizza restaurant to provide room service rather than providing it from within the hotel
- contracting the cleaning of common areas to a specialist cleaning agency. In some cases, hotels use agencies to provide room cleaners
- giving a concession to someone to run a shop, or florist or hairdressers within the hotel rather than running it oneself
- using a specialist car parking company to run the hotel car park
- in some cases, (see Box 7.6) bringing in a specialist restaurant company to run a hotel restaurant.

From the other perspective, many hospitality companies exist to provide "distanced" services for companies that do not want to look after that aspect of their business. Contract catering companies provide, amongst other services, food for people at work for companies that do not want to run their own staff canteen or restaurant.

Advantages of distancing

- The company can concentrate on the core elements of its business where it has most expertise. The hotel is focused on the business of managing its rooms: the managers do not have to waste too much time worrying about how the hairdressers is doing.

- The company can make use of the specialist expertise of other companies for whom the activity is their core business. The core activity of the takeaway pizza company is to cook and deliver food to people for consumption in their home or place of stay. Room service, by contrast, is an extra service provided in the hotel: it is not the hotel's main reason for existence.

- The company is transferring the risk and responsibility for an activity to the "distanced" operation. If the hotel shop is not profitable, it is the concessionnaire who suffers, not the hotel. At the same time, the concessionnaire is motivated to make the shop a success because it is his or her livelihood.

- The cost of operating the activity may be reduced if it is "distanced" out. A hotel might not be able to justify the extra staff costs required to provide room service if there was only an occasional demand for it. But for the local takeaway pizza company that was already doing business in the area, providing meals to the hotel would increase their business without necessarily increasing their costs.

Disadvantages of distancing

- The company loses direct control over an activity that affects its business. If a hotel guest sends some shirts to be washed and they are returned late and damaged, he will not blame the laundry, he will blame the hotel. As a last resort the hotel could terminate the contract with that laundry if problems persist. But what if there are no other laundries in the local area that the business could be transfrered to? "Distancing" can be a risky strategy.

- Because the "distanced" worker or contractor is not directly employed by the company, they are not likely to be as committed to the company as the "core" employees. They have their own motivations and agenda which may not be completely in line with those of the company.

Box 7.7   Employee or self-employed?

When is an employee not an employee? The concierge at an exclusive five-star hotel in London earns more than most of the managers but three-quarters of his earnings come from the tips given to him by his wealthy guests and only a quarter from the salary he is paid by the hotel. What is his relationship to the hotel? Is he really just another employee or is he essentially self-employed?

In summary, organizations have a number of choices about how to design the jobs that their staff do. They need to decide which activities they employ people directly to do and which activities they contract out to other agencies. For those activities managed directly by the organization, they need to consider if jobs should be designed to have responsibility, be interesting and offer career opportunities or if jobs should be simplified and designed to be "idiot-proof". I shall now explore some broader issues about how jobs can be linked together into organization structures.

Organizational structures

Box 7.8   Two organizational structures

A study by Hales and Tamangani (1996) compared two hotel companies in Zimbabwe.

Alpha arose from the privatization of a publicly-owned concern in 1990. It had four hotels and a non-hotel division and employed 400 people. It had a typically centralized structure. All important decisions were made by the managers at the corporate level. The hotel managers only had control over immediate and detailed operational areas. Communication flows were up and down the organizational hierarchy. There were extensive and tight formal rules and regulations. Jobs, including the jobs of managers, were specialized and closely defined. Managers were rewarded for conforming to the company standards and for demonstrating their loyalty to the company.

Omega was a subsidiary of a locally owned conglomerate. It comprised five hotels and employed 600 people. Omega was a relatively decentralized organization. Decision-making and operational planning were devolved to the hotel manager level. Information flowed not just up and down the hierarchy but also across the organization through informal contacts and consultation as well as through the formal reporting mechanisms. Managers were seen as generalists and given a broad remit. There were relatively few formal rules and regulations: people were expected to regulate themselves. Managers were rewarded for achieving performance targets.

These two companies were similar: both hotel companies, similar sized and based in the same country and yet they were structured in very different ways.

There are two key factors that need to be understood in relation to organizational structure: *differentiation* and *integration*. Differentiation is about how activities are split up between people in the organization. Integration is about how those activities are coordinated so that everyone is heading in broadly the same direction. The discussion above, looking at whether jobs should be simplified or enriched, has explored some of the issues to do with differentiation. But how can organizations solve the problems of integration, of bringing all the diverse activities together?

It is possible to distinguish between two broad approaches to solving these problems of differentiation and integration: the *mechanistic* model and the *organic* model; a contrast that was first explored by Burns and Stalker in 1961.

The mechanistic model

In a mechanistic organization, tasks are split up to make clearly defined specialized jobs. Standardized rules and procedures define what people should do. If a decision needs to be taken which is outside of these rules and procedures, it is referred up the hierarchy. The organization structure tends to be tall, i.e. there are many levels in the hierarchy. The organization is very *centralized*, in that the people at the top make all the important decisions. People are rewarded for conforming to the rules and procedures. Alpha (see Box 7.8) is an example of a mechanistic organization.

The mechanistic organisation is highly differentiated and activities are integrated through rules and regulations and through the centralized control exercised by the hierarchical chain of command. The mechanistic organization structure is the classical solution to the problem of structuring a large organization. The classical writers on organizations, such as Fayol and Urwick who were writing in the early part of the twentieth century, advocated this approach to organization. It is easy to find examples of organizations which used to be structured in this way. For example, Shamir (1978), describing a British hotel 20 years ago, claimed to have found no fewer than 23 different occupational titles and ten different hierarchical levels in the hotel kitchen alone. (Refer also to the Lake District hotels described in Box 7.1.) However, the example of Alpha (Box 7.8) demonstrates that mechanistic organizations are not just a relic of the past.

The organic model

In an organic organization, there is less emphasis on job specialization and people are expected to use their initiative to resolve problems, even if that is not in their formal job description, rather than always to refer them to a superior. The organizational structure tends to be flatter, i.e. there are fewer levels in the hierarchy. The organization is more *decentralized*: people at lower levels are given more authority and responsibility and it is not always assumed that those at senior levels know best. People are encouraged to become committed to the goals of the organization and are rewarded for their achievements and initiative, not just their loyalty. Communication flows across the organization, not just up and down. Omega (see Box 7.8) would seem to be an example of an organic organization.

The organic organization is less differentiated. Approaches to designing jobs such as job enrichment, empowerment, the use of autonomous working groups and the delayering of management hierarchies fit well within the organic model. The organization is integrated through the use of performance targets rather than through the use of rules and regulations.

Are organic structures better?

Is the delayered and decentralized organic structure better than the tall, centralized mechanistic structure? Is this the organizational form of the future? Certainly, some organizational theorists from Burns and Stalker (1961), through Lawrence and Lorsch (1967) and through to Tom Peters (1988) have argued that whilst mechanistic organizations operate well in stable environments, organic organizations are better suited to the conditions of rapid change and turbulence that modern companies face.

As always, it is not quite as simple as that. Whilst the trend generally in organizations is to decentralize, delayer and empower employees, that trend is not universal. As we have seen, in any one company it is quite possible to find simplified, formalized jobs existing alongside enriched, empowered jobs, that is to find elements of both the mechanistic and organic organizational types. Furthermore, just because an organization seems to have a decentralized structure does not necessarily mean that the people at the top exert less control over people lower down, merely that they exert control in a different way. Hales and Tamangani (1996) argue that the unit hotel managers at Alpha and Omega are subject to different control mechanisms; the former conforming to centrally determined operating procedures and the latter being held accountable for financial performance. "However, the managers subject to performance controls were not, in practice, significantly freer to choose what they did than those constrained by regulations, even though performance accountability carried the illusion of greater managerial autonomy" (p. 751). In other words, the real differences between Alpha and Omega may not be quite as large as they appear initially.

Hales and Tamangani do highlight the way in which differences in organizational structure affect what managers do. It is to the role of managers that I turn in the next chapter.

Summary

- There are two broadly opposing approaches that can be taken to the design of jobs. Jobs can be simplified, to make them as easy as possible to do, or jobs can be enriched, to make them intrinsically interesting and rewarding for the job holder.

- Jobs can be enriched by increasing the following characteristics: skill variety, task identity, task significance, autonomy and feedback.

- The characteristics of the job need to be matched to the characteristics of the job holder. Not all employees want an intrinsically interesting job: although some people who seem just to work for the money may respond well if they are given more responsibility. One needs to be careful that enrichment does not lead to employees taking on so much responsibility that they are being exploited by their employers.

- There are some cases of hospitality companies experimenting with job enrichment techniques: for example, by empowering employees, encouraging multiskilling and using autonomous working groups.

- At the same time, some jobs in the hospitality industry are being simplified and deskilled. This is frequently possible because of the introduction of new technology. The sociologist Braverman (1974) argued that new technology would inevitably lead to the deskilling or elimination of jobs because it is easier for managers to control the work process. However, it is probably more accurate to argue that the introduction of new technology leads to reskilling not deskilling: employees require different skills, not necessarily fewer skills.

- Atkinson (1985) proposed an ideal model of a flexible firm where a core group of functionally flexible staff was surrounded by a peripheral group of staff that was required to be numerically flexible. This type of structure can be seen in some hospitality firms. The core staff have interesting, enriched jobs and career prospects and the peripheral staff have simplified jobs and are not expected to stay very long. The danger is that the peripheral staff who are less committed to the organization may deliver a poorer quality of service to the customer.

- Another strategy that organizations can use to increase their flexibility is "distancing" : that is contracting out some of their activities to another company, agency or to someone who is self-employed. "Distancing" allows the organization to concentrate on its core activities where it has most expertise but it is harder for the organization to control an activity that has been distanced.

- When designing organizational structure, there are two key issues that need to be addressed: *differentiation* (how tasks are divided up to make jobs) and *integration* (how everything can be pulled together to meet the same goals and objectives). Two approaches to designing structures are the "mechanistic" model and the "organic" model.

- The mechanistic organization is highly differentiated: employees do specialized, tightly-defined jobs and there are many levels in the hierarchy. Integration is managed through centralized control exercised from the top of the organization through the chain of command.

- The organic organization has broader, less specialized jobs and a flat hierarchy. It is more decentralized with authority passed down the organization. Each separate division has to meet performance goals which integrate its activities with the other parts of the organization. There are communication flows across the organization, not just up and down.

- There seems to be a trend towards more organic forms of organizational structure as companies delayer and decentralize. It can be argued that such structures allow organizations to adapt better to changes in the environment. However, people working in an organic organization are not necessarily less tightly controlled than those working in a mechanistic structure: they are merely controlled in a different way.

The next stage

Experience

Try to build up a picture of the way in which jobs are split up and linked together in any large organization that you have contacts with (a hotel would be an ideal choice here because of the wide range of departments). Get hold of the organizational structure and any job descriptions which might be available. Can you identify any "core" jobs and any "peripheral" ones? To what extent are employees expected to be functionally flexible or numerically flexible? Identify any activities which are "distanced". How tall is the hierarchy? Are communications mainly up and down the organization or do they operate across it as well? Is the organization closer to the mechanistic model or the organic model?

Ask people who work in different departments about the work that they do: what skills do they need, what do they like best about it and what do they like least.

If possible, ask a manager about the organizational structure and the design of different jobs. What problems are there with the current structure? What would they change if they were able to?

Reflection

Reflect on a job that you have done. (If you have no work experience, you can reflect on your "job" as a student.) How would you score this job in terms of skill variety, task identity, task significance, autonomy and feedback? How did this affect how you felt about doing this job? Are there any ways in which the job could be enriched, i.e. the level of these job characteristics increased? How do you think this would have affected how you thought about the job? Are there any ways in which the job could be simplified (think particularly about the use of technology here)? How would this affect how you felt about this job?

Think about the broader structure in which the job exists. Was this a "core" job or a "peripheral" job? How did this affect how you felt about it? Was there a tall hierarchy or a flat hierarchy? Was the organization centralized or decentralized? How did this affect your attitude towards the job?

Theorizing

What is the theoretical case for and against job enrichment? In what conditions would a job enrichment strategy be most effective?

Atkinson's (1985) model of the flexible firm is an "ideal" model. To what extent does the ideal match reality? Why might one see a mismatch between Atkinson's model and the way organizations attempt to be flexible in practice?

When might a mechanistic organizational structure be more appropriate than an organic organization structure?

In practice

Think about the organization you considered under the "experience" section. How would you redesign any jobs which you think do not work well? How would you change the organization's structure?

You are about to open your own 50-room hotel. (You decide where it is, what market it serves and what facilities it will offer.) How many staff will you employ, what jobs will they do and what will your organizational structure be? Why?

A friend runs a successful chain of restaurants. The style of the restaurant and the market that it is aimed at fits well with the style of your new hotel. He does not have a restaurant near your hotel. He asks if he can take over your hotel restaurant and run it as one of his chain. He would lease the space from you, kit out the restaurant and kitchen in his style and put in his own staff and management team. What are the arguments for and against accepting his proposal? What would you decide?

Further reading

General organizational behaviour texts will include material on job design and organizational design, although not generally on the flexible organization. For a discussion of the latter refer to Atkinson (1984). For further information about the Braverman hypothesis refer to Pugh and Hickson (1996). For further discussion of organizational design, refer to Child (1984) or Hales (1993).

There is plenty of material looking at job and organization design in relation to the hospitality industry. See Leidner (1993) or Gabriel (1988) for an exploration of what it feels like to be stuck in a "simplified" job; Lashley (1997) for a discussion of new approaches to organizing work, and Guerrier and Lockwood (1989a) for a discussion of the application of the flexible firm model to the hotel industry.

References for further reading

Atkinson, J. (1984) Manpower strategies for flexible organizations, *Personnel Management*, 28–31 August.

Child, J. (1984) *Organization: A Guide to Problems and Practice* (Second edition), London: Harper and Row.

Gabriel, Y. (1988) *Working Lives in Catering*, London: Routledge and Kegan Paul.

Guerrier, Y. and Lockwood, A. (1989) Core and peripheral employees in hotel operations, *Personnel Review*, **18**, 9–15.

Hales, C. (1993) *Managing through Organisations*, London: Routledge.

Lashley, C. (1997) *Empowering Service Excellence*, London: Cassell.

Leidner, R. (1993) *Fast Food Fast Talk: Service Work and the Routinization of Everyday Life*, Berkeley: University of California Press.

Pugh, D. and Hickson, D. (1996) *Writers on Organizations* (Fifth edition), London: Penguin.

8 Managers and their roles

Box 8.1 What do managers do?

Management is neither art nor science nor skill, at base there is nothing to do. A manager is hired for what he (*sic*) knows other firms do, what he can find to do and what he can be told to do.

(Fletcher 1973, p. 136)

The work of the manager is less that of the captain of industry, coolly commanding from the bridge, than of the honey-bee flitting noisily from bloom to bloom.

(Thomas 1993, p. 48)

Introduction

Probably the majority of you reading this book will be doing so because you are interested in hospitality management. Perhaps you aspire to becoming a manager in the hospitality industry in future or perhaps you already work as a manager. But what exactly do hospitality managers do? And what do you need to know about and be able to do in order to be a good manager?

It is suprisingly difficult to answer that question. In some respects, managers do not do anything in that the function of management is to ensure that things are done rather than to do them directly oneself. As the old adage goes: "managers do things through people". So the food and beverage manager is not appointed to cook and serve the meal herself but to ensure that meals are cooked and served. Indeed, if she does start cooking and serving, she may be criticized for not organizing, planning and delegating effectively.

What do managers do?

Management is a recent activity. One hundred years ago management as we know it barely existed (Thomas 1993). Its development came with the Industrial Revolution and the growth of larger scale, more complex organizations which required "managing". In this context some of the earliest writers on management, who were usually practising managers themselves, tried to define some of the principles of effective management.

One of the founding fathers of management science, the French manager Henri Fayol, defined the management process as far back as 1916, writing that: "to manage is to forecast and plan, to organize, to command, to coordinate and to control". Fayol was trying to establish management as a worthwhile activity in its own right, which made a valuable contribution to organizational effectiveness and which should be ranked alongside other professional activities, for example engineering, in terms of prestige. His definition remains a good starting point and his ideas formed the basis of the Classical School of Management Thought.

However, from the 1960s onwards, management researchers started questioning whether the Classical School's ideas about what management should be like, which implied that management was a rational and scientific activity, bore any resemblance to the way managers actually behaved. The best way to study the reality of management work was to watch how managers spent their time.

The most famous study on management activities was conducted by Mintzberg (1973), who observed the work of a small number of American chief executive officers. But other studies, notably by Stewart (1967, 1976, 1982) of British managers and by Kotter (1982) in the United States drew similar conclusions. Their characterization of the reality of management work was very different from the image promoted by the Classical School.

According to these studies, real management work has the following characteristics:

- **Unrelenting pace**. Managers have to deal with a great quantity of work.

- **Variety, brevity and fragmentation**. Managers tend to spend relatively short amounts of time (about ten minutes) on any one activity. They flit from task to task and rarely have time for uninterrupted planning or thinking.

- **Preference for issues which are current, specific and non-routine**. Management is a seat of the pants activity and managers make most of their decisions on an *ad hoc* basis.

- **Preference for verbal rather than written means of communication**. Managers would rather sort out problems face-to-face or over the telephone rather than by writing memos or reports.

- **A web of internal and external contacts**. Managers spend most of their time talking to people and responding to their demands. They pay a lot of attention to developing networks, interpersonal relationships and organizational politics.

- **Is subject to heavy constraints but managers can exercise some control over their work**. It may seem that managers do no more than react to problems, crises and the demands of others. But by pursuing broad agendas of issues through their contacts, managers can be proactive as well as reactive.

What do hospitality managers do?

Box 8.2   Hotel management: an art or a science?

As recently as two or three decades ago the stature of a hotel man was often measured by the extent of his personal charm, the degree of his individual popularity and the number of people he could greet by name.

Today the axis is shifting. Maybe we are sacrificing some of the industry's picturesque glamour on the altar of hard facts, know-how and a familiarity with the tools of scientific management. But it is these latter that pay off when the monthly system or annual report is issued.

> A hunch sometimes pays off, but facts and knowledge pay bigger
> dividends. Modern competitive conditions demand a scientific approach.
> (Ernest Henderson of the Sheraton Corporation
> speaking in the 1950s, quoted in Vallen *et al.* 1978, p. 30)

Whilst hotels and restaurants have existed for centuries, the discipline of hospitality management is a relatively recent one, growing up in the United States with the development of new hotel and restaurant chains. As the quotation above demonstrates, by the 1950s the large hospitality corporations had been influenced by the ideas of Classical Management Theory and viewed hospitality management as a professional, scientific and rational activity. But is the work of the hospitality manager in practice any different from that of other managers?

There have been several studies of the activities of hospitality managers (Nailon 1968, Ley 1980, Ferguson and Berger 1984) and the picture that emerges is that their work is as fragmented, pressurized, messy and dominated by the demands of others as the work of Mintzberg's managers, if not more so. For example, Ferguson and Berger, studying restaurant managers, commented that their sample worked constantly in "interrupt" mode, were rarely at their desks and were spending much of their time monitoring the performance of the restaurant by being around and even helping out. For these managers ". . . planning seems to have been eclipsed by reacting; organising might be better described as carrying on; co-ordinating appears more like juggling; and controlling seems reduced to full time watching" (Ferguson and Berger 1984).

In the hospitality industry as in other industries the *image* of management as a rational and scientific activity does not seem to square with the *reality* of management as the messy, chaotic and *ad hoc* business of getting things done.

Controversies in hospitality management

The nature of the managers' role in the hospitality industry is controversial. Thomas (1993) presents three criteria for making an issue controversial:

1. The issue must be the object of dispute. If everyone agrees about some matter it cannot be regarded as controversial.
2. For an issue to be controversial it must be considered important.
3. For an issue to be regarded as controversial it must be the focus of a debate between those who hold opposing views.

As Thomas goes on to argue, engaging in controversy is stimulating and fun. The world would be very boring if we all agreed with each other about everything. But controversies are also important because although we debate about ideas, ideas affect actions. A lively debate about the pros and cons of feminism and the rights of women to equal opportunities in the workforce may be intellectually stimulating but, at the end of the day, the career opportunities of real women (and men) are affected by the way that dispute is resolved. Controversies are difficult to resolve. Ideally we look for a "public" resolution so that everyone comes to agree that one side in the debate is correct. This has perhaps happened in the debate about giving equal opportunities to women in the workforce; it is now broadly publicly accepted, at least in many countries, that women should have equal opportunities. But while we wait for a public resolution of other controversies we can at least try to come to a private resolution: we can decide which side of the debate we agree with as individuals.

There are two major and interrelated controversies about the nature of hospitality management:

- **Controversy 1:** Is hospitality management unique and substantially different from management in other industries?

- **Controversy 2:** To what extent do managers require craft-based skills, particularly food preparation and food service skills, or are business skills sufficient in themselves?

Controversy 1: Unique skills?

Box 8.3 Superhuman or only human?

The hotelier must have the diplomacy of a Kissinger, the social grace of the Queen Mother, the speed of a Concorde, the smile of a Greek God, the patience of a saint, the memory of an elephant, the thick skin of a rhinoceros, the strength of an Atlas, the staying power of a mother-in-law, the fitness of a centre forward, the grooming of a duke, the voice of an Olivier, the eye for profit of a Vestry, and last but not least the hotelier must have a love of humanity: for humans show their worst side when they are tired and hungry.

(Albert Elovic)

The hospitality industry is no longer seen to require the special management skills to the extent that it once did. The industry now has a greater reliance on specialist managers in personnel, marketing, sales, finance and computing and increasingly recruits these specialists from outside the hotel and catering sector. Similarly managers from the industry perceive they have the opportunity to move into other service based organizations.

(Gamble, Lockwood and Messenger 1994)

Are the skills required to be a hospitality manager unique; in terms of the quotation from Elovic above, do you need to be superhuman? This has implications for the career paths of managers. If the successful supermarket manager or factory manager could run a hotel or restaurant, why select hotel or restaurant managers only from those with a background in hospitality management? It also has implications for the training and development of managers. Why run separate hospitality management programmes if all prospective managers require is a general business and management education?

The case for hospitality management being unique

The argument is that the nature of the hospitality business, i.e. that it is about the provision of accommodation and/or food and drink away from home, places particular demands on the manager that are different from the demands on managers in other businesses. First, hospitality is about giving service to customers; customers with diverse needs who, as Elovic points out, are frequently tired and hungry and need care and attention. The management of service quality is therefore necessarily a major focus of the role of any hospitality manager. However, the hospitality manager has to simultaneously manage a service operation (restaurant, reception) and a production operation (kitchen). Further, hospitality managers are dealing with perishable products that require instant sale and there is a short lead time between the demand for the product and the requirement for service; the guest wants a meal now, not in three weeks' or even three hours' time. Thus most day-to-day business problems in hotels have extremely short lead times. The implication is that managers need an in-depth knowledge of the work of the people that they are managing in order to deliver good service quality and to resolve any problems; that the manager needs to be able to cook, wait, serve drinks, make the bed if he or she is going to ensure that this is being done correctly. (Thus Controversy 1 is linked with Controversy 2 about the extent to which managers require craft skills.)

The case against

The argument here is that many of the characteristics that are claimed to make the hospitality industry unique can also be found in other service sector industries, for example retailing or banking (see Chapter 3). Hospitality managers are not really so very different from other managers but their lack of contact with managers from other sectors makes them claim they are. Furthermore, portraying the industry as unique is often an excuse for managers to avoid confronting their poor management practice; the insularity of the industry means that it is "a sector dominated by the spirit of amateur management" (Parsons and Cave 1991) that fails to recognize that it can learn from best practice elsewhere. Baum (1989) sums up these arguments in a paper on hotel management in Ireland:

> The perception of uniqueness is translated into a very clear reluctance to acknowledge common ground with other business sectors, in terms of operating business practice, management tools and development needs. The priority given to customer satisfaction over and above the need for profit and other business objectives, does create a certain distinctiveness, albeit questionable. However, the consequences of insularity for the industry are considerable. In practical terms, it translates into a failure to perceive of business and product market place terms, in competition with other food and leisure sectors and, indeed, with alternative use of plant and space. It leads to low profit margins and the consequences this has for investment. Insularity also results in a reluctance to engage in significant "cross pollination" of ideas and experience with other business sectors or to participate in general management and business development programmes. (p. 139)

The argument is that what hospitality managers really need is a good grasp of general business and management principles and skills if the industry is to escape its amateur image. Thus people who support the case against for Controversy 1 also tend to support the case against for Controversy 2.

Stop

What is your opinion about this controversy? Which side do you support? (You will find my opinion at the end of the chapter.)

Controversy 2: Craft or business skills?

Box 8.4   Craft or business skills?

Managers should know how to make beds, know how to be a waiter, a barman, a butcher. A manager isn't a manager if he can't do every job in the hotel.

(Owner manager of an exclusive hotel)

At the end of the day it's the management skills of the person that are important. Whether the person knows how to cook the product or not is unimportant because we can tell them as much about the product as we want.

(Manager from a restaurant chain)

This controversy is particularly hotly debated. The two sides are represented by two different traditions of developing managers for the hospitality industry: the European tradition, especially that of the Swiss Hotel School, and the American tradition. In European hospitality schools, potential managers are provided with an in-depth knowledge of the technical skills needed to work in the hospitality industry. There is particular emphasis on the food and beverage skills needed to work at the top end of the market (in silver service restaurants). This emphasis would seem to mirror a general European approach, especially a Germanic approach, to management and the role of the manager where technical craft skills are highly valued (Warner and Campbell 1997).

The American tradition, on the other side, emphasizes the management skills. Nebel *et al.* (1994) describe the approach as: "long on management training and short on practical industry operational skills".

The case for managers having craft operational skills

The argument is that managers cannot possibly manage an operation if they do not have an in-depth knowledge of the jobs of all the people they are managing. A restaurant is a technically complex operation and therefore potential managers need particularly to focus on developing their understanding of food preparation and service. This is also true at the unit management level. A hotel manager, for example, in a hotel which operates a restaurant should also have this detailed knowledge if only because this is the only way of controlling the chef! In an earlier article I quoted an example of a hotel GM who had gained his first post as a general manager largely because his ability to carve smoked salmon impressed the chef (Guerrier 1987).

Further, the European system of developing hospitality managers has been demonstrably successful. Graduates of European hospitality schools are in prominent positions in the hospitality industry around the world. For example, a study by Nebel *et al.* (1994) of food and beverage directors in American four- and five-star hotels found that a high proportion were Europeans with European hospitality management qualifications. So the hospitality industry still seems to value managers who have operational skills.

The case that business skills are sufficient

The argument here is that business and general management, for example people skills, are more important. There are many examples of managers who manage staff without knowing their jobs in detail; any manager of a multifunctional team is unlikely to know in detail about the role of all members of the team. Indeed, there is a danger in knowing too much about the jobs of one's staff; you are tempted to step in and help them out rather than encouraging them to resolve their own problems (see Chapter 7 on empowerment) and focusing on managing the operation.

In an earlier article Andrew Lockwood and I described the following case example which illustrates this problem:

> Take (an) example from (a) 200 bedroom four star hotel. . . . This hotel was built in the late 1970s to a rather unusual design and the restaurant, although pleasant to eat in, was difficult to operate. Talking to the management team in the hotel, everyone identified the restaurant as causing the biggest headaches – "we've had problems with the restaurant since the hotel opened . . . it's never really worked properly." The result is that the food and beverage manager spends most of his time on duty in the restaurant (which may explain why the restaurant manager left), dealing with day to day problems – and clearing plates. He is happy to be active and to be seen to do something to help(?), rather than taking action to sort out the underlying problems. He is happy to cope with the *status quo* and be concerned with preventing complaints, rather than experimenting and focusing on achieving results.
>
> This lack of experimentation is again reinforced by the manager's presence as part of the operation. The manager is there to supervise the action and make sure things are done properly. The manager is there to control the detail of the operation – have the oyster forks been cleaned properly? Is the tablecloth the right way up? The manager's constant presence in the operational areas, therefore, ensures that "standards" are maintained but stifles opportunities for staff to try things out themselves.
>
> (Guerrier and Lockwood 1989, pp. 85–86)

In any case what is so special about food preparation and service skills? In a hotel, it is the rooms not the restaurant that makes the money so it is far more important for managers to know how to manage the rooms business. In restaurants, there has been a move towards different styles of service and of food preparation. In a McDonald's or a pizza chain, the preparation of the product is standardized and simplified. There is no need to employ a manager who knows how to prepare a bechamel sauce, or even what one is, or a manager who can silver serve. The emphasis on traditional food preparation and service skills that are central to European hospitality education is out of touch with the hospitality industry as it now is.

Finally, although many managers at the unit level have craft/operational management skills, these skills do not seem to be valued at the head office/directorate level. At the board level, large hospitality

companies seem to be run by accountants, not by people with operational management experience (see Roper *et al.* 1997).

Stop

*Where do you stand on this controversy? See the end of this chapter for my
opinion.*

Is management changing?

Box 8.5   The changing face of management

What it means to be a manager varies historically in relation to changing
conceptions of the activity of management.

(Du Gay *et al.* 1996, p. 265)

Most writers portray the middle manager as a frustrated, disillusioned
individual caught in the middle of a hierarchy, impotent and with no real
hope of career progression. The work is dreary, the careers are frustrating
and information technology . . . will make the role more routine, uninter-
esting and unimportant. The numbers and role of middle managers will,
therefore, decline.

(Dopson and Stewart 1993)

In the previous sections, the way in which the hospitality industry is
changing and the impact that this is likely to have on the skills and
approach required by managers has been discussed. It was traditionally the case, I have argued, that hospitality managers needed craft
skills but this may not still be true.

As the first quotation in the Box 8.5 indicates, what is required of a
manager today is not the same as was required of a manager 20 years
ago. As the second quotation indicates, many writers take the view that
the role of the manager, at least the middle manager, is becoming less
rewarding.

A book by Goffee and Scase (1989) which looked at male middle managers in the UK highlighted four major influences on managerial jobs that they argue make managers more dissatisfied with their career prospects and rewards:

1. A decline in organizational growth that has led to shorter, less predictable career paths.
2. Organizational restructuring leading to organic, flatter structures, where managers are expected to behave as risk-taking entrepreneurs and be measured against their performance.
3. Technological change that has affected the skill requirements of managerial jobs.
4. Socio-economic changes that have undermined the authority of traditional forms of management. There is a questioning of managerial prerogative and a rejection of more autocratic leadership styles.

Goffee and Scase argue that these changes mean that managers are no longer so emotionally committed to their companies. They are more detached and take a more instrumental view of their work; they will put effort in only if they think the rewards are worth it.

Other writers take a more positive view of these same changes. The management gurus, Rosabeth Moss Kanter (1991) and Charles Handy (1994), talk about the emergence of "new managerial work". Far from becoming redundant, they argue, the skills and personal attributes of the "new" middle manager are crucial to the success of the new delayered and decentralized organization, but what managers now need are "soft" skills (interpersonal and team-building skills) rather than "hard" technical skills. Furthermore, the disappearance of the lifetime career may have advantages. Life is not all about hard work and efficiency and is it really desirable that there should be female (or even male) business executives, argues Handy, who read bedtime stories to their children over international telephone lines? Future management careers, with the death of the lifetime career in a single company, may be less secure but, if they allow managers more choice in the way they balance work and non-work, they may be more fulfilling.

Goffee and Scase, Handy and Kanter were all discussing managers generally. Do the same patterns and issues emerge in the hospitality industry? A study by Gilbert and Guerrier (1996) looked at the way in which British managers in the hospitality industry thought that the management role had changed between the late 1970s and the 1990s. Some of the results are summarized in Box 8.6.

Box 8.6   The changing role of the hospitality manager

The manager of the 1970s	The manager of the 1990s
Management style	**Management style**
Autocratic/military	Considers staff when decision making
Made instant decisions	Less hands-on or involved
Almost theatrical	Team leader or facilitator
Distanced from staff	Only forces issues when required
Hardness of approach	More consultative/democratic
Leads by example	More office based
"Seat of the pants"	
Management status	**Management status**
Through craft skills	Through business skills
Being "mine host"	Having the right training and background
Having leadership qualities	Making good decisions
Ability to work long hours	
Poor decisions carried no stigma	
Expectations of managers	**Expectations of managers**
To give guest satisfaction	To carefully control costs while achieving quality
Not so profit accountable	Reaching financial targets
To work hard	To do well against other units
To have a high profile with guests	To be a management specialist
To be a craft/rule expert	To be open and honest with staff and be accessible
	Ability to provide assessment and appraisal systems
Management structures	**Management structures**
Functional	Flatter
Hirer of cheap labour	Team mentality
Tall hierarchies	Standardized ways of working
Lots of assistant managers	Empowerment
Considerable scope and flexibility given to senior managers	Head office creating rules
	More operational and less strategic control
	Branding constrains the scope for management
Management skills	**Management skills**
Good craft skills	The rise of the specialist
Ability to communicate well with guests	Need for communication and interpersonal skills

The manager of the 1970s	The manager of the 1990s
Limited financial understanding	Need to plan for training and
Ability to apply a hands-on	development of others
approach	Financial expertise
Good "figurehead"	Computer literate
Knowledge of food and beverages	Able to organize multiskilling
	Good commercial skills
Management background	**Management background**
Few formal qualifications and	Often recruited from other
distrust of those who had them	service-related occupations
Membership of a professional body	Better formal education with
was sufficient qualification	specialist qualifications
Belief in working one's way up	Management qualifications are
	now more important

(Adapted from Gilbert and Guerrier 1996, pp. 128–130)

This study would seem to suggest that managers in the hospitality industry have been affected by shifts in the nature of management work in the same way as have managers in other industries. They are working in delayered organizations where the number of levels in the hierarchy has been reduced; they are expected to deliver results against financial targets; they are expected to be better educated; they are expected to be team managers and facilitators leading empowered staff rather than autocratic managers. One interesting observation is the way that working within a brand may constrain what managers can do (see Box 8.7) and make it more difficult to motivate them. The study incidentally also provides some evidence relevant to the controversies discussed above as it seems to suggest that the skills of the hospitality manager are becoming more similar to those of managers in other sectors and that general business and management skills are becoming more important.

Box 8.7   Managing within a brand

There was considerable debate in most of the focus group interviews conducted for the Gilbert and Guerrier (1997) study about the way in which branding affected what managers did. Some respondents pointed out that branding constrained what managers did.

> There was more opportunity for individualism ten years ago where a manager would say "I'll have a go at that or I'll try that". Now the brand is all important and that is inhibitive. That is not to say that ideas are not accessed or trialled but now it is more professionally managed rather than run on the quiet or as a flyer with no approval.
>
> Other respondents pointed out that the "clever" brands built in some scope for individual initiative:
>
> You cannot change the menu (as a unit manager), you cannot change the way the dish is presented but you can adopt a different style of management to deliver the product. The end result is for a meal to be served in this time, or for a customer to get a drink within two minutes or to be greeted and seated within 30 seconds. How they achieve this is up to them. They are able to adopt their own systems. What really matters is that they meet the standard.

What conclusions can be drawn from this small study? Clearly it has a number of limitations:

- It is a study of managers' *perceptions* of the changes in management jobs; it did not actually look at the jobs themselves. So it shows that managers in the British hospitality industry have embraced the "rhetoric" of new management work, i.e. they think that they should have management and business skills, that they should use participative management styles and empower their staff etc. It does not demonstrate that they are actually more participative or actually have better management skills. Some writers are dubious about whether "new managerial work" is in practice very different from "old managerial work". Hales and Tamangani (1996) studied managers in hotel and retail companies in Zimbabwe (see Box 7.8). They argued that managers in companies that seemed to have moved towards new management practices by decentralizing were not necessarily less autocratic than managers in more centralized organizations. They were just autocratic for different reasons. Now they told their staff what to do because otherwise they were afraid they could not meet their unit's financial targets, whereas previously they told staff what to do because they were told what to do by their managers.

- What may be true of hospitality managers in the UK is not necessarily true of hospitality managers across the world. We have seen in Chapters 4 and 6 how writers like Hofstede argue that national culture influences leadership style. Similarly, it can be argued that culture influences broader management practices. A study by Pizam *et al.* (1997), for example, looked at hotel managers in Hong Kong, Korea and Japan. They claimed that there were significant differences in management practices between managers from these different national cultures to the extent that "it is possible to conclude that national culture has a greater effect on managerial behavior than the culture of a particular industry".

Even outside of differences linked with cultural values, it can be seen that the factors that Goffee and Scase (1989) argue have affected the roles of British middle managers have not necessarily affected the managers in all countries. The trend towards restructuring and delayering organizations has been a feature in most western countries but new management practices have not yet reached, for example, ex-eastern bloc countries (see Box 8.8).

Box 8.8   Management practices in Bulgaria

A study of the attitudes of British and Bulgarian hotel managers compared their responses to a range of attitudinal questions exploring their communication styles, readiness to delegate to subordinates and style of conflict-handling. The British managers described themselves as more participative, on the whole, where the Bulgarian managers tended towards a more autocratic style. The researchers comment that British management style has shifted over the last decade (reinforcing the findings shown in Box 8.6) but that although in Bulgaria it is appreciated that the old ways of doing things are inappropriate, managers have not yet achieved a different way of managing and rewarding employees.

(From Anastassova and Purcell 1995)

To summarize, what seems to be happening is that notions of what managers should do and know are changing. Management gurus argue that new managers should:

- be well educated and trained in business and management skills

- have highly developed "soft" skills: people management skills, creativity and risk taking

- be able to take control of their own careers and not expect the organization to provide them a lifetime career. Balance work and non-work activities

- act as facilitators and team-builders leading empowered staff.

However, the extent to which managers are actually like that will vary from country to country and company to company affected by national cultural values, national business culture and company culture.

Women managers: female travellers in a male world

In Chapter 3, the issue of the gender segregation of jobs was discussed. Although women employees form the majority of the workforce in the hospitality industry in many countries, they are concentrated in the lowest jobs. At the management level, women are universally under-represented (Purcell 1993), as indeed they are in management roles in all industries. Why is this? Marshall (1984) examines six propositions which are typically cited as reasons why women do not, and perhaps should not, succeed as managers. These are the propositions and her responses to them.

Proposition 1. Women are different from men, so they do not make good managers.

Response: The research evidence suggests that women are very much the same or very similar to men. Where there are differences, women seem to possess more of the characteristics that managers of the future are expected to need (for example, good interpersonal/team-building skills) (refer back to Chapter 6). So perhaps women would make better managers than men.

Proposition 2. Women do not have the same motivations towards work as men do.

Response: Research evidence suggests that many women have motivations towards work similar to those of men. (They want to work for similar reasons to men and want meaningful work.) Practical difficulties explain why some do not translate these into action (for example, concerns about caring for children, husband's attitudes to their work, availability of work, whether they have appropriate training).

Proposition 3: Stereotypes of women mean that companies are reluctant to employ them as managers. Asked to think of a good manager and most of us will automatically think of a man – "think manager, think male" (Schein 1975) is the typical reaction and one that is hard to break away from.

Response: But we know stereotypes are ill-founded. They are not an adequate excuse for excluding women from management.

Proposition 4: Women believe the stereotypes and behave accordingly. In particular, women suffer from a fear of success in work careers because they may be seen as aggressive and masculine, bringing with it social disapproval (Horner 1972).

Response: Stereotypes trap women and men. But we create them so we can change them. If attitudes towards women changed, their views of themselves and their behaviour would change too.

Proposition 5: Attitudes have not changed substantially – other people believe the stereotypes and do not want to work with or for women; if they have to they make women's lives difficult. There is substantial evidence to suggest that women tend to be evaluated less favourably than men (see Wilson 1995).

Response: If we gave women more freedom, they would demonstrate their abilities. Stereotypes would change and relationships get easier.

Proposition 6: When women go out to work, their children, husbands and homes suffer, and society suffers as a result.

Response: No they don't! But what is all this?

Marshall's refusal to give an argued response to the final proposition is based on her view that there are no fundamental reasons why women cannot be successful managers. The propositions are just attempts to justify the *status quo*. The problem is that the values of work organizations mirror wider societal values: men are "naturally" at the top and women at the bottom. So women managers are inevitably seen as imposters in what is normally a "male world". It is harder for women to succeed in management than men because (drawing from Kanter 1977):

1. **They lack opportunity**. Women can find themselves sidelined into jobs that offer fewer pathways for promotion. So women managers are more often found in human resource management or customer service although the promotion opportunities may be better for food and beverage managers. Women can also find themselves cut out of the informal networks that may be the route to success (see Chapter 2, Box 2.1 Case 3).

2. **They lack power**. Being a woman diminishes one's status (women managers are frequently mistaken for secretaries whilst male secretaries are likely to be mistaken for managers). Kanter (1977) calls this process status-levelling. Further, to the extent that women are seen as having limited advancement opportunities themselves, they are not seen as being able to help others in their careers. Kanter argues that the stereotype of the "mean and bossy woman boss" is the perfect picture of the powerless person.

3. **They become tokens**. Because there are relatively few senior women in most work organizations those there are are highly visible; so everything they do is noticed. Token women can feel a pressure to succeed not just for themselves but on behalf of other women. (In my first serious job in an all-male marketing department, one of the first things I was told was "We had a woman here once. She wasn't any good".) Token women can easily find themselves trapped in a stereotyped role as mother, seductress, pet or iron maiden.

Studies of women managers in the hospitality industry echo these points (Guerrier 1986, Hicks 1990). In these circumstances it is not surprising if, whilst more women than men follow degree programmes in hospitality management, they leave the industry at a much greater rate than their male counterparts (Purcell 1993, Brownell 1994).

What can be done to improve the opportunities in organizations open to women? Successful women executives in a study by Morrison, White and Van Veslor (1987) passed on the following "commandments" to other women wanting to emulate their success:

Commandment 1: Be able. There is no substitute for competence.

Commandment 2: Be seen as able. Don't let your abilities be discounted or ignored.

Commandment 3: Help others to help you. Find a mentor. Never stop networking.

Commandment 4: Prepare to be lucky. Train yourself beyond the job. Do lots of different things. Be flexible and open to opportunities.

Commandment 5: Know what you want out of life. A vice-presidency doesn't mean much to someone who would rather be doing something else.

At the same time, there are steps that organizations can take in order to become more women-friendly:

1. Ensure that their human resource practices are fair and treat women as equals. Rather than "think manager – think male", organizations should "think manager – think qualified person".
2. Modify current working practices for the benefit of women by providing childcare facilities, flexible working hours and opportunities for career breaks.
3. Ensure everyone in the organization is aware of women's issues and that traditional sex-role stereotypes are punished rather than rewarded.

Undoubtedly women's opportunities in many organizations have improved immeasurably over the last 20 or 30 years and women are widely represented at the junior and middle management level even if they have still, in great numbers, to break through the glass ceiling into senior management. However, the radical feminist perspective is that women will never truly be regarded as equals unless organizations change to reflect women's, not just men's, values.

Box 8.9   Male managers trapped in a male world

This section has focused on the way in which women managers are trapped by traditional sex-role stereotypes. But men can also feel trapped by a need to conform to the image of a "real man" who is tough, can "take it" (Morgan 1992) and succeed as a manager. Doing research in a UK hotel, I asked one assistant manager what he needed to learn in order to improve his skills as manager. He thought for a while. "The first thing I need to learn is how to give a good bollocking. The second thing I need to learn is how to take a bollocking." (A bollocking is slang for an aggressive telling off.) This type of traditional male culture is arguably as harmful to male managers as to women. A television fly-on-the-wall documentary series about the Adelphi Hotel, Liverpool (BBC 1997) showed the female general manager of the hotel regularly bollocking staff, demonstrating that women too can become adept at such stereotypically male behaviour!

Travellers in a white world

Many of the points that have been made about women managers are equally applicable to managers who are not from the dominant ethnic group within a company. For most US or European-based hospitality companies, it is not just a question of "think manager – think male" but "think manager – think white male". Charles and McCleary (1997) researched the few African-American general managers of hotels in the States and uncovered the following anecdotes:

A guest was surprised to see a black person in charge (the respondent sensed that the guest doubted that a black person could be capable of being the manager).

When voicing a complaint and realising that the hotel was run by a black manager, a guest remarked, "No wonder!"

A black general manager was going to a meeting for general managers of the properties in the chain for which he worked. He was stopped at the door and informed that the meeting was for general managers only.
(Charles and McCleary 1997, p. 27)

Even in their Asian and African properties there is some evidence that western companies favour white managers. Wise (1993) comments that despite the growth of the hotel industry in East Asia, there remains a suspicion that the big companies are like "a double layer cake, white on top, brown or yellow at the bottom" (p. 58). Dieke (1993) and Ankomah (1991) make similar points in relation to sub-Saharan Africa, despite the attempts of governments to ensure that locals are trained up for management positions (see also Chapter 10).

The advice given by Charles and McCleary's respondents about how to be successful as a black manager is strikingly similar to the advice given by successful women managers (see above):

- Have an appropriate mind-set. Believe there are opportunities for advancement.

- Be educated. A college degree is essential.

- Develop the right tools and skills. The ability to communicate, a strong work ethic, the ability to suppress ego and patience are important.

- Get the right work experience. Expect to work excessively long hours and be willing to relocate as and when asked to do so.

(Note though that black male managers are expected to sacrifice their home lives for their career. Women managers are expected to think about whether that is really what they want.)

Summary

- The role of a manager is difficult to define. Research into what managers do, however, indicates that management work is characterized by unrelenting pace, variety, brevity and fragmentation and face-to-face rather than written communication. Managers work through an extensive network of contacts. Although they may seem to have little control over their own work, effective managers use these networks to pursue their agendas. Research into what hospitality managers do shows a similar pattern of frenetic activity and constant interruptions.

- There is a controversy about the extent to which hospitality management is different from management in other industries and the extent to which hospitality managers require craft-based skills as well as business skills. Some writers argue that it is important that managers are familiar with every job in their operation in order to be able to manage it. Other people point out that the hospitality industry may lose out and not learn from practice in other industries by emphasizing this "uniqueness".

- The nature of management work changes over time. Some writers argue that the role of the middle manager is becoming less fulfilling as organizations delayer and the lifetime career disappears, technological changes deskill managers and socio-economic changes reduce management status and privilege. Other writers think that the "new" manager will need improved interpersonal skills to work in the new flatter organizations and will potentially have a more interesting role. Research indicates that the managers in the hospitality industry think that their role is very different from the role of managers 20 years ago.

- Women are still under-represented in management in the hospitality industry, as in other industries, especially at the senior management level. Research would indicate that there is no reason why women cannot be successful as managers in terms of their attitudes and skills but, while management is essentially a "male" world, they are always seen as imposters. There are actions that women can take to help them "break through the glass ceiling" and that organizations can take to become more women-friendly.

- Similarly managers from certain ethnic groups may find themselves under-represented in management. Once again there are actions that they can take and that organizations can take to redress the balance.

The next stage

Experience

If you work in a management job, try monitoring how you spend your time. Keep a diary noting down what you are doing at ten-minute intervals. (Do not try to remember what you have been doing at the end of the day – you will have forgotten the little interruptions.) How does your work match up with the pattern of management work described by writers like Mintzberg?

If you do not have a management role, try to interview a manager about what they do. Focus on the way in which they spend their time (if it is possible to shadow them for a while, do that), the way they define their role, the skills they think they need to do their role (do they have craft skills?). What are the best parts and the worst parts of their job? If they work in a branded operation, how does that affect their role? Ask them about their career development. Have they worked in sectors other than the hospitality sector? Where would they see their careers developing?

Reflection

Think of a manager you have worked for who you considered to be a good manager. What did he or she do? Think of a manager you have worked for who you did not consider to be a good manager. What did he or she do? In both cases, how do you think that the managers' managers expected them to behave? What type of managers were promoted and well regarded within the company? (What skills did they have to have? Did it help them or hinder them to be male or female, or of a particular ethnic background?)

Based on these reflections, what skills do you think a good manager in the hospitality industry should have? And what skills and attributes do you think help managers to develop their careers successfully in the hospitality industry?

Think of an example from your experience of a male manager doing a job which is normally done by a woman (a male head housekeeper for instance) or a female manager doing a job which is normally done by a male. How were these managers treated? How did their "token" status affect their behaviour?

In any organization that you are familiar with, where is the "glass ceiling"? What is the level of management where women are under-represented?

Theorizing

What is your position on Controversy 1 and Controversy 2, based on the research on managers and management? (See Appendix after you have thought about this.)

What will happen to middle managers? Will they increasingly become deskilled and finally redundant or will their work become more demanding and significant? (See Chapter 11 after you have thought about this.)

How does the shift towards more branded operations affect the role of managers in the hospitality industry, especially unit managers? How does the debate about branding and the role of managers link with the debate about centralized and decentralized organizational forms? (Make links between the material in Box 8.7 and that in Box 7.8.)

In practice

Think about a management job in any hospitality organization with which you are familiar. If you were recruiting a new manager to that job, what skills and experience would you look for? Why? Would you be prepared to recruit someone with no previous experience in the hospitality industry? Would you look for someone with craft hospitality skills?

Refer back to Box 2.1 case 3. If you were Eileen, how would you motivate Phil while ensuring that he sticks within the brand?

What advice would you give to a woman manager to help her to break through the glass ceiling? What can organizations do to help open up career opportunities for all?

Further reading

This is not a topic which is usually fully covered in general organizational behaviour textbooks. For a general review refer to Smith and Davidson (1991) or Wilson and Rosenfeld (1990). For information about the historic writers in this area refer to Pugh and Hickson (1996). Dopson and Stewart (1993), Goffee and Scase (1989) and Thomas (1993) are also well worth reading especially in relation to the debate about changes in what managers do.

For more information about the way in which what managers do varies around the world refer to Hickson (1997). For a discussion of the issues women face in management try Wilson (1995), for a review,

Marshall (1984) and Morrison *et al.* (1987). For a specific discussion of men as managers try Collinson and Hearn (1995).

For material specifically related to the hospitality industry, refer to the article by Gilbert and Guerrier (1997) and Nebel's (1991) book for general points and to the articles by Hicks (1990) and Brownell (1994) for the problems faced by women managers and to Charles and McCleary (1997) for a discussion of African-American managers.

References for further reading

Brownell, J. (1994) Women in hospitality management: general managers' perceptions of factors relating to career development, *International Journal of Hospitality Management*, **13**, 101–117.

Charles, R. and McCleary, W. (1997) Recruitment and retention of African-American managers, *Cornell Hotel and Restaurant Administrative Quarterly*, **38**, 24–28.

Collinson, D. and Hearn, J. (eds) (1995) *Masculinity and Management*, London: Sage.

Dopson, S. and Stewart, R. (1993) What *is* happening to middle management, in *Managing Change*, Mabey, C. and Mayon-White, B. (eds), London: Paul Chapman.

Gilbert, D. and Guerrier, Y. (1997) UK Hospitality Managers Past and Present, *The Service Industries Journal*, **17**, 115–132.

Goffee, R. and Scase, R. (1988) *The Reluctant Managers*, London: Unwin.

Hicks, L. (1990) Excluded women: how can this happen in the hotel world, *Service Industries Journal*, **10**, 348–363.

Hickson, D. (1997) (ed.) *Exploring Management across the World*, London: Penguin.

Marshall, J. (1984) *Women Managers: Travellers in a Male World*, Wiley: Chichester.

Morrison, A., White, R. and Van Veslor, E. (1987) *Breaking the Glass Ceiling: Can Women Reach the Top of America's Largest Corporations*, Reading, Mass: Addison-Wesley.

Nebel, E. (1991) *Managing Hotels Effectively: Lessons from outstanding general managers*, New York: Van Nostrand.

Pugh, D. and Hickson, D. (1996) *Writers on Organizations* (Fifth edition), London: Penguin.

Smith, M. and Davidson, L. (1991) Analysing jobs: the manager and the job, in Smith, M. (ed.) *Analysing Organizational Behaviour*, Basingstoke: Macmillan.

Thomas, A. (1993) *Controversies in Management*, London and New York: Routledge.

Wilson, D. and Rosenfeld, R. (1990) *Managing Organizations: Texts, Readings and Cases*, London: McGraw Hill.

Wilson, F. (1995) *Organizational Behaviour and Gender*, London: McGraw Hill.

Appendix: Controversies in hospitality management

Is hospitality management unique?

Controversies, as stated above, are matters of dispute about which there is no agreed right answer. So you will have to decide for yourself which case you support. To help you make up your mind, I present my opinion on the debate.

There is evidence that industry context affects management work. A study by Hales and Tamangani (1996) compares the work of hotel managers and retail managers in Zimbabwe. They found differences between the roles:

> In the hotel industry, the emphasis upon interpersonal service and the need constantly to accomplish simultaneous production and consumption of a complex service product produces an emphasis in the hotel managers' work upon routine problem solving, assistance with and monitoring of work processes, monitoring and improving service delivery, time management, networking and self-presentation. In contrast, the importance of merchandising and sales in retail operations makes control of stock, ensuring adequate supplies, managing display, handling cash and credit transactions and dealing with customers central to the store manager's work.   (p. 750)

So there is evidence to suggest that hospitality managers require different skills from other managers even within the service sector. However, in my opinion there is no evidence that the hospitality industry is "uniquely" unique, i.e. that a set of generic management skills are relevant to all industries except the hospitality industry. All industries can justifiably make a claim to need managers with industry-specific skills and it is as appropriate to offer, for example, programmes in retail management as programmes in hospitality management. Even within one industry, management skills may not be totally transferable. I have heard it argued that a good hotel manager is not necessarily a good restaurant manager (Thus, hotel managers should stop trying to manage their own restaurants and concentrate on managing rooms which is what they know about, contracting their restaurants out to specialist restaurant management companies. It is no surprise that a representative from a specialist restaurant company put forward this argument.)

At the same time, it is unreasonable to suggest that there are no generic management skills that cannnot be applied across a range of management roles. Of course, managers can and should learn from contact with managers in other sectors and I would support Baum's contention that traditionally the hospitality industry has been held back by being too insular and convinced of its own uniqueness.

So which of the cases do I support? Both and neither.

Do hospitality managers need craft food and beverage skills?

There can be no set of generic management skills that apply across the whole hospitality industry. I would argue that this relates to the hospitality industry as well. To be a food and beverage director of a four- or five-star restaurant, it is undeniable that anyone needs a certain amount of "time on the floor" (as Nebel *et al.* 1994, p. 7 put it). However, a detailed knowledge of food and beverage operations may be less important for a manager whose specialism is accommodation management, or human resource management or marketing. The key debate is whether you can become a unit manager, or whether you would be a worse unit manager, without a detailed knowledge of food and beverage crafts.

It certainly used to be the case, at least in the UK, that the general manager of a hotel would inevitably have served some time as a food and beverage manager (Guerrier 1987). However, in a more recent study conducted for the HCIMA (Gilbert and Guerrier 1997), several respondents strongly asserted that business skills were now becoming more important. Again this varied from sector to sector. Respondents from the contract catering sector believed that a knowledge of craft skills was important for unit managers, alongside business skills, and bemoaned what they saw as a skills shortage in that area. Similarly, the owner-manager of a small hotel may benefit from an in-depth knowledge of the jobs of all his or her staff.

Does a knowledge of craft skills inevitably make a person a less creative manager who is less prepared to "get out of the staff's way" and let them solve problems? An uncle of mine was a successful furniture designer who had started his career as a carpenter, a furniture maker. He said that his designs were always influenced by his knowledge as a carpenter; if he could not work out how he could make a piece of furniture that he had designed he would change the design. He often envied his fellow designers who did not have this craft knowledge and innocently set the furniture makers seemingly impossible problems, which frequently they found ways of solving. The lesson I would take from this is that a knowledge of craft skills inevitably influences a manager's approach and way of thinking (my uncle was a different designer because he had that knowledge) but not necessarily for the better or the worse (he was still an excellent designer).

Much depends on the way in which craft skills are taught. If they are taught as a series of prescriptions, for instance, about the right way to serve and clear, then the manager inevitably learns to be someone who makes sure things are done in the right way. This indeed is the advantage which the manager trained at a traditional Swiss school is claimed to have. According to a respondent for the HCIMA study (Gilbert and Guerrier 1997), the Swiss represented "the epitome of what standards were supposed to be", "they always did it correctly". If craft skills are taught instead as part of the process of managing a production and service operation which has to take into account the needs of the customer (who does not always want full silver service) then managers may learn to be more flexible – important in what is a fast-changing industry.

9 Serving customers

| Box 9.1 "Managing" a smile |

Box 9.1   "Managing" a smile

I know my receptionists don't smile. I know that they should smile. I don't need telling that. What I want someone to tell me is how to get them to smile.

(Hotel manager in Romania)

(In service industries) traditional methods of control (i.e. bureaucratic control) are too overtly oppressive, too alienating and too inflexible to encourage employees to behave in the subtle ways which customers define as indicating quality service, many of which – subtleties of facial expression, nuances of verbal tone, or type of eye-contact – are difficult to enforce through rules, particularly when the employee is out of sight of any supervisor.

(Du Gay and Salaman 1992, p. 621)

How do you "manage" a smile?

This chapter is about those staff who are in the "front line", i.e. in direct contact with customers – receptionists, waiters, porters, room attendants. This book is about hospitality organizations and the word "hospitality" conjures up images of warm, smiling welcomes. When, for example, guests book into a hotel they notice how the receptionist makes them feel – comfortable, cared for, welcome – as well as whether he or she is technically able to handle the reservation.

But, as the example in Box 9.1 demonstrates, one cannot tell someone to smile in the same way as one can tell them to clear a table or clean a bathroom. Indeed, it is usually apparent to customers if service staff are being pushed to behave in ways they do not find natural. The author was working in Woolwich, in south London, at the time (about 1980), when the first McDonald's hamburger restaurant opened in England. The staff were local Londoners, they had little experience of American service styles and, although willing, they were obviously uncomfortable with phrases like "have a nice day" which were not part of their natural speech. The author remembers eating in the store early one evening when a children's party was going on and the staff were required to gather round and sing "Happy Birthday". They went through the motions but it was clear from their faces and their body language that they felt acutely embarrassed.

Fifteen years on and staff in British McDonald's have learned to sing Happy Birthday without embarassment. However, in following the McDonald's' script, staff are submerging some of their own identity to the extent that they are not talking to customers in exactly the way that they would if they were free to make up their own script. Leidner (1993) points out that when companies try to control the behaviour of service staff they are "seeking to legitimate intervention into areas of workers' lives usually considered to be the prerogative of individual decision-making or to compromise aspects of individual character and personality" (p. 9). Outside of work, people make their own decisions about how they dress, how they relate to other people, what they say and think and the image they project to other people about who they are. But people working in customer service roles find their employers specifying how they act and dress, what they say and even what they should think or feel.

Box 9.2   Ridiculous hats

During a special promotion of "Shanghai McNuggets", (McDonald's workers) were forced to wear big Chinese peasant hats made of styrofoam. Most of the workers felt that the hats made them look ridiculous: "Katie says that McDonald's ought to pay another ten cents an hour for making them wear the hats. 'No one should have to wear those. It's TORTURE.'"

(Leidner 1993, p. 183).

There is an ethical issue here. What are the psychological costs for service staff of adopting an identity at work which they do not feel comfortable with? What are the boundaries that companies should work within in terms of what they should expect of their staff? The intrusion into personal life may not be so important if it is merely about insisting that staff say "have a nice day" or sing "happy birthday" to children having a party. But, as Box 9.2 shows, apparently innocuous requirements (to wear a Chinese hat for a special promotion) can cause resentment. Is Disney's insistence that male staff should not wear beards or moustaches acceptable? What about restaurants that ask female staff to wear short skirts or revealing costumes that may make them more vulnerable to unwanted attentions from customers?

Box 9.3   Short skirts and tips

Everyone I know wears shorter skirts – especially on Saturday nights – because you can guarantee better tips. . .I suppose you are slightly willing to compromise and I'm not as feminist about it as I know I should be. But unfortunately men tip and women don't.

(London waitress quoted in Cook, 1996, p. 27)

Box 9.3 raises some of these issues of identity and the conflicts that someone may feel when required to act at work in a way that they would not out of work. It is interesting that the pressure on this waitress to wear short skirts comes not from management but from her perception of what will please the customer and increase her tips. She has apparently made the decision herself even if she feels slightly uncomfortable about it. This raises another issue about customer service: the behaviour of service staff is influenced by customers as well as by managers. Indeed, when customers control the rewards of staff because they control their tips their influence is likely to be very strong. But while service staff are pleasing customers, they are not necessarily doing what is best from the point of view of their managers. Referring back to Box 9.3, all the waitress's attention goes on pleasing her male customers because she believes that is the way to maximize her tips. Presumably the restaurant management want their female customers to go away as happy as the men.

This chapter will explore the following issues:

- **The customer service role in hospitality organizations**. The next section will look at the service encounter and particularly at the power and status of service staff and customers. Are our expectations as customers changing, given that enterprise society places such emphasis on pleasing the customer? How can organizations balance the need to simplify and routinize service encounters with the need to treat each customer as an individual? How do organizations adapt service encounters to meet the needs of different situations and types of customer?

- **Service staff and emotional labour**. To what extent is it helpful to think of service work as a form of theatre, with service staff required to display appropriate emotional responses to make customers feel good? What are the consequences for staff of providing this emotional labour? Do gender and ethnic origin matter? How do uniforms affect the performance?

- **The downside of service work**. Following from the previous points, what are the negative elements of service work, for example, dealing with stress, dealing with difficult customers, dealing with harassment and, taken to extremes, with physical threat?

The sovereign customer

Box 9.4   Who do you serve?

I don't enjoy waiting on my peers. I feel if I am to occupy a position that's menial, let it be to someone perhaps a cut above me.
(Washroom attendant interviewed by Terkel, S., 1972, p. 154)

Waiters, receptionists, porters and so on are service providers whose work is mainly taken up with a series of *service encounters* with people who are not part of their organization, i.e. customers. They can be described as having *boundary roles* (or boundary-spanning roles) (Thompson 1962, Shamir 1980), working on the boundary between those inside and those outside the organization. Czepiel *et al.* (1985) note the following characteristics of service encounters:

1. **Service encounters are purposeful**. The purpose of the encounter between waiter and customer is to serve the customer a meal. The

purpose of the encounter between teacher and student is for the teacher to impart knowledge to the student. The encounter is goal-oriented.

2. **Service providers are not altruistic**. They do not serve customers just for the love of serving customers. The service encounter is work; it is part of the job for which the service provider is paid.

3. **Prior acquaintance is not required**. The service encounter is a socially sanctioned relationship between strangers. The fact that you have never met the waiter before does not stop you from talking to him.

4. **Service encounters are limited in scope**. The waiter is there to take your food order and serve the meal. You would not ask him to fix your plumbing or take your dog for a walk.

5. **Task-related information exchange dominates**. There may be some general chat but the task-related information is the most important.

6. **Client and provider roles are well defined**. Customers have clear expectations about providers' roles and have a role to play as well. Customers in a formal restaurant expect to be asked to choose starter and main course, to be presented with a wine list, to be asked to taste the wine. They would be taken aback if the waiter sat down at the table with them to take the order, as would the waiter if the customers insisted on going into kitchen to see the food before ordering. (Although both these behaviours might be acceptable or even expected in an informal local resort restaurant.)

7. **A temporary status differential occurs**. During the encounter the "normal" social status of each party is suspended and the service provider is working *for* (and is therefore subservient to) the customer/client. This can be problematic, as Box 9.4 indicates, in that it is difficult for each party to totally ignore their "normal" social status.

Compare the role of a waiter or receptionist with that of a teacher, doctor or lawyer. Both groups have boundary roles and have to manage service encounters. The seven characteristics of service encounters given above can be applied as easily to a teacher's encounter with a student or a lawyer's with a client as to a waiter's encounter with a customer. However, there are differences: the role itself is not the same.

Shamir (1980) describes the role of waiter and receptionist etc. as *subordinate service roles*. Waiters and receptionists are not considered to be experts or professionals in the way that lawyers and doctors are and are accorded a low status relative to their customers. They also have a low status relative to other employees in their organization; they are usually near the bottom of the organizational hierarchy. In addition, they are dealing with customers who do not *have* to use the service they provide but have to be motivated to do so. Customers can always go to another restaurant or hotel or indeed not use a restaurant or hotel at all. The power and status that customers have in relation to service providers are reinforced by maxims such as "the customer is always right".

Recently, "customers" and the provision of "quality customer service" have been emphasized by companies trying to gain an advantage over their competitors (refer back to the section on hospitality organizations in Chapter 3). Du Gay and Salaman (1992) discuss "the managerial attempt to reconstruct work organizations in ways which are defined as characteristically commercial and customer focused" (p. 615). On the one hand, organizations talk much more about *customers*. Hotels and restaurants encourage their staff to talk in terms of customers not guests, airlines and railways similarly refer to customers not passengers, academics are asked to think about their students as customers. We talk about one department in an organization as being the internal customer of another. This change of terminology brings with it a change of meaning. Guests and passengers (and students) are passive recipients. Customers are discerning and demanding; they have a choice. But it is not just about the use of language. The attempts to restructure and re-engineer organizations in this period (see Chapter 7) have also been done in the name of getting the organization closer to the customer. For example, Jan Carlzon's restructuring of Scandinavian Airline Systems (SAS) focused on "moments of truth", i.e. on the service encounters between front-line staff and customers (Carlzon 1987, Baum 1995). Similarly, the restructuring of British Airways in the early 1980s started with a campaign to "put the customer first" (Höpfl 1993).

This raises a number of dilemmas. To recap, the service encounter is by its nature difficult to manage. Service providers may feel resentful about being required to be, as they see it, servile to customers. Staff and customers may be unsure of their roles. In addition, much of the success of the encounter is affected by the subtle and intangible cues given by the service provider – whether their smile seems genuine or not – which are difficult for managers to control. Now, the importance of managing the service encounter well has increased in that companies are competing with each other on the quality of the service they provide. In response, customers are expecting higher standards of service. The people who have to deliver this are usually amongst the lowest paid and most junior in the organization.

So how can service encounters be managed? There are several options:

- **Eliminate the service encounter**. Should one necessarily assume that customers prefer personal service? Levitt (1972) argues that rather than focusing on improving the ability of service staff to manage service encounters, we should concentrate on ways to "eliminate or supplement them" (p. 52). Do hotel guests really want to order coffee through room service? The evidence would seem to be that many prefer coffee-making equipment in their rooms. Information technology provides increasing opportunities to replace people with machines. Most of us now happily draw money from an automatic bank machine. Why should we not learn to pay for our hotel room by machine? This technology is already in place in some hotels.

- **Routinize the service encounter**. If one cannot eliminate personal service, one can so script and programme the service provider that he or she has little scope to mishandle the encounter. This is an approach taken by fast-food operations like McDonald's. The problem with such scripting and tight control is that it is difficult for service workers to avoid sounding as if they are scripted and this can be a problem if the customer wants to be treated as a real person and is put off by routinized service. At the McDonald's in the States that Leidner (1993) studied, she observed that many customers were perfectly happy with routinized service. Indeed, as they simply wanted to get their food as quickly as possible, some "seemed to regard the forms of routinized service as intrusive, impertinent, or a waste of time" (p. 186). However, even in McDonald's, the tension between providing standardized service and personalized service persists, as the following quotation (again from Leidner) indicates:

> Organizations that routinize service interactions are acting on contradictory impulses. They want to treat customers as interchangeable units, but they also want to make customers feel they are receiving personal service. The tension inherent in this project was apparent when I asked one of the trainers at Hamburger University about McDonald's goals for customer service. He told me quite sincerely, "We want to treat each customer as an individual in sixty seconds or less – thirty seconds for drive-thru."
>
> (Leidner 1993, p. 178)

- **Personalize the service encounter**. For customer service staff to be able to respond to the needs of individual customers, they need a range of skills and techniques to help them recognize customer needs, deal with upsets and difficult customers, motivate them to do the best for their company and help them handle their own stress and emotion. Whilst some staff may have or be able to develop these skills naturally, increasingly companies have been looking to training initiatives as a way of improving customer service.

Generally, the longer and the more complex the service encounter, the more customers expect personalized service. Also the more we pay, the more we expect the service to be adapted to our particular needs. Short, routine encounters lend themselves more to being "scripted" or eliminated. At the very top end of the market, customers may be prepared to pay a premium to ensure that all their requests, no matter how idiosyncratic, are met. So prestigious hotels will make a particular selling point of their ability to provide the "impossible"; e.g. tickets that would normally be unobtainable for shows and events, and so on. Tensions between customer service staff and guests will surface if these high expectations are not met, as can be seen in Box 9.5 (see also Urry 1990).

Box 9.5   Customer expectations

I used to be a duty manager in a four-star chain hotel. In that hotel if a guest had a complaint, you could deal with the problem by offering them a voucher for a free meal or a free night's accommodation. The hardest adjustment moving here was that guests here don't want to be bought off with a free meal. They have plenty of money so free meals don't matter to them. They just want you to solve their problem. And that is much more difficult.

(Manager in a prestigious London hotel)

However, there are other problems to be faced in the medium-range establishment. Here there is an expectation that there should be some element of personal service and some attempt to meet the non-standard requests from customers. But at the same time such establishments do not have the resources to provide everything that customers might want. Their service has to be standardized to some extent. The issue then becomes that of drawing the boundaries. To what point should staff be encouraged to step outside the normal procedures to provide what the customer wants? And at what point do the customer's requests cease to be legitimate? This debate is closely linked with the debate about the "empowerment" of front-line staff (see Chapter 7). Staff cannot be completely empowered; so how much discretion do they have and how do they know how much discretion they have?

Box 9.6 Empowering customer service staff

In the UK there is a branded restaurant chain called Harvester restaurants that provides mid-range meals aimed particularly at families. Staff at these restaurants are expected to serve meals according to a standard set of procedures which are set down in manuals and which they are trained to follow. However, should a guest ask for milk rather than cream (the normal condiment offered) with her coffee, the waiter is expected to use his or her initiative to meet this request. The difficulty is to ensure that staff are clear about what is expected of them and where the boundaries of their authority lie. In Harvester, managers attempt to achieve this through the development of a strong organizational culture with a shared set of values. But Harvester is a relatively small chain with a relatively stable workforce. Would such an approach be possible in a larger operation or one with high levels of labour turnover?

(Adapted from Guerrier and Pye 1994)

To summarize, whereas in the past customer-service staff might have been exhorted merely to be "nice" to the customer, they are now more likely to be put through an elaborate training, monitoring and reward system to ensure that they are displaying the "correct" emotions and approach. But do the people writing the "scripts" and doing the training really know what customers want?

Box 9.7 What do customers want?

I travelled with some colleagues to a conference in Palm Springs in the USA. The day we arrived after a fourteen-hour flight from London, we went for a meal in the hotel's coffee shop. The waitress greeted us in the energetic and extroverted style that obviously worked well with the predominantly American guests in this resort hotel. However, because we were used to a more restrained and British style of service and because we were tired and disorientated after the flight, the waitress's enthusiasm was merely exhausting and irritating. Some years before I had similarly gone to eat in the coffee shop of a hotel in Jakarta, Indonesia. Once again I was exhausted after a long flight and, since I was travelling on my own and it was my first visit to Indonesia, feeling even more fragile and vulnerable. The waitress was quietly caring and helpful. She gently suggested some menu choices and I left feeling more secure and happy in my new surroundings and (of more importance to the hotel) having spent more on the meal than I had originally intended.

As this example illustrates, the style of service customers prefer will depend on factors such as their nationality, their personality, whether they are travelling on business or pleasure. Many hospitality companies are aware of this and have designed different styles of service to meet the needs of different groups of guests. Hilton, for example, attempts to adapt the service in its hotels to meet the needs of different nationalities of guests; it has a special programme designed particularly for Japanese guests. Other hotel companies encourage customer service staff to treat leisure guests differently from business guests to the extent of having different uniforms at the weekend and promoting a more relaxed and chatty style of service.

What does it mean for the staff to work in an environment where more and more is expected of them? The consequences have been examined by writers like Hochschild (1983) who is interested in the potentially adverse effects on staff of work which is primarily about delivering "emotional labour".

It's all an act

Box 9.8   The waiter going on stage

It is an instructive sight to see a waiter going into a hotel dining-room. As he passes the door a sudden change comes over him. The set of his shoulders alters; all the dirt and hurry and irritation have dropped off in an instant. He glides over the carpet, with a solemn priest-like air. I remember our assistant *maître d'hôtel*, a fiery Italian, pausing at the dining-room door to address an apprentice who had dropped a bottle of wine. Shaking his fist above his head he yelled (luckily the door was more or less soundproof): *"Tu me fais chier.* Do you call yourself a waiter, you young bastard? You a waiter! You're not fit to scrub floors in the brothel your mother came from. *Maquereau!"*

Then he entered the dining-room and sailed across it dish in hand, graceful as a swan. Ten seconds later he was bowing reverently to a customer. And you could not help thinking, as you saw him bow and smile, with the benign smile of the trained waiter, that the customer was out to shame by having such an aristocrat serve him.

(George Orwell, 1933, *Down and Out in Paris and London*)

Box 9.8 is taken from George Orwell's description of his experiences working as a *plongeur* (kitchen porter) in a top hotel in Paris in the 1930s. It is an illustration of the way in which theatre and acting may be used as metaphor for understanding customer service. The waiter here is an actor who adopts an appropriate role when he is "on stage", in the restaurant, giving a performance to the customers, quite different from his role "off stage" in the kitchen.

Certain types of service style are more obviously "theatrical" than others. Gardner and Wood (1991), for example, writing about an American theme restaurant where waiting staff need to be able to juggle glasses, sing and tell jokes as well as serve food, observe that many of the staff are also actors or singers and that "for a new store, a theatre is hired and new staff *auditioned*" (my emphasis). Disney employ "cast members" in their theme parks. But even in more prosaic service encounters, the metaphor of theatre is useful. I have discussed how customer service staff may be given "scripts" to use when talking to customers. They are required to put on a costume (a uniform) which indicates to the customer the role that they are playing. And they are required to display the emotions that are appropriate to the role. The assistant *maître d'hôtel* may be angry with the waiter. However, his skill lies in not displaying that anger to the customer but instead in appearing calm, pleasant and smiling.

Emotional labour

Hochschild (1983) uses the term "emotional labour" to describe the way in which customer service workers are required to "induce or suppress feeling in order to sustain the outward countenance that produces the proper state of mind in others" (p. 7). She argues that customer service workers are paid not just for their technical skills but for their "emotional labour", for keeping smiling whether they feel like it or not.

Customer service roles have always involved "emotional labour"; the example from Orwell dates back to the 1930s after all. Indeed, as customers, most of us do not want to deal with surly waiters or rude shop assistants. But nowadays, as has been discussed above, companies are becoming more sophisticated and demanding in terms of their expectations of staff. Hochschild raises some interesting issues about the costs of emotional labour for the staff concerned.

Faking in good faith and faking in bad faith

Central to Hochschild's argument is the notion that what service workers actually feel is not always the same as the emotions that they are required to display. So they have to *act* to display the "correct" emotion. She distinguishes between "surface" acting, where a waiter puts on a smile (for example) although he does not feel happy, and "deep" acting, where the waiter tries to make himself feel happy so he can smile. Whilst a waiter skilled at "surface" acting *can* seem genuine to the customer, (the *maître d'hôtel* in Orwell's example would seem to have been surface acting) the danger is that the smile seems false. So, many companies encourage their employees to use "deep" acting techniques to help them display the appropriate emotions: to practise an "inside-out" smile.

"Deep" acting is a technique that most of us engage in when we psych ourselves up to feel and therefore display appropriate emotions. It may involve trying to change the way we think about a situation, so we may try to sympathize with the problems of someone whose behaviour is otherwise irritating or angering us to try to make ourselves feel sorry for them.

Why do we try to display different emotions from those we actually feel? We can distinguish between "faking in good faith" and "faking in bad faith". I am "faking in good faith" when I work to display those emotions that I think that I should, although I do not actually feel them. I am trying to conform to my "internalized feeling rule". So when I try to look sad at the funeral of a distant acquaintance or relative, even though I do not feel sad, it is because I believe that I should look sad at a funeral, I am "faking in good faith". If, on the other hand, as a nurse or hospital porter, I try to look sad about the death of a patient because I know my superiors expect me to look sad, even if I do not feel sad and do not see why I should feel sad, I am "faking in bad faith" (i.e. I am conforming to the organization's feeling rules and not my own). I am being emotionally deviant if (like the hospital porter who said "Beam me up Scotty" when removing the body of a dead patient) I display the emotion I feel although it is out of line with the organization's and my internalized feeling rules. Such employees are usually described as having an "attitude" problem.

According to Hochschild, there are three different stances that a service worker can take towards her work:

1. She can identify totally with her work so she no longer sees it as acting. Although the service worker is in emotional harmony and this would seem desirable, for Hochschild this is the most dangerous stance because it brings with it the greatest risk of stress and burnout. Those readers familiar with Ishiguro's novel *The Remains of the Day* (or the film of the book) will find an extreme example of this problem. The main character, a butler, is so adept at managing his emotions for the good of his job that he loses touch with his true feelings and wastes his life.
2. She can make a distinction between herself and the role but blame herself for doing so and for being an actor who is not sincere. She "fakes in good faith" but feels guilty for not genuinely feeling the correct emotions.
3. She can distinguish herself totally from her role and see it as positively requiring acting, with the danger of being estranged from it and cynical about it. She "fakes in bad faith".

Hochschild emphasizes the negative side of service work. Other writers argue that she overstates her case. Ashforth and Humphrey (1993) point out that Hochschild's claim that service staff have to work to display the appropriate emotion is not necessarily true. In many cases, they may quite naturally feel what is expected of them without any danger of stress and burnout. One should also not forget that dealing with customers can be fun. Service workers can enjoy giving a good performance and doing the "right things well" even while being aware that they are acting (Fineman 1993). George Orwell's waiter in Box 9.8 illustrates some of the pleasure that staff and customers can derive from skilled service. Finally, it may not be that we are requiring service staff to "act" any more or less than people generally have to do at work and in life. Erving Goffman, the sociologist whose work on the theatrical nature of everyday life still offers some of the best insights in this area, writes: "Scripts even in the hands of unpractised players can come to life because life itself is a dramatically enacted thing. All the world is not, of course, a stage, but the crucial ways in which it isn't are not easy to specify." (Goffman 1959, p. 78).

Waiters and waitresses: the gender dimension

There is one further element to Hochschild's discussion: the gender dimension. She argues that service work is experienced differently by men and by women doing the same job. She claims that women are increasingly employed in subordinate service roles because they are thought to be better at providing the type of emotional labour that these roles require. Women have been socialized to look after other people's emotions outside work (see for example Dunscombe and Marsden 1993) so providing emotional labour at work comes more naturally to them. Other studies indicate that women smile more than men; the more feminine a woman is the more she smiles and the more masculine a man is the less he smiles (DePaulo 1992).

At the same time, customers treat women service workers differently from men. It is still true that women are accorded less status than men in society and these attitudes tend to spill over into the way that customers treat women service workers. So Hochschild says that the female flight attendants that she studied ". . . tend to be more exposed than men to rude or surly speech, to tirades against the service, the airline and airplanes in general. . . . Because her gender is accorded lower status, a woman's shield against abuse is weaker" (Hochschild 1983, p. 175).

Because her gender lowers her status women may also find it harder if they have to control customers' behaviour. So junior male flight attendants studied by Hochschild often found it easier than their more senior female colleagues to persuade passengers to move luggage, refrain from smoking where they should not and so forth. To the extent that women are emotionally more expressive than men, that is they are seen as friendlier and smile more, that also seems to decrease their credibility as technical experts. A study of female betting-shop cashiers, for example, found that the more they turned on their personality the less they were seen as technically competent (Filby 1992).

Furthermore, Hochschild argues that the female flight attendant is disadvantaged compared with a woman bus driver or a female accountant because a flight attendant is perceived as a female role. Flight attendants ". . . symbolize Woman. Insofar as the category 'female' is mentally associated with having less status and authority, female flight attendants are more readily classified as 'really' female than other females are" (Hochschild 1983, p. 175).

Many customer service roles are viewed as either male or female roles. We expect, for example, hotel porters to be male and chambermaids to be female. There may be some exceptions to this; it is possible now to find female hotel porters and there are parts of the world where room attendants are usually male (for example, Turkey). However, if you are a man in a predominantly female role or a woman in a predominantly male role, you will be "marked" as different or unusual.

Take, for example, waiting on table. This is a role in which both men and women are employed, however most people have a different image of a "waiter" compared with a "waitress".

> ### *Stop*
>
> *Without reflecting too much write down ten words that you would associate with the word "waiter" and ten words that you would associate with the word "waitress".*

"Waitress" is an example of what linguists call the "marked" form of the noun "waiter". The unmarked form of the word is male; with the "marked" (changed) form, in this case indicating that we are referring to a female, the associations change. Tannen (1994) in a book on gender and work relations comments that it is common in English for the unmarked form of a noun to be male and for the "marked" female form of a noun to bring with it more derogatory and lower status associations. Think also of actor/actress, adventurer/adventuress, poet/poetess, steward/stewardess.

Hall (1993) defines "waitering" and "waitressing" as totally different jobs using different scripts in different service settings: "Waiters, dressed as butlers . . . were expected to provide 'professional' service in upscale dinner houses whereas waitresses wearing 'sexy' uniforms were expected to give friendly service in family-style restaurants" (Hall 1993, p. 457).

Note here the emphasis on the way in which the waiter and waitress should be dressed. One of the key ways in which the masculinity or the femininity of a role is enhanced is through the use of appropriate uniforms.

What you wear tells me who you are

As actors wear costumes to help them define their role, so the dress of service workers helps their performance. Most customer contact staff in the hospitality industry are required to wear a uniform or, as a minimum, some dress code is prescribed. Uniforms serve a number of functions. At the simplest level, they help customers identify members of staff so they know who to approach and with what type of query. Uniforms can also help indicate to customers what the service encounter is going to be like: they help to set the tone. Thus we would probably expect a more informal encounter with a waiter wearing a tee-shirt and shorts than with one wearing a black tie and a dinner jacket. Uniforms can also help indicate the seniority of staff; supervisory and management staff often have different uniforms to operative staff.

Uniforms also help employees identify with the organization and conform to organizational requirements. When we put on a uniform we give up some of our individuality and we become a representative of the organization. Alison Lurie in an interesting book on the meaning of clothes states this strongly: "No matter what sort of uniform it is – military, civil, or religious . . . to put on such livery is to give up one's right to act as an individual. . . . What one does, as well as what one wears, will be determined by organizational standards" (Lurie 1983, p. 18).

This does not necessarily imply that people are reluctant to wear uniforms. In a recent business programme on television, staff whose contact with customers was on the telephone rather than face-to-face were shown requesting management to be issued with uniforms. One of the arguments that they put forward was that they wanted to be identified as members of the company to friends and family when they were travelling to and from work.

Most of us can think of examples of situations when we have been required to wear uniforms we have disliked and equally examples of situations where we have been proud to wear a uniform or follow a particular dress code. The difference between these two situations is related to our concepts of our own identity. If a uniform helps us become the person we want to be then we will wear it gladly. If the uniform identifies us with an organization that we do not wish to be identified with or implies a status which is different from our own view of our status, we may resist wearing it. Many hospitality degree and diploma students have put up with derogatory comments from fellow students on other courses when they are required to wear a uniform to work in a training restaurant. Similarly, those of us who were required to wear a school uniform can probably remember finding ways of adapting it or incorporating items that were not allowed (shortening skirts, wearing jewellery, wearing the wrong type of shoes). All of these minor adaptations are designed to let other people know that this uniform does not really say who "I" am. Returning to the example quoted at the beginning of this chapter, of the McDonald's employees required to wear styrofoam Chinese peasant hats, asking employees to wear clothes that they feel make them look ridiculous is not a minor matter as far as they are concerned.

Uniforms affect the way one acts out a role. The role of a waitress cannot be acted out the same way if one is wearing a sarong and high heels compared with wearing a white shirt, black trousers and flat shoes. As customer service roles have traditionally been gendered, so uniforms have tended to be designed for the dominant gender. Hotel commissionnaires have traditionally worn an adapted military uniform which is characteristically male. Similarly waiters in formal restaurants have traditionally worn an adapted version of a butler's uniform; again male clothes. The traditional solution for a woman working in a "male" occupation was to wear an adapted version of the male uniform. So female waiters in traditional establishments may wear a skirt rather than trousers and a bow rather than a bow tie. It is interesting to note the trend in certain restaurants now for women to wear exactly the same uniform as men (i.e. trousers, men's shoes and bow tie) rather than an adapted version of it. They do not avoid being "marked" by doing so; they are noticeable for being women wearing men's clothes. Of course, there are similar problems in reverse when men enter occupations that are traditionally female.

In the hospitality industry, uniforms may also be used to identify staff with a particular national culture. This is often the case in resort hotels where local staff are serving predominantly foreign tourists and an adaptation of local costume is used to create an appropriate atmosphere. So Balinese staff in a Balinese hotel will usually wear an adapted version of Balinese local costume, staff in Austrian alpine resorts will often wear local costume etc. As gender affects how staff behave towards customers and how they are treated by customers so nationality and ethnic background will also affect this, especially when staff and customers have different backgrounds and expectations. Uniforms that specifically identify staff with a national group will heighten the effect.

Smiling Thais and surly Bulgarians

> ### Box 9.9   Bulgarian receptionists
>
> "She answered my questions . . . as if giving information depended on her goodwill and was not part of her job. And she did not smile." (Drakulic, 1994 describing an encounter with a hotel receptionist in Sofia.)
>
> Service workers in eastern Europe have a reputation for providing inefficient and surly service, as the above quotation illustrates. A research study looking at hotel receptionists in Bulgaria investigated the extent to which this stereotype was accurate and, if so, why? The researcher made observations of receptionists in 12 three-, four- and five-star hotels in Sofia and the Black Sea resorts assessing their social skills, politeness, empathy and rapport with the guests. She also conducted a series of semi-structured interviews with hotel managers to look at their attitudes to service quality and their practices in terms of monitoring quality, motivating staff, training and selection.
>
> The results confirmed that quality of service was generally poor. Moreover, the quality of service seemed to depend on factors such as the receptionist's personality, mood, general pressure on the reception desk and whether the guest was liked or disliked. Receptionists were left to their own devices and given little guidance by management about how to treat guests. Of course, they had also grown up and worked under a Communist system that had fostered conformity, egalitarianism and submission to "party ideals" and in a environment where there was careful monitoring of all interactions with foreigners from "capitalist" countries.
>
> Managers were not interested in service quality. At the time of the research they were mainly preoccupied by forthcoming privatizations. Customer service skills were not assessed when new receptionists were selected. In any case, selection was generally determined by "who you

know". There were no appraisals or performance indicators. Firing of
staff was not encouraged.

A Bulgarian professor had the following comments to make about the
way in which Bulgarian culture tended to influence the behaviour of
customer service staff. She commented firstly that Bulgarians were
reluctant to smile because they associated smiling with not being serious.
To smile at someone implied that you were not to be taken seriously and
you were not taking them seriously. She also commented that a
distinction is made between personal guests who will be treated
wonderfully and paying visitors who are not highly valued in the culture.

(Adapted from Kassova 1995)

As one's gender affects how one behaves and how one is treated as a
service worker, so one's nationality or ethnic background is likely to
affect behaviour. Box 9.9 looks at the way in which hotel receptionists
typically behave in one eastern European country and demonstrates
the way that what in western terms might be decribed as "poor"
service attitudes may be explained by a range of factors that include
cultural attitudes about what are appropriate "display rules" (should
you smile at guests?) and about the status of hotel guests (are they
people to be treated well in any case?). Organizational culture also
influences behaviour. Many receptionists had previously worked
under a regime where they were positively discouraged from contact
with foreign guests. And they are working in organizations which do
nothing to reward good customer service. Taking all of these factors
into account, their behaviour seems perfectly understandable. Contrast
this with the situation in other cultures, where national values may
specifically encourage a friendly attitude towards customers.

Box 9.10   The land of the smile

A high value is placed in Thai society on "social smoothing" and "surface
harmony", i.e. achieving smooth, kind, pleasant, conflict-free, interpersonal interactions. They are the necessary means to function successfully
in the Thai society. The cognition that to respect another's ego and not to
hurt others, is the core behind the behavioural pattern of everyday social
interactions of Thai people. It is this value of smooth and pleasant
interpersonal interaction that gives Thai people the image of being very
friendly and Thailand, the "Land of the Smile".

(Adapted from Phornprapha 1996)

In tourist resorts, where staff and tourists come from very different cultures and often different class backgrounds and may have very little understanding of each other's culture and expectations, there is considerable scope for misunderstanding and mutual resentment. Krippendorf (1984) describes how locals in a Swiss resort distinguished between "guests", who stay longer, return to the same place and are people one knows, and "tourists", who are no more than merchandise to be treated with a mercenary smile and sterile politeness. Shamir (1980) quotes the example of a waiter unable to keep within his subordinate service role when faced with what he considered to be unreasonable behaviour from a guest:

> There was a guest from ___, one of those who think they are kings of the world. I brought him a fried egg. He said; "without a tip you are not doing anything", and threw twenty Agora at me. So I said to him: "here I give you honor, if you have honor, come outside with me."
> (Shamir 1980, p. 745)

The customer is not always right

Box 9.11   The customer is always wrong

Most of the time, as in any service industry, you come across a lot of people who are exceptionally demanding and exceptionally selfish in their requests and they don't take into account that you are not subservient nor are you there for their specific use. . . . The customer is not always right but unfortunately the service industry has been drummed into that . . . Rule one, the customer is always wrong.

(Nightclub employee quoted by Sosteric 1996, p. 301)

The modern focus on customer service and "being close to the customer" puts pressure on customer service staff to "be nice" and meet all customer expectations. Customer service staff, at the same time, are usually near the bottom of the organization's hierarchy and have a low status relative to their customers. However, there are occasions when staff cannot do what the customer wants; they have to say "no". Saying "no" creates its own problems and stresses.

Staff can find themselves having to say no to customers in the following circumstances:

- **The customer requests something which would be against the organization's rules or outside the organization's resources to provide**. Staff are placed under additional stress if they have to enforce rules which customers regard as unreasonable or the resources are not there to provide an acceptable level of service. Thus a receptionist who is always having to book guests out to other hotels or cannot provide rooms when the guest arrives because the room has not yet been cleaned is put under extra pressure. The same applies to the waiter who has to inform customers that there is a long wait for their meal or that a menu item is not available. Usually the customer contact staff have the responsibility of informing the customer about a problem which is not of their own making and which they have no power to resolve. The waiter has no direct control over what happens in the kitchen and the receptionist has no direct control over the housekeeping department. But customers will hold the waiter or receptionist responsible because the waiter or receptionist is the person there.

- **A customer behaves in a way which upsets other customers**. A customer who smokes in the non-smoking section of a restaurant may not be behaving in a way which the restaurant staff could not accommodate but if they are upsetting a majority of other customers, staff may need to intervene. As customers, when we buy a meal in a restaurant, stay in a hotel on holiday or on business, our satisfaction with that service can be as much affected by the behaviour of other customers as by the behaviour of staff. If you go out for a quiet meal with your partner and cannot hear yourself speak because of the antics of a noisy party at a nearby table or if you are kept awake all night because of a party going on downstairs, the good service of the staff will not be a compensation. But managing groups of customers with different motivations and deciding when to intervene for the sake of other people is not easy.

- **A customer behaves in a way which transgresses the rights of the member of staff**. He or she may be abusive or even physically violent. The boxed example below describes a situation in which an English court held that two waitresses had been subjected to unacceptable abuse by hotel guests and the court also took the view that the hotel management should have protected them from that abuse.

> ### Box 9.12   The protection of staff
>
> Two black waitresses in Derby, England had been working at a private function where the comedian Bernard Manning was appearing. Manning has a reputation for including racially abusive jokes in his act. During the course of the evening, he directly taunted the waitresses and members of the audience also subjected them to racist abuse. The waitresses took the case to an industrial tribunal, claiming that the hotel management had racially discriminated against them by failing to protect them from abuse. Their case against their employer was upheld on appeal.

One of the skills that good customer service staff acquire is that of controlling the customer. This can be done in a subtle way so that customers may hardly notice that they are being controlled and, indeed, are under the illusion that it is they that are in charge. Whyte (1946) in a classic study of a restaurant commented that ". . . the waitress who bears up under pressure does not simply respond to customers. She acts with some skill to control their behaviour" (p. 132). The need to have the skills to control customers may be most pressing in those settings where staff may be particularly vulnerable to abuse from customers, in nightclubs or rowdy bars or restaurants, and staff may feel that it is their individual responsibility to be able to handle difficult customers. Consider the following comment from a waitress working at a novelty restaurant in London which attracts groups of drunken "City boys".

> All the girls here are very broadminded. It goes with the turf. Inevitably you are going to be groped at some stage but it is up to you to control the situation. One comment is usually enough to stop them doing it again.
>
> (Cook 1996)

Sometimes groups of staff in this type of situation will actively support each other to control, and even to punish, difficult customers. Sosteric (1996) described how the established staff in a nightclub would "teach" new staff to handle customer problems.

An experienced bartender might relate a story about "this one guy" who had come into the bar and whistled and snapped his fingers for service. The bartender would go on to explain how he had identified this individual as "dry" to other members of staff who then supported the bartender's decision by not serving the customer.

(Sosteric 1996)

Because the examples quoted so far about dealing with abusive customers have related to waitresses, it should not be assumed that women are always more vulnerable than men to abuse from customers. The Suzy Lamplugh Trust does research into violence at work. Their studies indicate that seven out of ten problems of aggression or violence from customers, clients, patients, passengers or other service users are experienced by men. Because men are more likely to meet aggression with aggression, incidents are more likely to end in a confrontation. Women on the other hand are very good at defusing, coping with and avoiding aggressive incidents. In addition, men often do not report violent incidents as they are ashamed of being seen as wimps or cowards (Lamplugh 1996).

Summary

- The behaviour of customer service staff has a major impact on customer satisfaction. If the service is lousy even if the food is great, customers may not return. But the quality of customer service is difficult for managers to control because good service depends on subtle non-verbal and verbal cues. A manager may be able to "tell" staff to smile but customers can sense if the smile is not genuine.

- Over the last 15 years, companies have become more conscious of the need to be close to the customer and to compete by providing good customer service. This has led them to pay more attention to the way in which their service staff are dressed, how they behave, what they say and the image they project. There is an ethical issue about how far companies should be able to specify what their staff do, say and how they look. In any case, staff will become resentful if asked to behave in ways they feel uncomfortable with.

- Service encounters are goal-directed and closely defined meetings between customers and service workers; the waiter is there to take the customer's order and serve the meal. Customer service staff in the hospitality industry are those staff whose work mainly consists of a series of such service encounters. These staff can also be described as filling subordinate service roles. They have a low status relative to other people in the organization and a low status relative to customers.

- Service encounters may be either low contact or high contact. Low contact encounters are short, straightforward encounters, buying a hamburger in a fast food restaurant, for example. Such encounters lend themselves to being "scripted", so the service worker is told exactly what to say, or even eliminated through the use of technology. (The customer inputs their order into a computer rather than speaking it to a member of staff.) High contact encounters are longer, more complex and more personalized; the service one expects from a waiter in a top class restaurant. These encounters cannot be totally "scripted" as it is impossible to predict exactly what customers might want. Staff in "high contact" encounters have to be trained to manage a range of different situations and types of customers and to adapt their behaviour to the customer.

- A theatrical metaphor is often used to describe the work of customer service staff. Staff are like actors performing for the customer. They are even dressed in costume (uniform) to help them play their role. Like actors, they are required to manage their emotions and keep smiling even if they do not feel like they want to. The term "emotional labour" relates to this. Service staff are paid as much for their "emotional labour" as for their technical skills and several writers have drawn attention to the emotional cost of this type of work.

- The gender and ethnic origin of service staff also affect the service encounter. Women and certain cultural groups tend to be more expressive than men and other cultural groups. Gender and ethnic origin may also affect how customers treat service staff.

- The old adage that "the customer is always right" is not accurate ; there are occasions when the customer is wrong. Although saying "no" to customers is always difficult, skilled customer service staff develop ways of controlling customers whilst giving the impression that they are in charge. Managers have a responsibility for protecting their staff from unacceptable abuse but it is not easy to define the point at which abuse becomes unacceptable. Men are no less vulnerable to violent abuse from customers than women: indeed because they are more likely to match aggression with aggression they are more vulnerable.

The next stage

Experience

It is relatively easy to get personal experience of the issues discussed in this chapter. If you have never worked in a customer service role, you have, at least, plenty of experience of what it is like to be a customer. But for anyone considering a career in any area of the hospitality industry, it is essential to gain as much experience as you can of the perils and pleasures of working at the "sharp end" with customers. If you have experience of customer contact work in one type of establishment, seek out opportunities to work in a different type of setting. Try to gain experience with customers from different age groups, different nationalities, people on business and people on holiday etc.

Reflection

Think of a service encounter which you experienced either as a customer or a member of staff which you felt was managed particularly well. What were the factors which made it successful? Think of another service encounter which went wrong. What were the factors which made it go wrong?

If you have worked in a service role, can you identify with Hochschild's descriptions of the costs of providing "emotional labour"? Have you found it difficult to manage your emotions for the benefit of the customer? Do you think that you are in "emotional harmony", "faking in good faith", "faking in bad faith" or "emotionally deviant"?

Are women service workers treated differently from men? If you are male, do your female co-workers have a different experience of their role? If you are female, how are your male co-workers treated?

If you have had to wear a uniform for work, how do you feel about that? Do you wear the uniform with pride or reluctantly? Why? Observe the uniforms worn by different groups of service staff. How do their uniforms affect the way they "play" their role?

Have you ever suffered abuse or harrassment from a customer? How was the situation handled by yourself, your co-workers and your supervisor? In retrospect, what might have been done differently?

Theorizing

In most service encounters in the hospitality industry, staff have a low status relative to customers. But there are some occasions when the reverse may be true, for example school meal staff serving school children, staff serving inmates of institutions such as prisons. How will this reverse of status affect the service encounter?

Hochschild (1983) claims that women are more exposed to rudeness from customers than men. Lamplugh (1996) claims that men are more likely to be subject to physical violence from customers than women. Can you reconcile those two views?

What are the limitations of the "theatrical" metaphor as a way of understanding the behaviour of customer service staff? In what ways is being a "waiter" not the same as being an "actor"?

The Romanian hotel manager quoted at the beginning of the chapter complained that his receptionists did not smile. What would be your theory about why they do not smile?

In practice

What advice would you give to the Romanian hotel manager who wanted to get his receptionists to smile?

You are a supervisor working in a hotel bar. In the bar is a party of local business men who have been holding a meeting in the hotel. They have moved into the bar after dinner and are drinking quite heavily. You notice one of this party "touching up" one of the female bar staff. The woman is a new and young member of staff and looks confused and distressed. You recognize the guest as a prominent local doctor who is a regular in the hotel and a good friend of the general manager. He seems to be very drunk. What do you do?

Further reading

You will find a review of many of the issues discussed in this chapter in Urry (1990) Chapter 5 and in Baum (1995) Chapter 6.

For a more detailed understanding of the concept of "emotional labour" refer to Hochschild (1984). Leidner (1993) is also strongly recommended. Both of these books are very readable with plenty of examples about work in customer service occupations. Remember that both books are written by sociologists who look critically at management practices. The article by Sosteric (1996) is also recommended for its insight into the problems customer service staff working in a night-club have to face and the way that managers can make it more difficult for staff to cope. Hall (1993) is also recommended for her insights into the way the roles of "waiters" and "waitresses" differ and about "flirting" with customers.

If you want to read further about the "theatrical" metaphor, I would recommend reading Goffman (1959). This book may have been written nearly 40 years ago but it remains an entertaining and insightful guide to the way we are all actors at work and in life.

For advice on handling violence and aggression, refer to Lamplugh (1988) and Lamplugh (1991) or Breakwell (1989).

References for further reading

Baum, T. (1995) *Managing Human Resources in the European Tourism and Hospitality Industry*, London: Chapman and Hall.

Breakwell, G. (1989) *Facing Physical Violence*, London: Routledge.

Goffman, E. (1959) *The Presentation of Self in Everyday Life*, London: Penguin.

Hall, E. (1993) Smiling, Deferring and Flirting: Doing Gender by giving 'Good Service', *Work and Occupations*, **20**, 4: 452–471.

Hochschild, A. (1983) *The Managed Heart*, Berkeley: University of California Press.

Lamplugh, D. (1988) *Beating Aggression – a Practical Guide for Working Women*, London: Weidenfeld and Nicolson.

Lamplugh, D. (1991) *Without Fear – the key to staying safe*, London: Weidenfeld and Nicolson.

Leidner, R. (1993) *Fast Food Fast Talk: Service Work and the Routinization of Everyday Life*, Berkeley: University of California Press.

Sosteric, M. (1996) Subjectivity and the labour process: a case study in the restaurant industry, *Work, Employment and Society*, **10**, 2: 297–318.

Urry, J. (1990) *The Tourist Gaze*, London: Sage.

10 The wider environment

Box 10.1   Murder in Moscow

Paul Tatum was an American entrepreneur who went to the Soviet Union in the late 1980s and was responsible for transforming a pre-perestroika concrete skeleton of a hotel into Moscow's sleek Radisson Slavyanskaya hotel and business centre, a gathering place for foreign and Russian entrepreneurs, a steak house, Parisian fashion boutiques and a glittering lobby bar.

But by 1996, the Radisson had become a model of how severely such ventures could go wrong. The Russian stake had changed hands three times and was being administered by a charming young Chechen whom Tatum had suspected of having ties with the mob. Western lenders, fearful of Moscow's deteriorating business climate, had turned down Tatum's loan applications. . . .

So when a call came late on a Sunday afternoon last November from someone with information . . . Tatum leaped to the phone. After a rapid conversation in English, he grabbed his coat and headed with two bodyguards for the dingy metro station a stone's throw from the Radisson. . . .

The three men – Tatum in the middle, a bodyguard fore and aft – hustled out of the hotel gates and past the Kievsky train station's pageant of kiosks, cabbies and street vendors. They took the first steps down to the seedy underpass below, and in the darkening five o'clock hour, Tatum's killer, his Kalashnikov rifle wrapped in a plastic bag, took aim.

(Arvedlund, E. 1997, p. 87)

Introduction

Organizations do not exist in a vacuum. The case in Box 10.1 may be an extreme one but it illustrates vividly that the issues and problems that beset someone trying to run a hotel in late 1990s Moscow may not be exactly the same as the problems that would face someone trying to run a similar hotel in Geneva or Toronto. It is impossible to ignore the social, political and economic environment in which organizations operate. This chapter looks at some of the reasons why some organizations survive and others die, the processes by which organizations adapt to their environments and the way in which organizations may network together to try and influence their environment. Finally it looks at some of the ways in which organizations impact in a negative way on their environment and the extent to which they act in socially responsible ways.

The survival of the fittest

In Chapter 2, a range of different ways of understanding organizations was explored. One metaphor which is sometimes used is to think of organizations as living organisms or open systems. This way of thinking particularly focuses attention on the way in which organizations adapt to their environment and is thus relevant to this chapter.

In what ways are organizations like living organisms?

- A living organism has to interact with its environment in order to survive and maintain itself. Any organism goes through a continuous cycle of inputs, transformation, outputs and feedback. So an animal has to ensure it has air to breathe, water to drink and food to eat. It transforms those inputs into energy, outputs waste products. Feedback from its experience means that it learns strategies to make it more effective at finding the inputs it needs in the future. Similarly, a hotel takes in raw materials, finance, a labour force and customers from the environment and transforms these inputs to provide services for customers and outputs (hopefully) satisfied customers and richer employees into the environment. Feedback from the experience can make the hotel better at finding the inputs it needs in the future.

- Organisms have self-regulation mechanisms that help them maintain a steady state. If an animal becomes too hot its body reacts to help it cool down, for example, by breathing heavily. Similarly a work organization requires such self-regulation mechanisms. For example, if labour turnover suddenly rises far above its normal levels, it needs to find a way of correcting this problem.

- Organisms are born, grow, develop, decline and die. Similarly new organizations are being formed all the time and unsuccessful ones are going out of business. Existing organizations need to transform themselves if they are to survive.

- Organisms have to fight for survival in difficult and crowded environments and the weaker ones do not survive. Similarly, organizations have to fight for survival and only the strongest will win through.

The population ecology view of organizations argues that the processes that determine which organizations survive and flourish and which decline and die are similar to the Darwinian processes of natural selection. In essence, the argument is that those organizations which are best fitted to their environment will be the ones that survive.

The process has four stages:

1. **Variation**. There has to be some variation between the organizations in a population. Take the population of restaurants in one town, for example. They are not identical: they will offer different menus, different service styles, be managed in different ways and use technology differently. Some of these variations will offer some restaurants an advantage in the environment over others. For example, the first Harry Ramsden's Fish and Chip Restaurant outside Leeds in England provided something different from the competing local fish and chip restaurants in terms of a higher quality product and environment, which was attractive to people who might not normally have eaten fish and chips.
2. **Selection**. Over a long period, only some of the restaurants in the town may be expected to survive and be reasonably prosperous. Others will come and go. Harry Ramsden's survived and flourished.

3. **Retention**. Over time these successful restaurants may use their
   success as a platform for further modifications and become a new
   type of institution. The success of the first Harry Ramsden's
   allowed the development of a chain of upmarket fish and chip
   restaurants in a context where the population of independent fish
   and chip restaurants is probably declining.
4. **Modification**. The success of Harry Ramsden's might encourage
   other people to try to develop chains of fish and chip restaurants
   with slightly different characteristics, allowing the process of selection and adaption to continue.

One of the assumptions of the population ecology perspective is that
ultimately it is the environment which is critical in deciding which
species of organization survives and which is doomed to extinction
and there is little that an individual member of the species can do to
buck the trend. If the characteristics of the environment mean that a
chain of fish and chip shops is selected in preference to an independent
fish and chip shop, although certain independent fish and chip shops
may be stronger and able to survive longer than others in the long run
this species of restaurants may die out.

Box 10.2   Hotels around Niagara Falls

Ingram and Inman (1996) studied the founding rates and failure rates of
hotels on both the US and the Canadian sides of Niagara Falls between
1885 and 1991. From the early 1800s when tourists started visiting the
falls, peddlers, hucksters and conmen, on both sides of the falls, were
extremely aggressive in their attempts to profit from the tourists and
made it difficult for anyone to get a free, undisturbed view of the natural
scenery. Local hoteliers and businessmen banded together on the New
York side to promote the development of a park that would limit the
activities of these hucksters. A similar pressure group was developed on
the Ontario side, which had always seen itself as in competition with the
New York side hotels. The New York park opened in 1885, three years
before the Ontario park, but the latter was more elaborate and wealthy.
   The establishment of the parks benefited the populations of hotels on
both sides of the falls with an increase in founding rate and a decrease in
failure rate. However, the failure rate was lower and has remained lower
for hotels on the Ontario side. Within each population of hotels, larger
hotels were more likely to survive, hotels closer to the falls were more
likely to survive and, after controlling for the effects of size and location,

the humbler motels and inns were more likely to survive than establishments styled "hotel" or "house".

Thus although some hotels in this population were "fitter" than others
the whole population of hotels on both sides of the fall was helped to
survive and prosper because of the collective action they took to establish
the parks. However, the Ontario "species" gained a competitive advantage over the New York "species".

Competition and collaboration

The example in Box 10.2 demonstrates that, although there may be little
that individual organizations can do to influence the environment, by
banding together they may be able to improve the conditions for the
survival of their "species". Although hotels or restaurants in the same
location are, on one level, competing with each other, they can also
often benefit from collaborative action. Whilst two hotels on the
Canadian side of Niagara Falls compete with each other for guests, it is
in the interests of both that tourists come to Niagara Falls rather than
stay in Toronto because at least then they can compete for the business.
As well as collaborating through informal networks, trade and professional associations are often developed to lobby on those issues that
are of shared concern to a group of organizations. Box 10.3 describes
some typical activities of a trade association for the hospitality industry.

Box 10.3   The activities of trade associations: Ireland

In Ireland, as in many other countries, the hospitality industry is represented by a number of trade associations including the Irish Hotels
Federation and the Restaurants Association of Ireland. Their activities
include lobbying the Government on behalf of their members about such
issues as VAT (sales tax) levels, licensing regulation, smoking regulations,
hygiene and food handling regulations and employment regulations. The
trade associations also work to improve the quality of practice in the
industry through initiatives such as the Hotel Federation's Quality
Employer Initiative and the Restaurants Association's Restaurant and
Customer Charter. The argument is that improving the quality of practice
in the sector as a whole benefits everyone.

The examples so far have stressed the benign ways in which organizations can influence the environment. No-one, surely, can argue that clubbing together to develop a park at Niagara Falls or to improve the management practices of hotels in Ireland are other than desirable activities. But what is best for organizations or groups of organizations is not necessarily in the best interests of everyone in the community. The current debate about smoking in restaurants is a good example of the potential conflicts of interest between the organizational perspective on an issue, the government perspective and the interests of members of the community, specifically in this case smokers and non-smokers (Box 10.4).

Box 10.4   Banning smoking in restaurants: the US experience

Smoking was first declared a health risk in the United States in 1964 and since then the tobacco industry has been ever more tightly regulated. In 1993 The Environmental Protection Agency (EPA) produced a report showing a link between secondhand smoke and smoke-related illnesses in non-smokers. This raised the stakes on the smoking debate and promoted legislation restricting smoking in public places. Whilst in many states and cities, the legislation has taken the form of requiring restaurants to set by a proportion of their seats for non-smokers, in some places a complete ban has been enacted.

The general view of the restaurant industry is that legislation is to be resisted and that restaurateurs should be free to decide their policy to smoking in response to consumer preferences. The restaurant industry has played up the negative consequences of a smoking ban. For example, it is claimed that as a result of a law passed in 1993 preventing smoking in Los Angeles' restaurants, business dropped 10–15% in the first four months, a national trade association cancelled its convention plans and one in six of 300 restaurants surveyed had had to lay off staff. The industry has also claimed that with good ventilation and planning the preferences of both smokers and non-smokers can be accommodated without the need to resort to complete ban.

Some researchers (Bojanic 1996) have argued that restaurateurs may be worrying unnecessarily about the negative consequences of a complete ban. 75–80% of the population of the US do not smoke and a decrease in patronage by smokers may be compensated for by an increase in patronage by non-smokers. Further a complete ban, rather than partial restrictions, may be to the restaurateurs' advantage in that it will protect them against possible litigation from their employees who could claim that they had not been protected from exposure to a hazardous substance at work, namely customers' cigarette smoke (Young 1997).

Two companies, McDonald's and Dunkin' Donuts, have prohibited smoking in all their outlets.

The smoking example pulls together a number of issues that are relevant in considering how organizations interact with their environment.

- **Monitoring the environment**. It demonstrates the need for organizations to monitor the environment to pick up changes in public tastes (changing attitudes to smoking) and government legislation.

- **Representation**. It demonstrates the need for organizations to present their perspective on an issue to people in the wider environment, in this case to argue that a smoking ban might harm the restaurant trade.

- **Networking**. It shows how, particularly for small organizations, these processes of monitoring and representation may be most effectively managed by networking with other organizations. In the US the trade association, the National Restaurant Association, is extremely powerful. It has 30 000 members representing over 170 000 restaurants and is able to employ over a dozen specialists initiating and coordinating governmental lobbying in Washington DC. One of its action groups supports pro-business, pro-restaurant candidates for US Congress.

- **"First mover" advantages**. Certain companies may choose to adopt a different strategy from the rest of the industry to provide themselves with a competitive advantage. In this case McDonald's and Dunkin' Donuts chose to impose a complete smoking ban. (They are, of course, operating in a sector of the restaurant trade where a smoking ban is less commercially risky.)

- **Conflict of values and interests**. The commercial interests of the restaurants are in conflict with the values and interests of other groups in society, notably the health lobby.

The discussion so far has been based on a model of organizations as natural organisms trying to survive in their environment. This angle yields some interesting insights into the way organizations adapt and develop in response to environmental pressures and into the ways different organizations network together. But it is only one way of seeing organizations and it also has its limitations.

When we talk about organizations adapting to their environments, it is easy to forget that an organization cannot literally adapt. An organization may be like a natural organism but it is not a natural organism: it is a collection of buildings and resources and people. It is the people within the organization who make the choices and decisions, not the organization itself. When we talk about *the organization* adapting we are in danger of assuming that everyone in the organization has the same objectives and interests whereas, as has been shown in other chapters of this book, this is not necessarily the case. Taking the smoking example, restaurant owners, managers and employees may be variously smokers and non-smokers, one person's partner may work for a tobacco company, another's father may have died from a smoking-related disease. Will these personal circumstances really have no effect on their attitudes and choices about whether smoking should be banned?

So the next part of the chapter shifts to using a different metaphor about organizations: one which emphasizes some of the negative effects that work organizations, especially the largest organizations, have on the community.

Organizations as instruments of domination

Another of Morgan's (1986) ways of looking at organizations (see Chapter 2) is as instruments of domination. This image focuses on the ways in which organizations try to impose their will on others in the community, often against the community's best interests. Corporate profits are put above the interests of employees and consumers (as some might argue has happened with the smoking example).

Some of the ways in which hospitality organizations may be accused of acting against the best interests of the community are by:

- polluting the physical environment, literally by, for example, polluting the sea and figuratively, by developments that are unsympathetic to the environment (see Box 10.5);

- exploiting staff, for example by providing minimum pay and poor work conditions. (The reputation of the hospitality industry as a low-pay, low skill employer is discussed in Chapters 3 and 7);

- encouraging crime and socially undesirable behaviour, for example by turning a blind eye to drug taking, prostitution, overconsumption of alcohol and so forth;

- destroying the local culture through turning it into a sanitized version of itself suitable for tourists (see Chapter 3) or by replacing it with the type of establishments that cater only for the tourists. So British bars and clubs drive out local bars and restaurants in British-dominated resorts in Spain.

Box 10.5   Planning and the law

Vietri sul Mare (in Italy), at the western end of the spectacular Amalfi coast, is a colourful spot packed with shops selling the town's favourite ceramics. But it has been overshadowed by a seven-story hotel complex, built without planning permission. The local council has ignored court orders to bulldoze it. Green MPs are pushing a special law through parliament, giving the environment ministry power to override local authorities and send its own demolition experts in.

(Hanley 1998, p. 15)

Whilst there are many examples of organizations exploiting people in their own local environments, many people argue that this "ugly face" of organizations is particularly seen in the way in which multinational organizations, from developed countries, behave in developing countries.

The new colonials

Advocates of multinationals often see them as positive forces in economic development, creating jobs and bringing capital, technology, and expertise to communities or countries that might have difficulty developing these resources on their own account. Their critics, on the other hand, tend to see them as authoritarian juggernauts that are ultimately out to exploit their hosts for all they can get.

(Morgan 1986, p. 305)

When Hilton Hotels originally expanded internationally, Conrad Hilton saw this as an opportunity to promote world peace and promote American values internationally: "Each of our hotels is a 'little America', not as a symbol of bristling power, but as a friendly center where men of many nations and of good will may speak the language of peace" (Hilton 1957, p. 265 in Nickson 1997, p. 186).

According to Nickson (1997), Hilton originally considered locating outside the US on the suggestion of the US State Department and Department of Commerce who thought that this would make a substantial contribution to the government's foreign aid programme by stimulating trade and travel, bringing American dollars into the economies of countries needing help, creating international goodwill and transferring American management practices.

The 1970s, 80s and 90s have seen a massive expansion of multinational hotel corporations and rounds of mergers and acquisitions as the major corporations try to ensure that they are represented in all the key markets around the world. Multinational hotel corporations have the following advantages over their domestic competitors (see Go and Pine 1995):

- Their trademark guarantees customers a certain desired level of quality: helpful especially if the environment is unfamiliar. The Hilton, Sheraton, Marriott or Mandarin label will be reassuring to someone from the developed world staying in a developing country.

- These corporations bring with them management and organizational expertise which allow them to run and maintain hotels better.

- Multinational hotel companies with headquarters in America, Europe or Japan have favoured access to their domestic market. They know what their customers want and have strategic links with the airlines and tour operators in their countries.

As Box 10.6 illustrates, the presence of multinational hotel companies in developing countries does not always bring all the benefits to the host country that Conrad Hilton predicted. Trade is increased but the profits of tourism often return to the developed world rather than benefiting the host country. Locals do not always have the opportunity to develop management expertise as the top jobs continue to be held by expatriates and contact with foreigners, rather than transferring the positive aspects of the visitors' culture, creates social problems. Finally, multinational companies are fickle: they will pull out of a location if there are problems, leaving the locals to pick up the pieces.

In the case of the Gambia, it may be argued that the "villains" (if there are such) are the tour operators more than the hotel companies. Further, it can be argued that the Governments and ruling elites in the developing countries have some responsibility for the problems caused by the activities of multinational companies as they often encourage these companies to enter the country and fail to find a way of controlling their activities (Morgan 1986). Finally, it can be argued that there are also risks for the multinational company in trying to operate in certain environments and that they are therefore entitled to reap the rewards when they are successful (refer back to Box 10.1 for an extreme example of a case where it is the international entrepreneur who is the victim).

Box 10.6   Tourism in the Gambia

The Gambia is a small country in West Africa. It was discovered as a tourist destination in the mid-1960s and gradually increased the number of tourist arrivals through until the early 1990s. It was very reliant on British tourists but following concern in Britain about the safety of tourists and the internal stability of the country (the British Foreign Office advised tourists not to visit the country) the tourist industry was almost completely destroyed in 1994/5. Tourist numbers have subsequently increased, and the Gambia is less dependent on the British market, but this experience highlights the fragility of the industry.

So how has tourism affected the Gambia?

Tourism has brought in foreign earnings but, because most visitors come on "package tours", they use foreign air carriers and perhaps stay in foreign-owned and managed hotels. Therefore, the use of the facilities and services has been pre-paid overseas (Dieke 1993). There is a joke in the Gambia that some tourists arrive with no extra spending money to make purchases outside the hotel. Thus only a modest amount of the income created by tourism trickles down into the Gambian economy. Furthermore, the benefits of tourism are confined mainly to the coastal periphery of the country and there is a danger that inland rural areas become further disadvantaged.

Tourism has created jobs in the Gambia: an estimated 10% of the workforce are employed either directly in hotels and restaurants or indirectly benefit from tourists, e.g. as taxi drivers, making and selling handicrafts, "following the tourists". But many of these jobs are unskilled and expatriates still hold many of the senior posts. One problem is the lack of training and education facilities in the Gambia to prepare Gambians for skilled and managerial roles. A further problem is that as tourism is seasonal, many staff are laid off out of season. Theoretically they could return to farm work, but the tourism development areas are close to the urban and peri-urban rather than the rural areas. An increasing number of Gambians are living in the urban areas.

Tourism has brought social problems with it and the Gambian government is concerned about the impact contact with tourists has on the host community. There is the lure of foreign money in the face of endemic poverty. There is increasing petty crime and prostitution in a mainly Moslem country. Gambia has developed a reputation as a place where western women can seek a "holiday romance" and, for many local men, the prospect of a ticket to Europe or being helped to set up a business in the Gambia by a grateful client encourages them to offer their services.

The Gambian government is seeking ways to redress these problems but it is clear that the presence of international companies in the Gambia has not brought unequivocal benefits.

(Sources: Ministry of Tourism and Culture 1995, Dieke 1993)

Social responsibility

The previous section emphasized the most negative aspects of the impact a company has on its environment. Should we, as citizens, expect companies to behave in a way which attempts to minimize these negative impacts: that is, to be socially responsible?

Social responsibility may be defined as: "the firm's consideration of, and response to, issues beyond the narrow, technical, and legal requirements of the firm . . . (to) accomplish social benefits along with the traditional economic gains which the firm seeks" (Davis 1973, p. 312). Wood (1991) makes a useful distinction between social responsibility and social responsiveness. Social responsiveness is the capacity of a company to respond to changing customer expectations. So a restaurant is being socially responsive when it recognizes that non-smokers increasingly object to the cigarette smoke near their table and introduces a non-smoking area. A restaurant may be being socially responsible if, taking the view that smoking is bad for the health of customers and employees, it bans it. What is regarded as socially responsible behaviour varies between cultures and over time. It might be socially responsible to ban smoking in the US in the late 1990s when it would not have been in the 1950s. Social responsiveness is about making business decisions that take into account customers' values; social responsibility is about the company's values and what it stands for.

Some people take the view that it is not the business of business to be socially responsible. Friedman (1989) argues that ". . . there is only one social responsibility in business and that is to engage in activities to increase its profits as long as it stays within the rules of the game". However, there are many examples of companies taking initiatives which aim to put something back into the community and in some cases, particularly with small companies with strong community links, they may act as if the well-being of the community is more important than that of the narrow economic goals of the company (see Box 10.7).

Box 10.7 "Aggie's" – a business in the community

Aggie's is one of the best known hotels in the South Pacific and a major source of exchange for the Samoan government. It began as a modest two-room guesthouse that Aggie Grey began in the 1930s after her husband's business went bankrupt. It has developed into a multi-million complex with 154-room hotel, gift shop, tours and an extensive farm developed to meet the hotel's food needs.

Aggie is thought of as chief of a large house. She employs over 250 – "we could run the hotel on fewer but you don't fire family". She provides her staff with more than wages, acting like a parent, "when they were in trouble she stuck by them; and when they had a *faalavelave* (family obligations) she was generous" (Alailima 1988 p. 294). As fitting its "chiefly" status, the Grey family gives generously to national and local fund-raising efforts. These gifts reinforce the relationships between the enterprise and the people as in traditional times, true wealth is displayed in giving.

(Adapted from Fairbairn-Dunlop 1994)

In what areas is there now an expectation that organizations should be socially responsible? The rise of "green" values in the community means that actions to protect the environment, by conserving energy, controlling waste and using environmentally friendly products, are becoming more important. This is an example where actions which benefit the community are often also in the interests of the organization. The Royal York Hotel in Toronto, for example, claimed to save over a quarter of a million US dollars in waste removal costs by compacting and where possible recycling garbage (McDermid 1993). Employment policies are another area where organizations can "put back": by making particular efforts to employ and develop local staff, by employing staff from all sections of the community (abled and disabled, males and females, all ethnic groups and age groups) and by adopting local schools and colleges. It may also be argued that hospitality organizations have a responsibility to take a stand against crime and disorder that may, even inadvertently, happen on their premises. Box 10.8 gives an example of some initiatives which the hospitality industry has taken to combat one crime: child sex tourism.

To balance the negative view of organizations as instruments of domination, therefore, there are also more positive examples that can be cited where organizations have made positive contributions to the community. The key message from this chapter is that hospitality organizations exist within a wider community environment. They are influenced by their environment and also influence that environment and the influences each way may be both positive and negative. Organizations also exist at a particular point in time and in the final chapter I will speculate about some of the ways in which hospitality companies may change in the future.

Box 10.8   Child sex tourism: the responsibilities of the hospitality industry

Over two million children under the age of 16 are victims of commercial sexual exploitation and often hotels, no matter how inadvertently, are the scene of the crime. The International Hotel and Restaurant Association launched a campaign against the sexual exploitation of children and has produced guidelines for all its members worldwide. The IHRA resolution on this matter:

> observes with great concern that the sexual exploitation of children (prostitution, production of pornographic material etc.) is on the increase worldwide

> recognizes that, unfortunately, child sex abusers may attempt to use hotels as the location where they commit their crimes.

Hospitality operators are urged to train security staff and concierges to spot and report suspicious incidents, not let unsupervised children wander around the bar/lounge/reception areas and report to the relevant authorities anything that indicates sex trade with children, making sure the perpetrator, not the child, is held responsible.

Whilst this is a worldwide problem some countries are particularly affected. Thailand has long had an image as a sex tour destination attracting a high proportion of single male tourists. Workers for the sex industry (child and female prostitutes) have predominantly come from the marginal rural areas of north and north-east Thailand where many families and villages are economically dependent on these ill-gotten earnings. Since the late 1980s, when the spread of AIDS and other sexually transmitted diseases became recognized as a problem, the Thai Public Health Ministry has started campaigning against prostitution and the promotion of Thailand as a sexual paradise (Hall 1994). One south-east Asian hotel company has developed a programme designed to provide an alternative for young women who would otherwise have been "sold" into prostitution, paying their families and providing training for them in hotel work.

Summary

- Hospitality organizations, like all organizations, exist in a social, political and economic environment which impinges on what they do.

- One way of thinking about organizations is to see them as living organisms which have to interact with their environment in order to survive. Organizations take in inputs from the environment, process them and export them into the environment.

- The population ecology perspective on organizations uses the Darwinian model of natural selection to understand organizations. The environment selects those organizations that are best fitted to it to survive and thrive. Over time, some species of organization may become extinct.

- By banding together, organizations may be able to improve the chances of survival of their species. Trade associations provide one forum through which organizations can work together to promote common interests.

- There may sometimes be conflicts of interest between what actions are best for the organization and what might be in the best interests of the community. The current debate about smoking restrictions and bans in restaurants is one such conflict of interest.

- Another way of seeing organizations is as instruments of domination that want to control and exploit their environment and have a negative effect on it: for example, hospitality organizations may be accused of polluting the environment, exploiting staff, turning a blind eye to crime and undermining the local culture. Particular concerns have been expressed about the operation of multinational companies in developing countries.

- From a more positive perspective, there are also some examples of hospitality organizations behaving in a socially responsible way and attempting to "put something back" into the community.

The next stage

Experience

Collect information about the "births" and "deaths" of hospitality organizations in your local area (over the last five years if possible). What species of hospitality organization seems to be thriving and what becoming extinct?

Take one hospitality organization that you have contact with. What aspects of the economic, social and legal environment are likely to affect it in the near future? Is there any new legislation that will affect it? What about changes in social attitudes? Ask one of the managers for their views, if possible.

How is that hospitality organization trying to affect the environment? Does it collaborate with any other businesses in the area? Is it a member of any trade associations? If so, what campaigns are these trade associations engaged in?

Does the hospitality organization contribute anything to the community in terms of environmental practices, employment practices, charity work etc?

Reflection

If you have identified any patterns in the "births" and "deaths" of hospitality organizations in your local environment, why do you think these have occurred? Why are the organizations that are thriving better fitted to their environment than the ones that have died?

Can you identify any negative impacts that any hospitality organization that you are familiar with has on its environment? Could that organization do anything to minimize these negative effects? If it could, why do you think it does not?

If you have identified any ways in which a hospitality organization you are familar with "puts something back" into the community, why do you think it does this? Is the organization being socially responsive or socially responsible?

In theory

Taking a population ecology perspective, when is it in the interests of organizations to collaborate with each other? (Try to identify some examples of these collaborations.)

Would population ecologists agree with Milton Friedman that the social responsibility of business is to make profits? Why?

Do multinational companies inevitably exploit developing countries? What is the case for the prosecution and the case for the defence?

In practice

You run a small restaurant in the US. The neighbouring state has just banned smoking in all restaurants and many smokers are now crossing the border to eat in your restaurant where smoking is still allowed. You are getting more complaints from your non-smoking customers bothered by the smoke. What do you do?

You have been asked to advise the Gambian Minister for Tourism about how to maximize the benefits of tourism for Gambians. What is your advice?

Further reading

Morgan (1997) is a good starting point for the material in this chapter: his sections on organizations as organisms and organizations as instruments of domination particularly. The population ecology approach is discussed in a number of the general texts on organizational behaviour (for example Vecchio 1995). Sims *et al.* (1993) consider the organization in the community more broadly (Chapter 15).

The debate about smoking in restaurants is a good illustration of the way social issues are played out in organizations. See Bojanic (1996) and Young (1997).

Baum (1995, Chapter 10) considers the social responsibility of tourism organizations, particularly in relation to the management of human resources.

Beyond this much of the discussion of the impact of hospitality organizations on the host community takes place in the tourism rather than the hospitality literature. Refer to Urry (1990), Kinnaird and Hall (1994), who emphasize the impact on women, and Dieke (1993) and Ankomah (1991) for a discussion of issues in sub-Saharan Africa.

References for further reading

Ankomah, P. (1991) Tourism skilled labor: the case of sub-Saharan Africa, *Annals of Tourism Research*, **18**, 433–442.

Baum, T. (1995) *Managing Human Resources in the European Tourism and Hospitality Industry*, London: Chapman and Hall.

Bojanic, D. (1996) The smoking debate: a look at the issues surrounding smoking bans in restaurants, *Hospitality Research Journal*, **20**, 1: 27–38.

Dieke, P. (1993) Tourism and development policy in the Gambia, *Annals of Tourism Research*, **20**, 423–449.

Kinnaird, V. and Hall, D. (1994) *Tourism: A Gender Analysis*, Chichester: Wiley.

Morgan, G. (1997) *Images of Organization* (Second edition), California and London: Sage.

Sims, D., Fineman, S. and Gabriel, Y. (1993) *Organizing and Organizations: an Introduction*, London: Sage.

Urry, J. (1990) *The Tourist Gaze*, London: Sage.

Vecchio, R. (1995) *Organizational Behaviour* (Third edition), Orlando: Dryden.

Young, K. (1997) Environmental tobacco smoke and employees, *Cornell Hotel and Restaurant Administrative Quarterly*, February, 36–42.

Into the future

> **Box 11.1 The hotel on the moon**
>
> The year is 2050. Anna is about to take up her new job as a manager in the Sea of Tranquillity Hotel and Leisure Complex. As the shuttle craft carries her away from the earth, she wonders what her new life on the moon will be like.

There are two points that need to be made about any attempt to predict the future. First, it is likely to be proved completely wrong. Second, it tells one more about the problems and issues of the present than those of the future. Should anyone chance on a copy of this book in some junk shop 50 years from now this chapter will, no doubt, provide them with considerable amusement.

This final chapter reviews the main points made in the rest of the book and tries to pick up some of the trends which may change hospitality organizations in the future. What will the hotel on the moon be like?

Ways of seeing organizations

Imagine that Anna has just completed a hospitality management degree course. Would she have studied organizational behaviour? Would her course bear any relationship to an organizational behaviour module now?

Assuming that Anna will be working with other people on the moon and that the hotel and leisure complex is welcoming human guests, many of the issues that have been discussed in this book – how to motivate staff, how to work in groups, how to lead other people, how to design jobs and organizational structures, what managers should do, how to manage customer service staff – will be as relevant to her as it is to us. So my prediction would be that organizational behaviour will still be studied in some form in 50 years' time. But will they have all the answers then? Will Anna be the perfect manager because people in 50 years' time will have much better ways of solving organizational problems?

If they are building hotels on the moon in the future then our knowledge of the natural sciences will have increased. But the social sciences and the natural sciences do not work in exactly the same way. Although some organizational theorists might argue that we are working towards a common paradigm for understanding organizations, others take the view that this subject area will always consist of contradictory models and ideas. In 2050 organizational behaviour will not necessarily be better but there will certainly be new solutions proposed to both familiar problems and new problems.

For an indication of how far a subject matter can progress in 50 years it is instructive to look back 50 years. Organizational behaviour was in its infancy then: almost all the theories and research discussed in this book are post-1950 (the majority post-1970). But there was some research conducted in the late 1940s and early 1950s that still has relevance. Whyte's (1945) study of human relations in the restaurant industry raised issues about group working and inter-group working (how to prevent conflicts between waiters and kitchen staff) that are still current. Similarly the early Tavistock studies in the Yorkshire mines (Trist and Bamforth 1951) raised issues about job design and the impact of technology on job design that are still fresh (although the specific technologies and indeed most of the jobs they studied have long disappeared).

The organizational theorist in 1950 would have had a good understanding of basic individual and group psychology and how this affected behaviour at work. He or she would not have been able to predict the social, economic and technological changes that have affected organizations since then. Women at work were studied in the 1940s (Whyte's waitresses for example) but it was assumed that the world of work was fundamentally a male world: as late as 1973 it was still possible to publish a book called *Men and Work in Modern Britain* (Weir 1973) on the assumption that women's work did not matter. There was little or no discussion of cultural differences and their impact on management and organizations. The organizational theorist in 1950 would not have predicted the rise of Asian economies and the interest in Japanese approaches to management and organization. There was also an assumption that most people's work would involve making things (in factories and heavy industry). He or she would not have predicted the service revolution.

We may be sure that Anna in her hotel on the moon in 2050 will face issues that we cannot imagine now. Perhaps her organizational behaviour course will extol the value of Russian or Brazilian approaches to management and organization, just as we now study American and Japanese management.

Ways of seeing hospitality organizations

From the earliest times, people have found ways of accommodating travellers away from home and providing them with somewhere to sleep, food, drink and be entertained. A hotel on the moon will have the same basic functions as a hotel anywhere else even if, in this case, the traveller is a very long way from home. The hotel will need to provide a safe and comfortable environment for the guest as hotels do everywhere and at all times.

But what service will guests in a hotel on the moon expect? We do not know whether the hotel is designed for people working on the moon, in which case fairly basic services may be all that are provided. But perhaps the moon has become the ultimate holiday destination and the Sea of Tranquillity Hotel and Leisure Complex offers the most lavish and state-of-the-art accommodation. Or perhaps the hotel caters for both work and holiday visitors.

We can be sure that technology will have advanced and that there is even more scope to replace people with product. Perhaps there are no receptionists in this hotel: people check in through an interface with a computer. Perhaps there are no room attendants, as cleaning is carried out by robots. Perhaps meals are pre-prepared and guests heat them up themselves. Perhaps Anna is the sole member of staff.

Alternatively, perhaps, if this is the ultimate holiday destination, customers will demand personal service. Technology may be used to store more information about customer preferences and to provide a more individualized service. Perhaps the Hotel and Leisure Complex will have assigned a butler to every room. Perhaps staff are expected, even more than now, to look wonderful, to dress in the most fashionable clothes, to contribute to the atmosphere and the entertainment. Perhaps guests will be able to savour cuisines from around the world in absolutely stunning surroundings.

What type of world will Anna be leaving? Now about one in ten of the global workforce is employed in the tourism and hospitality industry. By 2050, will that proportion be smaller, larger or about the same? It could be argued that there will be fewer jobs in this sector as the hospitality sector may be just as prone to replacement of labour by technology as the manufacturing and other service industries such as retail banking have proved to be. It may be argued that the only reason the hospitality sector provides so many jobs currently is that labour is used unproductively.

Or it may be that consumers will have even more discretionary income than they do now and will want to spend more of this on eating out, entertainment and holidays. And, especially if they have little direct contact with people in the rest of their lives, perhaps working at home, shopping on the Internet and so forth, they may want direct contact with service staff when they are having fun. So the proportion of people employed in the hospitality sector may grow as our spending on leisure grows.

Much depends on what the future of work generally will be like. Since the time of Karl Marx, sociologists have discussed the soul-destroying nature of much work in modern society (Box 11.2). In the lowest level jobs, people may be required to work long hours doing work which is not intrinsically interesting. At the other end of the scale, top managers may earn huge rewards but have to work such long hours they have no life outside work. Will this pattern continue to the mid-21st century or will people demand more freedom and control over their lives?

Box 11.2 Marx and the alienation of labour

In what does this alienation of labour consist? First, that the work is *external* to the worker, that is it is not a part of his nature, that consequently he does not fulfil himself in his work but denies himself, has a feeling of misery, not of well-being, does not develop freely a physical

> and mental energy, but is physically exhausted and mentally debased. The
> worker therefore feels himself at home only during his leisure whereas at
> work he feels homeless.
>   (Karl Marx, *Economic and Philosophical Manuscripts*, 1844)

Writers like Handy (1994) point out that work does not have to mean a
full-time job with one employer. He argues that people should build
up a "portfolio" of activities and interests in their lives: a balance
between those things that they do in order to survive and those
activities, even "work" activities, which we do because they are fascinating or fun or because they serve a cause. In many societies, young
people are delaying starting work longer to stay on in full-time education and older people are retiring from work earlier (although they
are living longer), so we are already aware that there will be times in
our lives when we may be without paid work. Perhaps Anna has taken
the job on the moon with the intention of working for a few years to
make some money before she realizes her ambition to live in the
country and become a painter. Perhaps Anna is in her 60s and has
decided to take up this job purely for fun and the fascination of being
on the moon and she is not being paid at all.

   This is the optimistic scenario. Perhaps the hospitality industry in
2050 will still have a poor image and Anna comes from one of the
poorest parts of the world where jobs are hard to come by and incomes
are low. Perhaps she has taken this job not because she thinks it will be
particularly interesting or rewarding but because she needs the money
and is desperate for any job, even if it means leaving her children
behind on earth to be cared for by her parents.

The many faces of culture

Wherever she comes from, Anna will bring a set of cultural beliefs
and assumptions with her. But how far will her cultural beliefs and
assumptions be influenced by her national identity? If we assume
that in the next 50 years the world will have become "global" with
even more contact across national boundaries and nations themselves

becoming less important, will the cultural differences between people from different parts of the world have become less marked? Will people have become more similar in their beliefs and assumptions?

Hofstede's response to this would be a resounding "no". He argues that:

> Research about the development of cultural values has shown repeatedly that there is very little evidence of international convergency over time. . . . For the next few hundred years countries will remain culturally diverse.
>
> (Hofstede 1991, p. 238)

Adler (1991) agrees, arguing that although there is some evidence that organizations across the world are superficially becoming more similar to each other, the people inside those organizations still behave in different ways. So a hotel in Korea and a hotel in Australia might look similar from the outside, but inside, the Koreans and Australians still behave in different ways (see also Pizam *et al.* 1997). Anna's beliefs and assumptions will, probably, still be influenced by her national identity.

But of course there will, as yet, be no distinctive "moon" culture. So the culture of the hotel on the moon will be influenced by the cultural background of its owners, managers and employees. Will there be a dominant national cultural influence, because the ownership and management are largely drawn from the same nationality or will this be an example of a truly multi-cultural organization?

What type of organizational culture will the Sea of Tranquillity Hotel and Leisure Complex have? However high-tech this hotel may be, it will still have its "rituals" and "ceremonies", its ways of socializing newcomers, its shared values and assumptions. Indeed, as an isolated organization where people are separated from normal home and friends and are living as well as working together, it might be predicted that these cultural elements would be strong as they often are in relatively closed organizations (for example the Army).

We do not know who owns this hotel: perhaps it is branded a Marriott or a Holiday Inn or a Hilton. In this case, perhaps its culture will still be influenced, even if in a small way, by the background and values of the company founders: Bill Marriott, Kemmons Wilson or Conrad Hilton.

Motivation, job performance and satisfaction

Will Anna be motivated to work hard in her new job by the same factors that would motivate a hotel manager today? One view is that there are certain aspects of human psychology that are universal: as Mendonca and Kanungo (1994, p. 286) claim:

> the employee's performance in *any* culture will improve through the practices of goal setting, performance feedback and valued rewards. The underlying psychological principles of work motivation incorporated in these practices are universally valid.

Thus it will still be important that Anna understands what her job is, that she knows what she should achieve and is given feedback on how well she is doing and that her performance is linked with rewards that she values.

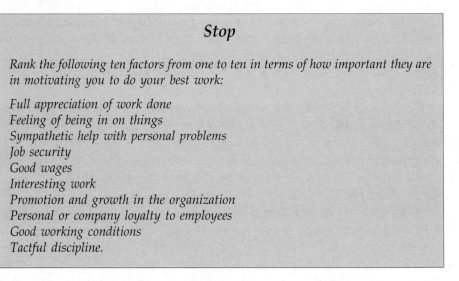

Stop

Rank the following ten factors from one to ten in terms of how important they are in motivating you to do your best work:

Full appreciation of work done
Feeling of being in on things
Sympathetic help with personal problems
Job security
Good wages
Interesting work
Promotion and growth in the organization
Personal or company loyalty to employees
Good working conditions
Tactful discipline.

But what rewards will she value from work? There is some evidence that the rewards people want from work change over time within the same culture, as it varies from culture to culture. Wiley (1997) compared surveys of what employees thought motivated them to do their best work conducted in the US in 1946, 1980, 1986 and 1992, using the ten criteria listed above. In 1946, respondents ranked "full appreciation of work done" first, in 1980 and 1986 "interesting work" was ranked first, but in 1992 "good wages" was ranked first. Wiley points out that the early 1990s were a period of recession in the US, with organizations downsizing and cutting labour costs. In those circumstances, it was not surprising that basic needs, for money and security, assumed more importance.

We do not know whether jobs, work and money will be easy or hard to come by in 2050; whichever it is will affect the rewards people seek from work. Take the scenario that Anna is in her 60s, well off, and has taken up this job purely for the interest and pleasure of being on the moon. Money, job security, company loyalty might mean nothing to her: indeed she could be quite hard to motivate if all she really wanted to do is stare out of the window at the scenery and the stars. Alternatively, we could imagine a scenario where Anna is totally motivated by money, working on the moon because it offers really high wages, and if it were not for the money would much sooner be back on earth.

Will hotel staff on the moon receive tips? Research suggests that the level of tips is only weakly associated with customers' evaluations of performance and therefore only provides a weak incentive (Lynn and Graves 1996). If pay is still an important incentive at work in 2050, it may be that, especially by making use of information technology, companies can come up with more elaborate ways of linking pay and performance. Perhaps tips will be a relic of an earlier age of hospitality.

Groups and leading groups

As our basic models of human motivation may still be valid in 2050, so may our basic models of the psychology of group behaviour. Anna will still have to cope with working with a team of people that will have developed their own norms, will have had to find ways of working together despite the diversity of their backgrounds and will be more or less cohesive. But will groups be used and led in the same ways in organizations in 2050?

Mainstream research into leadership over the last 50 years has yielded rather disappointing results (Smith 1991, Knights and Wilmott 1992). Will the future bring a better or different understanding of what leaders do and should do? One possibility is that we will abandon leadership as a concept altogether. Wilson (1995) comments that "perhaps we should consider giving up . . . organization based on hierarchy and therefore surrender the use of concepts such as leader and follower" (p. 177). Perhaps in the typical organization in 2050, people are organized on more collectivist–democratic principles in autonomous self-managed groups and more traditional and more directive forms of leadership have disappeared. Some would argue that Anna, as a woman, would feel very much at home in this type of organization. Quoting Wilson (1995) again:

> Women have more co-operative behaviour, something important in terms of consultation and democratic decision-making processes. They perceive power differently to men, less as domination or ability to control and more as a liberating force in the community.   (p. 174)

Alternatively, it may be argued that influencing others and exerting power are basics of human social behaviour. Even in the most "democratic" of groups, there are always some people who will take the lead and, when pushed to deliver by their leaders, women, as well as men, often resort to more directive styles of leadership.

Designing jobs and organization structures

If organizations develop according to current trends, one scenario would be that a typical hotel in 2050 would employ fewer staff than today. The simplest, least skilled jobs would have disappeared, replaced by technology. For example, there would be no more room attendants as robots would clean rooms. The operative staff still employed would have enriched jobs, be empowered to use their initiative and work in autonomous teams. Their role would be to provide a high quality service to guests. The organizational structure would be flat and there would be less division than now between managers and operative staff. Functional divisions would also break down. In this scenario, Anna would be working with a highly skilled and highly professional group of people in an organization which could truly be decribed as "organic". Technological advances would mean that jobs were reskilled, and functional areas might have changed in their significance. Perhaps the key functional area in the Sea of Tranquillity Hotel will be computer engineering, in order to maintain the high-tech facilities.

Will all the staff and managers in such an organization be "core" staff committed to long-term careers in the organization? It may be that companies will still recognize the value of building up a "core" workforce and that the staff in the Sea of Tranquillity Hotel will have all been transferred from other hotels run by the same company and will expect to move on to other roles in the company. However, it may be that companies in 50 years' time will have moved even further down the line of "contracting out", "distancing" and using peripheral staff and that the Sea of Tranquillity Hotel is staffed by skilled people working on a self-employed basis and contracted to work for a fixed term on this project. Many of these staff may be literally "distanced", for staff in certain functions may no longer need to be physically present in the hotel to perform their tasks.

The alternative scenario is that, however technology has progressed, it still may remain cheaper and easier to use people rather than computers or robots. But technology will allow for jobs, at all levels, to become even more standardized and simplified so the people doing them are easier to control, require less training and are easy to replace. Why will we need the judgment of a skilled chef, for example, if a computer system can determine the precise ingredients for a recipe, their measurements and the timing of the cooking? But it may still be helpful to have a human being to take the dish out of the oven! The staff of the Sea of Tranquillity Hotel, rather than being skilled professionals with demanding roles, may be relatively low-skilled operatives following procedures and obeying the computer systems.

> **Box 11.3   The technology of the future and the job of the future**
>
> Tom Peters tells this story about the aircraft cockpit of the future. In the cockpit are a man and a dog. The man is there to look out of the window. The dog is there to bite the man if he tries to touch any of the instruments.

Managers and their roles

What will the role of a hospitality manager be in 2050? It is clear that what it means to be a manager has changed in the past 50 years and it seems likely that it will change again in the next 50 years.

Will there still be a separate area of study called "hospitality management" or will general management skills be sufficient? One scenario would be that as technology advances, the need for the specific technical skills associated with hospitality management will decrease. There will no longer be any need to know in detail about food preparation and service because technology will have made these processes easier to control. The business of managing room supply and pricing will be controlled by computerized decision-making systems. Managers will need to know about managing staff (but there will be fewer of those to manage) and managing customers (and that process will have become more standardized and systematized).

So according to one scenario the prospects for the middle manager are bleak. The pessimistic view is presented by Dopson and Stewart (1993):

> The work is dreary, the careers are frustrating and information technology . . . will make the role more routine, uninteresting and unimportant. The numbers and role of middle managers will, therefore, decline.

A more optimistic scenario is that, freed of its more routine elements, management work may become more creative and satisfying. There may be more flexibility about where one works. Anna may be able to manage the Hotel on the Moon based mainly at her home on earth, using communications technology, and perhaps only needs to visit occasionally to check that everything is running well and for interest. So perhaps the pattern of management work, now based on frenetic activity, long hours and frequent face-to-face contacts, will change radically in the next 50 years. Anna's key role may be as a boundary spanner, searching for ideas in the business environment which she will be able to utilize to improve the hotel. Although in some ways technology will have made Anna's role easier, she will have to access to much more information than managers nowadays and will have to be skilled in ways of filtering and using information.

If present trends continue in 2050, women managers may be as accepted as male managers. Will this have changed what organizations are like? Will the woman-friendly organization be less hierarchical and control based and more based around networks and collaboration? Or will women, subject to the same pressures and environment as men, behave in very similar ways to men?

Serving the customer

It is likely, as has been discussed, that some of the simpler service-contact roles in the hotel of 2050 will have disappeared, replaced by technology. Electronic concierges using expert systems may replace the human concierge. Travel plans and reservations will be managed by computer. Communications ports to the outside world will give guests contact with business information and entertainment. What need will the guest have for contact with a real person?

Perhaps living in such a high-tech environment will make people crave face-to-face contact with real human beings. The role of the service staff may become even more about entertaining the guest and helping them select a customized package of services from those available in the hotel rather than providing information or a standard-ized service, which can more easily be done through technology. The capacity of service staff to provide "emotional labour" rather than technical labour, in this context, becomes even more crucial. Guest information systems will allow staff to customize their "performance", being friendly and informal to guests who prefer that approach, and to customize the products and services offered to guests. Perhaps cus-tomer service staff will actually have more time to get to know guests. How will customer service work be viewed in this context? Freed of its more routine elements, it may become viewed as a more professional and attractive career option.

But alternatively, perhaps guests will be happy to interact entirely with computer screens and expert systems and not miss interaction with real people at all. As technology has replaced many manufactur-ing jobs, so it may replace most service jobs.

The wider environment

When Peters and Waterman published *In Search of Excellence* in 1982 they identified companies as "excellent" which subsequently faced severe problems. Many of the brands and companies which are well known and well regarded now may have disappeared in 50 years' time, or so transformed themselves that they are virtually unrecognizable to us. There will be new names and hotel and restaurant concepts that we have no knowledge of that have developed because they fit well into the environment of 2050.

Organizations will still have the potential to both benefit or harm the environments in which they operate. Presumably there would be some debate on earth about whether a hotel facility on the moon should be built at all. Environments, as Haigh (1995) points out, can be seen in different ways by different groups of people: "as a resource to be developed, an heirloom from previous generations, a precious natural habitat, a workplace for people, or a gift from God that must not be despoiled" (p. 195). The way in which the environment of the moon is perceived, by the people who have constructed the hotel, will affect how the hotel operates. Is the moon a resource to be developed, with the hotel a first stage in the development process, or a precious natural habitat, keeping the hotel as unintrusive as possible?

Final thoughts

We do not know if there will be a hotel on the moon in 50 years. But speculating allows one to think about other possibilities and other ways of structuring hospitality organizations. Organizations may seem solid and permanent but they are human creations and they can be created in different ways.

So what do *you* think the hotel on the moon will be like?

Bibliography

Adams, J.S. (1963) Towards an understanding of inequity, *Journal of Abnormal and Social Psychology*, **67**, 5: 422–436.

Adams, J.S. (1965) Inequity in social exchange in L. Berkowitz (ed.) *Advances in Experimental Social Psychology*, New York: Academic Press, **2**, 267–299.

Adler, N. (1991) *International Dimensions of Organizational Behavior* (Second edition), Boston, Mass: PWS-Kent.

Alailima, F. (1988) *Aggie Grey: a Samoan Saga*, Hawaii: Mutual Publishing.

Anastassova, L. and Purcell, K. (1995) Human resource management in the Bulgarian hotel industry: from command to empowerment, *International Journal of Hospitality Management*, **14**, 171–185.

Ankomah, P. (1991) Tourism skilled labor: the case of sub-Saharan Africa, *Annals of Tourism Research*, **18**, 433–442.

Argyris, C. and Schon, D. (1978) *Theory in Practice*, San Francisco: Jossey Bass.

Arvedlund, E. (1997) Murder in Moscow, *Fortune*, 3 March, 87–91.

Ashforth, B. and Humphrey, R. (1993) Emotional labour in service roles: the influence of identity, *Academy of Management Review*, **18**, 88–115.

Atkinson, J. (1984) Manpower strategies for flexible organizations, *Personnel Management*, August, 28–31.

Atkinson, J. (1985) Flexibility, uncertainty and manpower management, *Institute of Manpower Studies Report No 89*, Brighton: University of Sussex.

Bass, B. (1985) *Leadership and Performance Beyond Expectations*, New York: Free Press.

Baum, T. (1989) Managing hotels in Ireland: research and development for change, *International Journal of Hospitality Management*, **8**, 131–144.

Baum, T. (1995) *Managing Human Resources in the European Tourism and Hospitality Industry*, London: Chapman and Hall.

Belbin, R.M. (1981) *Management Teams*, Oxford: Butterworth-Heinemann.

Belbin, R.M. (1993) *Team Roles at Work*, Oxford: Butterworth-Heinemann.

Björkegren, D. (1996) *The Culture Business: Management Strategies for the Arts-related Business*, London: Routledge.

Blanchard, K. and Johnson, S. (1982) *The One-Minute Manager*, Englewood Cliffs, New Jersey: Prentice Hall.

Bojanic, D. (1996) The smoking debate: a look at the issues surrounding smoking bans in restaurants, *Hospitality Research Journal*, **20**, 1: 27–38.

Bowen, D. (1998) Consumer behaviour in tourism with specific reference to consumer satisfaction and dis-satisfaction on long-haul inclusive tours, PhD thesis, Oxford Brookes University.

Braverman, H. (1974) *Labor and Monopoly Capital*, Monthly Review Press, New York.

Breakwell, G. (1989) *Facing Physical Violence*, London: Routledge.

British Hospitality Association (1998) *British Hospitality: Trends and Statistics 1998*, London: BHA.

Brown, A. (1995) *Organisational Culture*, London: Pitman.

Brownell, J. (1994) Women in hospitality management: general managers' perceptions of factors relating to career development, *International Journal of Hospitality Management*, **13**, 101–117.

Bryson, B. (1996) *Notes from a Small Island*, London: Black Swan.

Buchanan, D. and Huczynski, A. (1997) *Organizational Behaviour: an Introductory Text*, (Third edition), Hemel Hempstead: Prentice Hall.

Burnett (1966/1979) *Plenty and Want: a Social History of Diet in England from 1815 to the Present Day*, London: Scolar Press.

Burns, J. (1978) *Leadership*, New York: Harper Row.

Burns, T. and Stalker, G. (1961) *The Management of Innovation*, London: Tavistock.

Buzan, T. (1995) *Use your Head* (Revised edition), London: BBC Books.

Carlzon, J. (1987) *Moments of Truth*, Cambridge, MA: Ballinger.

Charles, R. and McCleary, W. (1997) Recruitment and retention of African-American managers, *Cornell Hotel and Restaurant Administrative Quarterly*, **38**, 24–28.

Child, J. (1984) *Organization: A Guide to Problems and Practice*, (Second edition), London: Harper and Row.

Cook, E. (1996) Stocking up on indignities, *The Guardian*, 13 July, 27.

Czepiel, J., Solomon, M, Suprenant, C. and Gutman, E. (1985) Service encounters: an overview, in Czepiel, J. (ed.), *The Service Encounter: Managing Employee/Customer Interaction in Service Businesses*, Lexington MA: Lexington Books, 3–15.

Dansereau, F., Graen, G. and Haga, W. (1975) A vertical dyad linkage approach to leadership in formal organizations, *Organizational Behaviour and Human Performance*, **13**, 46–78.

Davis, B. and Lockwood, A. (eds) (1994) *Food and Beverage Management*, Oxford: Butterworth-Heinemann.

Davis, K. (1973) The case for and against business assumption of social responsibilities, *Academy of Management Journal*, **16**, 312–322.

Deal, T. and Kennedy, A. (1982) *Corporate Cultures: the Rites and Rituals of Corporate Life*, Reading, Mass: Addison-Wesley.

DePaulo, B. (1992) Nonverbal behavior and self-presentation, *Psychological Bulletin*, **111**, 2: 203–243.

Dieke, P. (1993) Tourism and development policy in the Gambia, *Annals of Tourism Research*, **20**, 423–449.

Dodson, B. and Kilian, D. (1998) From port to playground: the redevelopment of the Victoria and Alfred Waterfront, in Tyler, D., Guerrier, Y. and Robertson, M. (eds), *Managing Tourism in Cities: Policy, Process and Practice*, Chichester: Wiley, 139–162.

Dopson, S. and Stewart, R. (1993) What is happening to middle management, in Mabey, C. and Mayon-White, B. (eds), *Managing Change*, London: Paul Chapman.

Drakulic, S. (1994) At the tender mercy of the unsmiling Sofia sphinx, *The Observer*, 24 July.

Du Gay, P. and Salaman, G. (1992) The cult(ure) of the customer, *Journal of Management Studies*, **29**, 5: 615–633.

Du Gay, P., Salaman, G. and Rees, B. (1996) The Conduct of Management and the Management of Conduct: Contemporary Management Discourse and the Constitution of the "Competent" Manager, *Journal of Management Studies*, **33**, 263–282.

Duncombe, J. and Marsden, D. (1993) Love and Intimacy: the Gender Division of Emotion and "Emotion Work", *Sociology*, **27**, 2: 221–241.

Easterby-Smith, M., Thorpe, R. and Lowe, A. (1991) *Management Research*, London: Sage.

Evenden, R. and Anderson, G. (1992) *Making the Most of People*, Wokingham: Addison-Wesley.

Fairbairn-Dunlop, P. (1994) Gender, culture and tourism development in Western Samoa, in Kinnaird, V. and Hall, D. (eds), *Tourism: a Gender Analysis*, Chichester: Wiley, 121–140.

Fayol, H. (1949) *General Industrial Management*, London: Pitman.

Ferguson, D. and Berger, F. (1984) Restaurant Managers: What do they really do? *Cornell Hotel and Restaurant Administrative Quarterly*, **25**, 24–34.

Fiedler, F. (1967) *A Theory of Leadership Effectiveness*, New York: McGraw Hill.

Filby, M. (1992) The figures, the personality and the bums: service work and sexuality, *Work Employment and Society*, **6**, 1: 23–42.

Fineman, S. (1993) Organizations as emotional arenas, in Fineman, S. (ed.), *Emotion in Organizations*, London: Sage.

Fineman, S. and Gabriel, Y. (1996) *Experiencing Organizations*, London: Sage.

Fleishman, E. (1973) Twenty years of consideration and structure, in Fleishman, E. and Hunt, J. (eds), *Current Developments in the Study of Leadership*, Illinois, Southern Illinois University.

Fletcher, C. (1973) The end of management, in Child, J. (ed.), *Man and Organisation*, London: Allen and Unwin.

French, J. and Raven, B. (1960) The bases of social power, in Cartwright, D.

and Zander, A. (eds), *Group Dynamics* (Second edition), Evanston Ill: Row Peterson.

Friedman, M. (1989) The social responsibility of business is to increase profits, *New York Times Magazine*, 13 Sept., 30.

Gabriel, Y. (1988) *Working Lives in Catering*, London: Routledge and Kegan Paul.

Gabriel, Y. and Lang, T. (1995) *The Unmanageable Consumer*, London: Sage.

Gamble, P., Lockwood, A. and Messenger, S. (1994) European management skills in the hospitality industry, paper presented at CHRIE conference, Palm Springs.

Gardner, K. and Wood, R. (1991) Theatricality in food service work, *International Journal of Hospitality Management*, **10**, 3: 267–278.

Gilbert, D. and Guerrier, Y. (1997) UK hospitality managers past and present, *The Service Industries Journal*, **17**, 115–132.

Go, F. and Pine, R. (1995) *Globalization Strategy in the Hotel Industry*, London and New York: Routledge.

Goffee, R. and Scase, R. (1988) *The Reluctant Managers*, London: Unwin.

Goffman, E. (1959) *The Presentation of Self in Everyday Life*, London: Penguin.

Goldthorpe, J., Lockwood, D., Bechhofer, F. and Platt, J. (1968) *The Affluent Worker: Industrial Attitudes and Behaviour*, London: Cambridge University Press.

Graen, G. and Scandura, P. (1987) Toward a Psychology of Dyadic Organizing, in Cummings, L. and Staw, B. (eds), *Research in Organizational Behavior Vol. 9*, Greenwich CT: JAI Press, 175–208.

Guerrier, Y. (1986) Hotel management: an unsuitable job for a woman? *Service Industries Journal*, **6**, 227–240.

Guerrier, Y. (1987) Hotel managers' careers and their impact on hotels in Britain, *International Journal of Hospitality Management* **6**, 121–130.

Guerrier, Y. and Lockwood, A. (1989a) Core and peripheral employees in hotel operations, *Personnel Review*, **18**, 9–15.

Guerrier, Y. and Lockwood, A. (1989b) Developing hotel managers – a reappraisal, *International Journal of Hospitality Management*, **8**, 2: 82–89.

Guerrier, Y. and Pye, G. (1994) Managing human resources in restaurant and catering outlets, in Davis, B. and Lockwood, A. (eds), *Food and Beverage Management: a selection of readings*, Oxford: Butterworth-Heinemann.

Guerrier, Y., Baum, T., Jones, P. and Roper, A. (1998) *In the World of Hospitality . . . Anything They Can Do, We Can Do Better*, London: Joint Hospitality Industry Congress.

Gummesson, E. (1992) *Quality Management in Service Organizations*, New York: SQA.

Hackman, J. and Oldham, G. (1980) *Work Redesign*, Reading, Mass: Addison-Wesley.

Haigh, M. (1995) World views and environmental action: a practical exercise, in Guerrier, Y., Alexander, N., Chase, J. and O'Brien, M. (eds), *Values and the Environment*, Chichester: Wiley.

Hales, C. (1993) *Managing through Organisations*, London: Routledge.

Hales, C. and Tamangani, Z. (1996) An investigation into the relationship between organizational structure, managerial role expectations and managers' work activities, *Journal of Management Studies*, **33**, 6: 731–756.

Hall, C.M. (1994) Gender and economic interests in tourism prostitution, in Kinnaird, V. and Hall, D. (eds), *Tourism: a Gender Analysis*, Chichester: Wiley, 142–160.

Hall, E. (1993) Smiling, Deferring and Flirting: Doing Gender by giving "Good Service", *Work and Occupations*, **20**, 4: 452–471.

Hall, E.T (1956) *The Silent Language*, New York: Doubleday Anchor Press.

Hall, E.T (1976) *Beyond Culture*, Garden City New York: Doubleday Anchor Books.

Hall, E. and Hall, M. (1997) The Americans, in Hickson, D. (ed.), *Exploring Management Across the World*, London: Penguin, 56–68.

Handy, C. (1978) *The Gods of Management*, London: Penguin.

Handy, C. (1994) *The Empty Raincoat*, London: Hutchinson.

Hanley, A. (1998) Tourist industry is outraged at Italy's belated attempt to clean up filthy seas, *Independent on Sunday*, 13 September, 14–15.

Harrison, R. (1972) How to describe your organization, *Harvard Business Review*, 50: May/June, 119–128.

Herzberg, F. (1966) *Work and the Nature of Man*, Cleveland: World Publishing Co.

Heskett, J. (1986) *Managing in the Service Economy*, Boston: Harvard Business School Press.

Hicks, L. (1990) Excluded women: how can this happen in the hotel world, *Service Industries Journal*, **10**, 348–363.

Hickson, D. (ed.) (1997) *Exploring Management across the World*, London: Penguin.

Hilton, C. (1957) *Be My Guest*, Englewood Cliffs, New Jersey: Prentice Hall.

Hochschild, A. (1983) *The Managed Heart*, Berkeley: University of California Press.

Hofstede, G. (1980) *Culture's Consequences: International Differences in Work Related Values*, Beverley Hills: Sage.

Hofstede, G. (1991) *Cultures and Organizations*, London: McGraw Hill (paperback version HarperCollins Business 1994).

Hofstede, G. (1998) Attitudes, values and organizational culture: disentangling the concepts, *Organization Studies*, **19**, 3: 477–494.

Honey, P. and Mumford, A. (1992) *The Manual of Learning Styles* (Third edition), Peter Honey: Maidenhead.

Höpfl, H. (1993) Culture and commitment: British Airways, in Gowler, D., Legge, K. and Clegg, C. (eds), *Cases in Organizational Behaviour and Human Resource Management*, London: Paul Chapman.

Horner, M. (1972) Towards an understanding of acheivement-related conflicts in women, *Journal of Social Issues*, **2**, 2: 157–175.

Hotel and Catering Training Company (1994) *Employment Flows in the Catering and Hospitality Industry*, London: HCTC.

Hotels (1996) Balance of power shifts at Hilton, Holiday Inn, *Hotels*, 3 April.

House, R. (1971) A path-goal theory of leader effectiveness, *Administrative Science Quarterly*, **16**, 321–338.

House, R. and Mitchell, T. (1974) Path-goal theory of leadership, *Journal of Contemporary Business*, **3**, 81–97.

Hubrecht, J. and Teare, R. (1993) A strategy for partnership in total quality service, *International Journal of Contemporary Hospitality Management*, **5**, 3: i–iv.

Ingram, P. and Inman, C. (1996) Institutions, intergroup competition and the evolution of hotel populations around Niagara Falls, *Administrative Science Quarterly*, **41**, 629–658.

Ishiguro, K. (1989) *The Remains of the Day*, London: Faber and Faber.

Ivancevich, J. and Matteson, M. (1993) *Organizational Behavior and Management* (Third edition), Homewood Ill.: Irwin.

Janis, I. (1972) *Victims of Groupthink*, Boston: Houghton Mifflin.

Jones, C., Nickson, D. and Taylor, G. (1994) 'Ways' of managing the world: manging culture in international hotel chains, in Seaton, A. (ed.), *Tourism State of the Art*, Chichester: Wiley, 626–634.

Jones, P. and Pizam, A. (eds) (1993) *The International Hospitality Industry: Organizational and Operational Issues*, London: Pitman.

Kanter, R. (1977) *Men and Women of the Corporation*, New York: Basic Books.

Kanter, R. (1991) *When Giants Learn to Dance*, London: Unwin Hyman.

Kanungo, R. and Mendonca, M. (eds) (1994) *Work Motivation*, New Delhi: Sage.

Kassova, M. (1995) Quality service and its role in retaining guests: a case study of hotel receptionists in Bulgaria, MBA dissertation, South Bank University, London.

Kinnaird, V. and Hall, D. (1994) *Tourism: A Gender Analysis*, Chichester: Wiley.

Knights, D. and Willmott, H. (1992) Conceptualizing leadership processes: a study of senior managers in a financial services company, *Journal of Management Studies*, **29**, 6: 761–782.

Knowles, T. (1998) *Hospitality Management: An Introduction* (Second edition), Harlow: Longman.

Kokko, J. and Guerrier, Y. (1994) Overeducation, underemployment and job satisfaction: a study of Finnish hotel receptionists, *International Journal of Hospitality Management*, **13**, 375–386.

Kolb, D., Rubin, I. and McIntyre (1979) *Organizational Psychology: an Experiential Approach* (Third edition), Englewood Cliffs, New Jersey: Prentice Hall.

Kolb, D., Osland, J. and Rubin, I. (1995) *Organizational Psychology: an Experiential Approach* (Sixth edition), Englewood Cliffs, New Jersey: Prentice Hall.

Kotter, J. (1982) *The General Managers*, New York: Free Press.

Krippendorf, J. (1984) *The Holiday Makers*, Oxford: Butterworth-Heinemann.

Kuhn, T. (1970) *The Structure of Scientific Revolutions*, Chicago: University of Chicago.

Lamplugh, D. (1988) *Beating Aggression – a Practical Guide for Working Women*, London: Weidenfeld and Nicolson.

Lamplugh, D. (1991) *Without Fear – the Key to Staying Safe*, London: Weidenfeld and Nicolson.

Lamplugh, D. (1996) Gender and personal safety at work, in *Gender and Life in Organizations*, Occasional Papers in Organizational Analysis No 5, Department of Business and Management, University of Portsmouth.

Lashley, C. (1997) *Empowering Service Excellence*, London: Cassell.

Lawrence, P. (1997) If not now, when? in Hickson, D. (ed.), *Exploring Management Across the World*, London: Penguin, 188–201.

Lawrence, P. and Lorsch, J. (1967) *Organization and Environment*, Cambridge Mass: Harvard University Press.

Lee-Ross, D. and Johns, N. (1995) Dimensionality of the job diagnosis survey among distinct sub-groups of seasonal hotel workers, *Hospitality Research Journal*, **19**, 2: 31–42.

Leidner, R. (1993) *Fast Food Fast Talk: Service Work and the Routinization of Everyday Life*, Berkeley: University of California Press.

Levitt, T. (1972) Production-line approach to service, *Harvard Business Review*, Sept–Oct, 41–52.

Lewin, K. (1938) *The Conceptual Representation and the Measurement of Psychological Forces*, Durham N.C.: Duke University Press.

Ley, D. (1980) The effective GM: leader or entrepreneur, *Cornell Hotel and Restaurant Administrative Quarterly*, November, 66–67.

Locke, E. (1975) Personnel attitudes and motivation, *Annual Review of Psychology*, **26**, 457–480.

Locke, E. (1976) The nature and causes of job satisfaction, in Dunnette, M. (ed.), *Handbook of Industrial and Organizational Psychology*, Chicago: Rand McNally, 1297–1349.

Lucas, R. (1995) *Managing Employee Relations in the Hotel and Catering Industry*, London: Cassell.

Lundberg, C. and Woods, R. (1991) Modifying restaurant culture: managers as cultural leaders, *International Journal of Contemporary Hospitality Management*, **2**, 2: 4–12.

Lurie, A. (1981) *The Language of Clothes*, New York: Random House.

Lynn, M. and Graves, J. (1996) Tipping: an incentive/reward for service, *Hospitality Research Journal*, **20**, 1: 1–14.

MAFF (1994) *National Food Survey 1993*, London: HMSO.

Mars, G., Bryant, D. and Mitchell, P. (1979) *Manpower Problems in the Hotel and Catering Industry*, Farnborough: Saxon House.

Mars, G. and Nicod, M. (1984) *The World of Waiters*, London: Allen and Unwin.

Marshall, J. (1984) *Women Managers: Travellers in a Male World*, Chichester: Wiley.

Maslow, A. (1943) A theory of motivation, *Psychological Review*, **50**, 370–96.

McDermid, K. (1993) Going green, *Hospitality*, April, No 137, 14–18.

McGregor, D. (1960) *The Human Side of Enterprise*, New York: McGraw Hill.

Mead, R. (1994) *International Management: Cross Cultural Dimensions*, Cambridge MA: Blackwell.

Medlik, S. (1994) *The Business of Hotels* (Third edition), Oxford: Butterworth-Heinemann.

Mendonca, M. and Kanungo, R. (1994) Conclusion: the issue of culture fit, in Kanungo, R. and Mendonca, M., *Work Motivation: Models for Developing Countries*, New Delhi: Sage.

Ministry of Tourism and Culture (1995) *National Policy for Tourism Development*, The Gambia: Banjul.

Mintzberg, H. (1973) *The Nature of Managerial Work*, New York: Harper Row.

Morgan, D. (1992) *Discovering Men*, London: Routledge.

Morgan, G. (1986) *Images of Organization*, California and London: Sage.

Morgan, G. (1997) *Images of Organization* (Second edition), California and London: Sage

Morrison, A., White, R. and Van Veslor, E. (1987) *Breaking the Glass Ceiling: Can Women Reach the Top of America's Largest Corporations*, Reading, Mass: Addison-Wesley.

Mühlmann, W.E. (1932) Hospitality, in Seligman, E. (ed.), *Encyclopedia of the Social Sciences*, New York: Macmillan.

Mumford, E. (1972) *Job Satisfaction*, London: Longman Group.

Nailon, P. (1982) A study of management activity in units in a hotel group, Unpublished MPhil: University of Surrey.

Nebel, E. (1991) *Managing Hotels Effectively: Lessons from Outstanding General Managers*, New York: Van Nostrand.

Nebel, E., Braunlich, C. and Zhang, Y. (1994) Career paths in American luxury hotels: hotel food and beverage directors, *International Journal of Contemporary Hospitality Management*, **6**, 6: 3–9.

Nickson, D. (1997) "Colorful stories" or historical insight? – a review of the auto/biographies of Charles Forte, Conrad Hillton, J.W. Marriott and Kemmons Wilson, *Journal of Hospitality and Tourism Research*, **21**, 1: 179–192.

Noon, M. and Delbridge, R. (1993) News from behind my hand: gossip in organizations, *Organization Studies*, **14**, 1: 23–36.

Northedge, A. (1990) *The Good Study Guide*, Milton Keynes: Open University.

Novarra, V. (1980) *Women's Work, Men's Work*, London: Marion Boyars.

Nuttley, M. (1997) Introduction, in *The Leisure Industry Report*, London: Leisureweek.

O'Brien, R. (1977) *Marriott: The J. Willard Marriott Story*, Salt Lake City: Desert Book Company.

Orwell, G. (1933) *Down and Out in Paris and London*, London: Penguin.

Parsons, D. and Cave, P. (1991) *Developing Managers for Tourism*, London: NEDO.

Pedler, M., Burgoyne, J. and Boydell, T. (1996) *A Manager's Guide to Self-Development*, (Third edition), London: McGraw Hill.

Peters, T. (1988) Restoring American competitiveness: looking for new models of organization, in Ivancevich, J. and Matteson, M. (1993) *Organizational Behavior and Management*, Homewood Ill: Irwin, 526–531.

Peters, T. and Waterman, R. (1982) *In Search of Excellence: Lessons from America's Best Run Companies*, New York: Harper and Row.

Phornprapha, S. (1996) The preferences of restaurant operative staff concerning leadership style: a study in Thailand, unpublished PhD thesis, University of Surrey.

Pizam, A., Pine, R., Mok, C. and Shin, J.Y. (1997) National vs industry cultures: which has the greatest effect on managerial behavior, *International Journal of Hospitality Management*, **15**, 347–362.

Porter, L. and Lawler, E. (1968) *Managerial attitudes and performance*, Homewood Ill: Irwin-Dorsey.

Porter, L., Lawler, E. and Hackman, J.R. (1975) *Behavior in Organizations*, Singapore: McGraw Hill.

Powers, T. (1995) *Introduction to the Hospitality Industry* (Third edition), New York: Wiley.

Prais, S., Jarvis, V. and Wagner, K. (1989) Productivity and Vocational Skills in Services in Britain and Germany: Hotels, *National Institute Economic Review*, November, 52–74.

Pugh, D. and Hickson, D. (1996) (Fifth edition), *Writers on Organizations*, London: Penguin.

Purcell, K. (1993) Equal Opportunities in the hospitality industry: custom and credentials, *International Journal of Hospitality Management*, **12**, 2: 127–40.

Ramsay, R. (1966) *Managers and Men: Adventures in Industry*, Sydney: Ure Snith.

Riley, M. (1991a) *Human Resource Management: A Guide to Personnel Practice in the Hotel and Catering Industries*, Oxford: Butterworth-Heinemann.

Riley (1991b) An analysis of hotel labour markets, in Cooper, C. and Lockwood, A. (eds), *Progress in Tourism and Hospitality Management Vol 3*, London: Belhaven.

Ritzler, G. (1993) *The McDonaldization of Society: An Investigation into the Changing Character of Contemporary Social Life*, Thousand Oaks, California: Pine Forge Press.

Robbins, S. (1998) *Organizational Behaviour*, (Eighth edition), New Jersey: Prentice Hall.

Roper, A., Brookes, M. and Hampton, A. (1997) The multi-cultural management of international hotel groups, *International Journal of Hospitality Management*, **16**, 2: 147–159.

Rosener, J. (1990) Ways Women Lead, *Harvard Business Review*, Nov–Dec, 119–125.

Rotter, J. (1966) Generalized expectancies for internal versus external control of reinforcement, *Psychological Monographs*, 80, No. 609.

Saunders, K. (1981) *Social Stigma of Occupations: the Lower Grade Worker in Service Occupations*, Farnborough: Gower.

Schein, E.H. (1985) *Organizational Culture and Leadership*, San Francisco, CA: Jossey Bass.

Schein, V. (1975) Relationships between sex role stereotypes and requisite management characteristics, *Journal of Applied Psychology*, **57**, 95–100.

Shamir, B. (1978) Between bureaucracy and hospitality – some organizational characteristics of hotels, *Journal of Management Studies*, **15**, 285–307.

Shamir, B. (1980) Between service and servility: role conflict in subordinate service roles, *Human Relations*, **33**, 10: 741–756.

Shamir, B. (1983) A note on tipping and employee perceptions and attitudes, *Journal of Occupational Psychology*, **56**, 255–259.

Sims, D., Fineman, S. and Gabriel, Y. (1993) *Organizing and Organizations: an Introduction*, London: Sage.

Sinha, J. (1995) *The Cultural Context of Leadership and Power*, New Delhi: Sage.

Smith, M. (1991) Leadership and supervision, in Smith, M. (ed.), *Analysing Organizational Behaviour*, Basingstoke: Macmillan.

Smith, M. and Davidson, L. (1991) Analysing jobs: the manager and the job, in Smith, M. (ed.), *Analysing Organizational Behaviour*, Basingstoke: Macmillan.

Smith, P.C., Kendall, L. and Hulin, C. (1969) *The Measurement of Satisfaction in Work and Retirement*, Chicago: Rand McNally.

Smith, P. and Peterson, M. (1988) *Leadership, Organizations and Culture*, London: Sage.

Sosteric, M. (1996) Subjectivity and the labour process: a case study in the restaurant industry, *Work, Employment and Society*, **10**, 2: 297–318.

Stewart, R. (1967) *Managers and their Jobs*, London: Macmillan.

Stewart, R. (1976) *Contrasts in Management*, Maidenhead: McGraw Hill.

Stewart, R. (1982) *Choices for the Manager*, Englewood Cliffs, N.J.: Prentice-Hall.

Tannen, D. (1994) *Talking from 9 to 5*, London: Virago.

Tayeb, M. (1997) English culture and business organizations, in Hickson, D. (ed.), *Exploring Management Across the World*, London: Penguin, 21–38.

Taylor, F.W. (1911) *Principles of Scientific Management*, New York: Harper and Row.

Telfer, E. (1996) *Food for Thought: Philosophy and Food*, London: Routledge.

Terkel, S. (1972) *Working*, New York: Aron Books.

Thomas, A. (1989) One-minute management education: a sign of the times, *Management Education and Development*, **20**, 1: 23–38.

Thomas, A. (1993) *Controversies in Management*, London and New York: Routledge.

Thompson, D. (1962) Organizations and output transactions, *American Journal of Sociology*, **60**, 309–324.

Tolman, E.C. (1932) *Purposive Behavior in Animals and Men*, New York: Appleton-Century Crofts.

Trist, E. and Bamforth, K. (1951) Some social and psychological consequences of the longwall method of coal-getting, *Human Relations*, **4**, 1: 6–24 and 37–38.

Trompenaars, F. and Hampden-Turner, C. (1997) *Riding the Waves of Culture* (Second edition), London: Nicholas Brealey.

Tuckman, B. (1965) Development sequence in small groups, *Psychological Bulletin*, **63**, 384–399.

Urry, J. (1990) *The Tourist Gaze*, London: Sage.

Urwick, L. (1943) *The Elements of Administration*, New York: Harper.

Vallen, J., Abbey, J. and Sapienza, D. (1978) *The Art and Science of Managing Hotels/Restaurants/Institutions* (Second edition), New Jersey: Hayden.

Van Maanen, J. (1991) The smile factory: work at Disneyland, in Frost, P., Moore, L., Reis Louis, M., Lundberg, C. and Martin, J. (eds) *Reframing Organizational Culture*, California: Sage, 58–76.

Vecchio, R. (1995) *Organizational Behaviour* (Third edition), Orlando: Dryden.

Warner, M. and Campbell, A. (1997) German management, in Hickson, D. (ed.), *Exploring Management Across the World*, London: Penguin.

Weir, D. (ed.) (1973) *Men and Work in Modern Britain*, Glasgow: Fontana.

Whyte, W. (1946) *Human Relations in the Restaurant Industry*, New York: McGraw Hill.

Wiley, C. (1997) What motivates employees according to over 40 years of motivation surveys, *International Journal of Manpower*, **18**, 3: 263–280.

Wilson, D. and Rosenfeld, R. (1990) *Managing Organizations: Texts, Readings and Cases*, London: McGraw Hill.

Wilson, F. (1995) *Organizational Behaviour and Gender*, London: McGraw Hill.

Wise, B. (1993) The Far East and Australasia, in Jones, P. and Pizam, A. (eds), *The International Hospitality Industry: Organizational and Operational Issues*, Chichester: Wiley.

Wood, D. (1991) Corporate social performance revisited, *Academy of Management Review*, **16**, 4: 691–718.

Wood, R. (1992) *Working in Hotel and Catering*, London: Routledge.

Wood, R. (1994) Hospitality culture and social control, *Annals of Tourism Research*, **21**, 65–80.

Wright, P. (1991) Motivation in organizations, in Smith, M. (ed.), *Analysing Organisational Behaviour*, Basingstoke: Macmillan.

Young, K. (1997) Environmental tobacco smoke and employees, *Cornell Hotel and Restaurant Administrative Quarterly*, February, 36–42.

Index

Related titles of interest..

The Handbook of Contemporary Hospitality Management Research

Edited by BOB BROTHERTON

0471 983950   April 1999   576pp   Hardback

Introduction to Management in the Hospitality Industry

Fourth Edition

TOM POWERS

0471 252441   March 1999   480pp   Paperback

Introduction to Management in the Hospitality Industry

Sixth Edition

TOM POWERS

0471 252034   March 1999   608pp   Hardback

Strategic Management in the Hospitality Industry

Second Edition

MICHAEL D. OLSEN, ELIZA CHING-YICK TSE
and JOSEPH WEST

0471 292397   October 1998   450pp
Hardback

WILEY

FEB 19 2001